DISORGANIZED CHRISTIANITY

By Keith H. McIntosh

To Dan,
Glad to meet
and chat with you.
enjoy! Namaste!

Disorganized Christianity
© 2020 by Keith H. McIntosh

ISBN: 978-1-09831-827-7

CONTENTS

DEDICATION

To my Mother, Marlene 19

ACKNOWLEDGEMENTS

George Carlin,

And always remember, life is not measured by the number of breaths we take, but by those moments that take our breath away. This quote has been my mission, from the first moment I heard it.

To Peter Messerschmidt my editor. At the time I didn't really know what I needed or wanted and you said:

My job as an editor is to take your words and your ideas and make them "look as good as possible." That means not only proofing for typos, but also editing "flow," changing word orders and word usage, sometimes rewriting sentences to avoid excessive repetition, editing for logic, concept and semantic consistency across chapters, basic grammar editing and spotting "problems."

Peter, you did all of this superbly and let me keep my voice. Thank you sir. I look forward to collaborating with you for book two, *"Are You Kidding Me!"*

Thank you Sam Del Russi for giving me your original painting of *"The Quest,"* that I used for the cover of this book. Rest in Peace my friend, we will share again.

I would like to say *"thank you"* to a few very special people that have been my *"teachers of life."* Seymour W., we helped our friend, Robert, pass comfortably and then started a brother to brother bond that will last forever and a day. Christopher P., each day and each journey validates even more how much our friendship is worth. Mark B., I know you wanted to defend me and stand by my side, when this adventure began, but taking care of your family came first. I believe that, thank you. Mr. Clarence J., you were my first hero and when you wrote to clarify *organized religion* and they condemned you, little did I know, I would follow in your footsteps. RIP (Mine fit inside yours.) Bill B., to the humblest and one of the best men I have had the privilege to have known. RIP

To Sarah Nash, my *spiritual Goddess.* The things you have taught me have made it possible to finish this project, start the next one and to lead a life that I never thought I was worthy to have. You have shown me how to be the best, spiritually, that I can be and how to help others along my journey. My prayer is that everyone will find their *"spiritual Goddess."*

INTRODUCTION

L ast week, I was singing "Amazing Grace," and listening to the pastor tell me how much Jesus loves me. This week, I am not allowed in *his* building. That is *my* story, what is yours?

For the millions upon millions of displaced Christians in this world, *Disorganized Christianity* is the gavel of justice with the power of redemption for our souls. I will, throughout this book, substitute the phrase *organized religion* in place of *Disorganized Christianity*. *Organized religion* will refer to the faith of Christianity in its many forms, but does not include in any way the Jewish faith, Muslim faith, Buddist faith or any other non-Christian faith. We all can be spiritual without being part of "the church," no matter what *organized religion* says.

This book includes a compelling critique of Christianity, hope for the disillusioned who have left their church, and suggestions for those who want to leave, but still hold onto their faith in a God, or higher power. It combines common sense insight with scriptural references and personal experiences. *Disorganized Christianity* isn't bitter, but it is biting. It contains concrete information that other books on the topic fail to include.

Growing up, I was the only one in my family to attend church regularly. I enjoyed it and started preaching in my mid-teens. After high school,

I became a Baptist lay minister and spent decades teaching the scriptures to thousands of people. I, then, had a falling out with some *mean spirited and intolerant* Christians in my local church.

After a disagreement with the pastor of the local church I was attending and serving in, I decided to reread the Bible, with the sole purpose to find enough valid reasons to not have to settle with *organized religion's* continual damnation of my eternal soul. My *Why!* for writing *Disorganized Christianity* is to give others, from the strongest charismatic church leader to the most gullible, but sincerely spiritual; "want to be saved from Hell," individual, enough biblical common sense and correct spiritual answers to withstand *organized religion's* condemnation for anyone who disagrees with their dogma.

For years, I did not like *organized religion's* vagueness and shallow answers to my questions. Responses like, "Have faith, God will reveal His plans and His will for your life, in His perfect timing," and "We are NOT to question God," were not, and are not good enough anymore.

Romans 10:17 *So, then, faith coming by hearing, and hearing by the word of God* and **2 Timothy 3:16** *All scripture is given by inspiration of God, and is profitable for doctrine, for reproof, for correction, for instruction in righteousness.* My only source for biblical references while writing *Disorganized Christianity* has been the *New Scofield Reference Bible, Authorized King James Version* copyrighted 1967. It is the same Bible I used from 1967, the beginning of my ministry, to 1986, the end of my ministry. Many of the notes I had handwritten in the margins of my Bible are some of the very stances that I am challenging with *this* book.

There are plenty of people like me who did not get truthful answers to our questions, and we *all* still had more questions that were never even answered, so we left *organized religion.* I have labeled us, *converted non-Christians,* because we have seen the light, and it does not include *organized religion.* Since my departure from *organized religion,* I have grown in my absolute belief that, "I *Believe in God. I just don't know who he is, or she is, or they are or we are.*" I did not set out to prove there is no God, but I cannot prove there is a God, either! My *choice* is to believe there is a God, and maybe we *can* find the true kind of loving God we *all* believe in our hearts, he or she or they or we should be.

When I challenged *organized religion* they were vague and dismissive and demanded that I not question God, but they wanted exactness in details and full responses from me for *my* actions when they condemned me. While writing *Disorganized Christianity* I found my answers to my questions, now it is truly their time, for their own credibility to find their answers to our questions. The old guard *organized religion* members that used to challenge me, are silent and no longer test me. This is my goal for anyone that wants to say to them, "Keep your brand of *organized religion, we do not want it anymore.*"

When religious misunderstandings get cloudy and the solutions are not completely transparent or exactly defined as right or wrong, sometimes good, kind, and loving Christians are over-powered by the few *mean spirited and intolerant Christians* with their own agenda. These few use God's word as their authority, even though these authoritative solutions based on present Bible dogma are not biblically correct. After being chastised, we are told we are wrong and then told that we have to accept their decisions as God's will, just because they said so, but not anymore!

When I left *organized religion* I encountered extreme hatred from a select few *mean spirited and intolerant* Christians. I just wanted to leave the church. When they verbally, using scripture tried to condemn me; I said I will challenge them. I reread the Bible with a new set of eyes and then understood verses with a different heart. I have not made it my goal to destroy *organized religion.* I have set out to intellectually and spiritually redefine many basic biblical doctrines.

Some simple and exact beliefs *organized religion* has about an apple, a whale, bunny rabbits laying chocolate eggs in church, three wise men at Jesus' birth, why Noah was the best man God could have chosen to repopulate the earth after the great flood, the treatment of women, slaves/ Blacks, and homosexuals, and many other false *organized religion* dogmas will be exposed in this book. *Disorganized Christianity* will also address some lesser-known events like angels ("host of them") having sex with Eve's daughters, what *could* be the origin of the anti-Christ's number 666, that Eve NEVER sinned in the Garden of Eden, and the fact Jesus CAN NOT BE the Messiah. It is time for people to wake up to their own divinity, not to rule others but to love one another.

With these new understandings all we *converted non-Christians* are demanding is, "We no longer have faith in your dogmas, so just leave us alone!" We do not care or have an interest to convert you to anything, and we do not want to have you convert us to anything. Your spiritual wellness and completeness actually has nothing to do with whether we are saved by you from a fiery hell. If you believe our actions are detrimental to our well-being, realize that they are *our* actions. Spend your time exorcising your own demons instead of inventing and then worrying about ours. All we are asking is that you few *mean spirited and intolerant Christians* concentrate and take care of your own lives.

I got tired of the story; I am a dirty, rotten sinner and only worthy of Hell and before I get there I have to make sure I obey a bunch of rules that if I don't follow, I will be deserving an even worse *Hell on earth.*

I now believe in **John14:12** *Verily. Verily, I say unto you, He that believeth on me, the works that I do shall he do also: and greater works than these shall he do, because I go unto my Father.* Jesus is actually saying we can be and do even better than himself.

Jesus said to turn the other cheek, but pretty soon all four of my cheeks got sore, and when there was no more cheek to turn, I perceived the next action coming was to have my cheeks nailed to a tree or cross. No, thank you! If you sincerely want to get my attention about what God and Jesus really want me to do, and you feel that if only I would obey God and turn the other cheek, I will experience Jesus' love and God's forgiveness, I have a test for you. Let me actually witness you lose in a court of law to a scam artist or a swindler or maybe even in divorce court. After the judge rules you to pay thousands of dollars, especially when you know in your heart of hearts that the judgment is unfair, double the judgment. **Matthew 5:40** *And if any man will sue thee at the law, and take away thy coat, let him have thy cloak also.* Your Bible commands you to pay more than the judgment. After you have willingly and lovingly paid this evil person twice the judgment, only then can you preach to me, "Turn the other cheek."

Another objective for writing *Disorganized Christianity* was to reveal and be able to declare, to the few *mean spirited and intolerant Christians* that had to prove with their truly limited understanding of Biblical scriptures and dogmas they used against anyone who were not in complete agreement with them, that they are wrong. All *organized religion* members are not *mean spirited and intolerant* and *Disorganized Christianity* was not written for *them. Organized religion* fervently condemns anyone who stands up to their biblical interpretations. Please believe whatever translation of the Bible you want to, and live a peaceful and loving life. But, if you change for any reason and believe that it is your mission to correct us, then we will use the words in *Disorganized Christianity* to put you in your place.

With *Disorganized Christianity* we *converted non-Christians* now have a better reasoning for our stand to not believe the Bible and its controlling authority.

I have challenged them. I took note of *their* condemnations as well as *their* commandments and then decided to read the Bible again. I had concerns about the many verses I reread and now understand them in a different way. I was now for the first time challenging the Bible and saying, "No, I am not believing it anymore!"

My soul-saving verse that I read with a "different set of eyes and a different heart" was John 20:1. You can read it and understand its new meaning in the chapter *Resurrection*! I didn't write the verse, I just reread the verse, and now others will also!

With my new found revelations, I compared what *organized religion* was saying in comparison to what the Bible said, and the two did not match up with each other. With these new understandings, I wrote a little study guide to defend myself from a few *mean spirited and intolerant Christians*. When other battle weary Christians started asking me for help, I started writing *Disorganized Christianity*.

I wrote this book to give all *converted non-Christians* a source of strength and recourse from the manipulation of biblical dogma to *control and condemn us on this earth and then declare our damnation in the hereafter*. *Disorganized Christianity* is not condemning or labeling all Christians as *mean spirited and intolerant,* but most of us have experienced plenty of Christians with their own agendas and prejudices. *Mean spirited and intolerant Christians* have an absolute belief in the Bible as they read and understand it. I am not here to tell them what to believe and what to understand. I am here to tell them what they believe and understand as their dogma, is not exactly correct.

I have been blessed by many loving Christians who stood tall when I needed them, and I tried to stand tall for them when they needed me. Christianity can be a very wonderful experience.

I have met some exceptional Christians who really do Love the Lord, Jesus, the Messiah, the Bread of Life, the Comforter, the Chief Shepherd, the Day Star, the Deliverer, the Lamb of God, the Prince of Peace, the Redeemer, the Savior, the Vine, and the Word. These additional names for Jesus are found in your Bible.

My life is full of memories of great Christians. I have had Christians love me and understand my sorrow when my mother died in the Pacific Ocean. Christians felt my grief that we never recovered her body. When my son Sean Michael died, I was devastated. I experienced love and compassion from a Christian couple that I respected and never even knew they had gone through the same pain as I.

From the first day I met Dawn J., she reminded me that Jesus still loved me and that she wanted me to come back to church and fellowship with other Christians again. Dawn was as sincere as anyone I have ever met with her faith in God and Jesus and in her absolute belief that I would one day come back to church. Sorry Dawn, it just isn't going to happen. I am very glad that you are happy in God and Jesus. I could see the strength you gathered from your faith. That faith is all right. My point is that you never tried to guilt me or shame me into coming back to church. You left the decision entirely up to me. You actually acted like the Bible says a Christian should act: with love and compassion for a lost soul. Dawn, I have no quarrel with you.

Tom B. is a third generation preacher who is not fully on board with my findings, but does have more than a few Bible questions of his own. Tom was a business associate, and he has never let our biblical differences cause us any other problems. Tom, I have no quarrel with you.

Mike C., a very recently ordained preacher that I had a business relationship with, will be shocked by *Disorganized Christianity* because we only talked about his preaching and my "used to be" preaching. We never discussed the details of my Christian faith or lack of Christian faith because I was always supportive of his decision to be called to the ministry. Mike believes in the Bible and loves God and Jesus, and I am not here to take that away from him. Mike, I have no quarrel with you.

Jeri P-F. is one of my most beloved people on this planet. Her faith is generational and her stubbornness is absolute. I truly believe there are not enough explosives on the planet to shake her faith. *Disorganized*

Christianity will certainly not shake her faith, and it is not intended to shake any Christian's faith. My faith was Baptist and Jeri's faith was Mormon and that was about as opposite as you could get. According to my true loving faith, she was in a cult. We grew to be friends and then my loving faith told me to stay away from her and her kind. In *Disorganized Christianity* I will document how biblical characters and current people have allowed themselves to be swayed by *organized religion* mistranslating God's word and using earthly situations to convince us they know what is better for our personal and spiritual life.

Sometimes the most loving of our Christian brothers and sisters believe that God has given them a special understanding into *our* everyday lives.

The Christian Army Is The Only Army That Spiritually Shoots Their Wounded, Sometimes Fatally! Bang! Bang!

I was diagnosed with malignant cancer of my thyroid in 1986. While I was recovering from my cancer surgery, I actually had a person from one of my churches come into my hospital room and say, "The thyroid cancer was God's punishment for my behavior and that since I was still alive, God was willing to let me repent and come back to church." I thought, "Here come the guns! No, thank you! No Bang! Bang!" Jeri and her family took me in and helped me survive my cancer battle. I love her and her family. Jeri, I have no quarrel with you. There are many Dawns, Toms, Mikes and Jeris in this world and I have no quarrel with these very real Christians.

This is about where the love and peace ends and the quarrel begins. To the Christian who cannot have a simple conversation without letting me know how great they are and how great their faith is, I have a quarrel with you. To the Christian who wants to engage me in a conversation and their motivation is to tell me what a sinner I am, and where they think I am going if I don't repent, I have a quarrel with you. For the Christian who puts a little fish on their business card and then cheats me on a business deal, I have a quarrel with you. A number of Christians that have read a pre-published copy of *Disorganized Christianity* stated they never saw this bad side of *organized religion* in their own church. These folks should be glad, because a lot of us have experienced *mean spirited and intolerant* Christians in *our* churches.

Disorganized Christianity was not written with an extreme motivation to destroy any *organized religious* group or the Christian faith of anyone. It was written, though, with a strong hand now capable and ready to do battle, if necessary, with anyone's punitive dogma against us.

Our weapon of choice in this spiritual battle will be *organized religion's* own Bible. **Revelation 22:18-19** *18 For I testify unto every man that heareth the words of the prophecy of this book, If any man shall add unto these things, God shall add unto him the plagues that are written in this book; 19 And if any man shall take away from the words of the book of this prophecy, God shall take away his part from the tree of life, and out of the holy city, and from the things which are written in this book.* Even though by Christianity's own declaration the Bible is complete and *infallible* "as it is," preachers, evangelists and certain religious personalities continually receive yesterday's, today's, and tomorrow's *new* dogma personally from God.

When any person thinks their translation and interpretation gives them the power to take away *my* hope, *my* joy, *my* blessings and declares what *my* salvation should look like, I will question them and hopefully now, others can, and will, too.

I believe when you read *Disorganized Christianity* you will discover some startling new revelations. Bible verses will mean something different now. Some of your most basic Bible beliefs *will be* challenged.

Genesis 1:26-27 *26 And God said, Let us make man in our image, after our likeness; and let them have dominion over the fish in the sea, and over the fowl of the air, and over the cattle, and over all the earth, and over* *every creeping thing that creepeth upon the earth. 27 So God created man in his own image, in the image of God created he him; male and female created he them.* I strongly disagree with this verse and believe that man actually has made God into man's own image. My reasoning is that if God did in fact make man and woman in his own image, why do we have so many different images and dogmas of God.

On April 15, 2018, I performed an Internet search for the *"largest world religions"* and got back 117,000,000 results. The five most consistent listings named: Christianity, Islam, Hinduism, Buddhism, and Sikhism. I then did a similar search for *"number of religions in the world"* that revealed a broad number ranging from 3,000 to 4,200 names of minor religions and followings. With this many salvation possibilities, how can any of them with absolute certainty declare their dogma alone will get anyone into Heaven?

While the overwhelming majority of the top five religions in the world do not even believe in Jesus Christ and the "pathway to Heaven through his virgin birth, death, and resurrection," and then having thousands of minor religions that may acknowledge Jesus Christ, but do not agree on a solid, consistent "Jesus doctrine," we have uncertainty and chaos.

I have spent many days and nights in heart-felt agony after talking to people about the biblical fact their loved ones, who have already passed away are not in Heaven, and that they will not ever be in a place called, Heaven.

I cannot tell you what is out there after we die. At this moment, I am not able to say where these loved ones are, even *my* mother. But I am confidant, without reservation in my mind, and with *King James Bible* verses backing my conclusions to declare, "I am absolutely able to say where they are not!"

I believe my interpretation of Jesus' non-existent biblical resurrection means that their loved ones are not in Heaven, but it also means they are not in a place called Hell.

I can assure anyone, with my Bible-based guarantee, after writing *Disorganized Christianity*, there is NO HELL! With all of the misinformational propaganda about almost every major biblical doctrine, I am saying there is no absolute basis for an eternal damnation in a place called Hell, proven in the Bible.

A very dear friend of mine shared with me the concept that in everything, we must strive for "balance" in our lives. My Balance: We *converted non-Christians* give *organized religion* the right to believe such stories without ridicule. Now, you *mean spirited and intolerant Christians* give us the right to not believe such stories, without your condemnation.

CHAPTER 1

In the beginning...

For most people it is getting easier than ever to imagine life without church. According to the Pew Research Center, 106 million Christians are expected to leave their *organized religion* between 2010 and 2050. Why? They are disillusioned. They are tired of punitive dogma. They sense that the Bible is filled with contradictions and man-made fables that are basically crossovers from the teachings of many different cultures that existed long before Christianity.

If we are to believe the Bible, then we must believe the following: There is one supreme being, GOD, who is loving and just and yet willing to condemn every living soul on this planet for the sin of eating an apple (actually a piece of unidentified fruit), committed by either Adam or Eve. *Disorganized Christianity*'s declaration is absolute: "Neither Adam nor Eve was the first of God's creations to sin and Eve NEVER sinned in the garden of Eden!"

The Bible asserts that there was a man/God named Jesus who led a sinless life, he died, was buried, and then rose again on the third day, and that these acts — if believed — could get you into a place called, "Heaven!"

Disorganized Christianity's declaration: "According to the Bible, this just didn't happen!"

The Bible states that the entire universe, including earth, was created in six days and six nights. God rested on the seventh day. The universe in its entirety is less than six thousand years old! *Disorganized Christianity's* declaration: "The universe, including the earth, moon and stars, is very much older than six thousand years."

Genesis 1:1-2 *1 In the beginning God created the heaven and the earth. 2 And the earth was without form, and void; and darkness was upon the face of the deep. And the Spirit of God moved upon the face of the waters.*

Nowhere in the Bible does it say that heaven and the earth was without form and void for a billion years and THEN the Spirit of God moved upon the face of the waters. The Bible says "God created the heaven and the earth in six days and six nights."

The entire premise of the Bible from Creation to the Great White Throne judgment seat is based on one action; Eve sinning in the Garden of Eden.

Disorganized Christianity will prove that there is not one verse that absolutely proves *that* dogma. Eve did not EVER *sin* in the Garden of Eden. *Disorganized Christianity* will offer an explanation for why it may *seem* she did, but the Bible gives no definitive proof that Eve willfully and knowingly sinned in the Garden of Eden. *Organized religion* took a unique situation and turned it into an absolute reason why we need their dogma. Those of us who identify as *converted non-Christians* do not need *organized religion* because there was no "first sin!"

It should be simple. God created us and loves us. God wants us to be in heaven with Him for eternity. *Organized religion* then had to create an *original sin* to condemn us all and make us *need* a Savior.

1 Corinthians 15:22 *For as in Adam all die, even so in Christ shall all be made alive:* **1 Timothy 2:14** *And Adam was not deceived, but the woman, being deceived, was in the transgression.*

The Bible asserts that Eve was in the transgression which led to mankind's spiritual death. Because of this transgression, we are now needing a Savior. Then we read in **Romans 15:14** *Nevertheless, death reigned from Adam to Moses, even over them that has not sinned after the similitude of Adam's transgression, who is the figure of him that was to come.*

Could the *"figure of him that was to come"* be Jesus because of Adam's transgression? I understood 1 Timothy 2:14 to say that the *woman* was in the transgression, not Adam. Hang on, it is going to be a bumpy ride!

To further confuse everyone, *organized religion* then devised a pathway to God that included a salvation message including a Jesus figure most major world denominations will not accept, and the smaller denominations can't or won't even agree on.

Organized religion then added a bunch of *"thou shalt nots"* for the purpose of keeping us in a constant state of guilt. *Organized religion* also blessed us with a bunch of *"thou shalts"* to keep us beholden to them for our daily walk with God.

Using *Disorganized Christianity* as our guide through the punitive dogma and selective service laid before us, we *converted non-Christians* will now say, "Not anymore!"

Whereas the biblical verses being taught today *could* have been accurate from the beginning of time, those verses have been mistranslated and misinterpreted by so many people with personal agendas centered on *proving their own position, and then using the Bible to serve their own purpose.*

I will not be a party to such translations and interpretations. I have no position to *prove*; my only purpose is to inform and expose.

Unlike *organized religion,* I do not hide behind any double meanings or catch phrases like *"that's not exactly what we meant,"* or *"you are taking the verse out of context,"* or *"God knows the real answer and will reveal it in God's own time,"* or the most famous deflection of all-time: *"we need to read that from the original text."*

Where *is* this original text?

Too many people talk as if there actually is a complete word for word "original text" available.

An easier question to answer than *where* the original text can be found, might be to consider *which* of the known "original texts" we should use? Do we reference the Hebrew 500 BCE Tanakh text, the Greek 250 BCE Septuagint text, the Dead Sea Scrolls, or do we give credence to the Latin and Early Vernacular Translations, or perhaps the Lindisfarne Gospels, or the Vulgate, or the Church of England version of the *King James Bible,* or just the earliest actual *King James Bible* we can find?

With each version claiming it is the "real" original, the world is left pondering the question of which writing *could* be the real original text?

The alleged absolute perfection of the entire Bible is not my main concern. The way *organized religion* manipulates translations, misinterpretations, and contradictions of its most crucial biblical events to *prove its own position, then serve its own purpose* and subsequently manipulate other Bible verses with an absolute punitive dogma to complete its *control of our condemnation on this earth and then declare the damnation of our souls in the hereafter is* my primary concern.

With all the conflicting biblical translations made by man in the course of the last 2000-plus years, I do *not* believe that the Holy Bible is God's *infallible* word to man. Once God gave the message to man, the mistranslations and misinterpretations began. My personal Christian faith was defined by what I believed and what I preached. I believed Jesus was born of a virgin. I believed that because Jesus led a sinless life he could be the only sacrifice to God for me. I believed that after Jesus was buried, he rose from the dead on the third day, and I *especially* believed — the best thing of all — that I would be raised from the dead also!

Nice and simple. Neat and tidy. No matter what age you are, this scenario could — and should — be believed even as a child.

Luke 18:17 *Verily I say unto you, Whosoever shall not receive the kingdom of God like a little child shall in no way enter it.*

As long as this scenario was maintained between me and a few chosen *King James Version Bible* verses and hopefully I didn't get challenged by *The Book of Mormon*; (Church of Jesus Christ of Latter-day Saints), *The Watchtower*; (Jehovah's Witnesses), the *Koran, The Christian Science Monitor* or worse, even another interpretation of the *King James Version Bible*, then I was pretty secure in my faith.

I was "saved" when I was 14 years old. At that time I did not know about any other Bible version than the *New Scofield Authorized King James Version* of God's word. I believed that the Bible my pastor was preaching from was the *only* Bible in the world. Why would there even *be* another Bible?

At 33 years of age, after preaching and teaching from that same *King James Bible*, I had heard there were a couple of Protestant versions of God's word around, but that the differences were very minor.

At 9:00 PM on September 18, 2012, I typed in the single word "Bible" into an Internet search. In less than 20 seconds, I got 449,000,000 results! I was amazed that there was an Internet database of 449,000,000 differing opinions on the Bible, which was — after all — declared to be the infallible word of God.

At 14, I believed there was only one Bible and I believed there was only one translation of the Bible. But if we are to believe that the Bible is God's inspired, infallible word, then we have a couple of troubling puzzles we must examine.

Our first puzzle has God verbally talking to man. We don't know *when* God spoke, nor to *whom* exactly God spoke, but we are supposed to believe that God *did* speak to man, and on a daily basis gave man what would eventually become the Bible. With all the different translations we have today, we can easily conclude that God's words were not memorized accurately.

The second puzzle is that man — hundreds of years later — wrote down the words spoken by God from memory, after they had been *verbally* passed from one generation to another. The most famous passing of scripture from one to another was when Moses was given the Ten Commandments personally by God, along with some help from a burning bush.

If the *basis* of any information is flawed, how can the *conclusions* of that information be anything but flawed?

I will show, using the *King James Version Bible*, that Bible conclusions are flawed because the very *basis* for the Bible information is flawed! By the time you finish reading *Disorganized Christianity,* you will understand that I am not trying to ruin or judge *your* Christianity. I just can't allow your Christianity to falsely condemn those who question, any longer. You keep your faith, we will find ours!

Many years ago, in 1985, I had a personal conflict with the *organized religion* church I was attending, and our differences could not be resolved. To achieve that separation was easier said than done. I was told "how bad a person" I was and that God would never bless me or answer another of my prayers ever again. My major problem, back then, was that I believed what I was being told. I simply didn't know any better.

In a reasonable world, I should have been able to leave the church in peace. I can still remember how I felt when I sincerely believed that God would never bless me again. It was a desperate feeling of loneliness and an abandonment that I firmly believe no one should ever have to feel.

I have stated I was a believer, but also that I had concerns. At that time, I did not want to be a Christian anymore for emotional reasons. Let me add, however, that now I also do not want to be a Christian for intellectual reasons. Whichever reasons I choose, then or now, and whatever reasons I base my decisions on, the Bible reads, "*but God hath called us to peace.*"

1 Corinthians 7:15 *15 But if the unbelieving depart, let him depart. A brother or a sister is not under bondage in such cases; but God hath called us to peace.* Even if I was a true *unbeliever*, I should have been able to leave in peace.

When I decided to walk away from Christianity, I had absolutely no intention of taking anyone with me. I just wanted out of the building, away from the parking lot, off the softball field, and for "anyone" to stop shooting. Bang! Bang! *Organized religion* would not let that happen.

When I left, *organized religion* had to make sure that I was driven out, because, as one pastor said, "Who in their right mind would ever leave us?"

Organized religion would not allow me to just walk away. *Organized religion* did not understand that I just wanted to go quietly. *Organized religion* would not let me go quietly. These particular Christians had to gossip and gossip, and then vomit some more gossip! Gossip can be true, and gossip can be false. But why gossip at all? Don't you have souls to save? Don't you have potlucks to prepare? Don't you have Bible commandments to memorize and then teach to others with your valuable time? Sadly, it seems those few *mean spirited and intolerant* Christians, although they do not outnumber loving Christians, often seem to have the loudest voices.

When I would not repent from what *organized religion* declared my sin(s) to be and "do the right thing," they decided that I needed some persuasion. This persuasion came in the form of judgments and condemnations. They actually had no clue as to the *real* motives for any of my actions that year, and nobody took the time to actually *ask* for a reason. Instead, everyone just guessed and judged!

Before Jesus was crucified, the Apostle Peter was told by Jesus that he, Peter, would deny Jesus three times. Understandably, Peter rejected Jesus' declaration. After fulfilling the prophesy and denying Jesus three times, Peter felt bad, but I don't believe it helped Jesus very much at the time. My best Christian friend at that time knew that *most* of the things being said about me were not true. My best Christian friend knew *some* of the things being said about me were true. Fully knowing both sides, my best Christian friend said he would stand by my side and get me through the tough time ahead. We had both seen what even loving Christians and *organized religion* could do to anyone who was found to be out of favor. My friend was told *not* to stand by me or he would be financially punished. He then chose to take care of his family.

I truly respected his decision, and I told him so, but I still felt crushed when he left. He was my hero. Another Bang! Bang!

That wasn't my first confrontation with *organized religion* though. The first incident happened when I was in my mid-teens, and it was over a *Blue Sequin Dress*. To my subsequent shame and sadness, I did not stand up for what I should have at the time. Maybe I was too young, or without enough self-worth or maybe I just felt too weak to want to make a stand. In hindsight *The Blue Sequin Dress* was the moment — the beginning — of *organized religion* telling me what was right and wrong by *their* standards, but not necessarily God's standards.

THE BLUE SEQUIN DRESS

I was a teenage preacher in my *organized religion's* youth group. Preaching was a little scary, but I did enjoy it. I preached my first sermon in a little church in Northern California. I actually have no recollection of what the exact salvation-themed sermon words were, but I do remember very vividly that when I had finished preaching, my friends congratulated me on my sermon, and one friend then asked me about the fly that kept landing on my nose. She said that she would have been very distracted if that had happened to her. It turns out the fly was a big drop of sweat that just attached itself to the end of my nose and every once in awhile, would drop off and another drop of sweat took its place. Oh, the things we remember.

I preached a couple of times in our church, and one day decided that I wanted my mother to come to church and hear *Her Son, The Preacher*. I desperately wanted my mother to be saved, and I thought that if she came to church and heard me preach, then she would accept Jesus as her personal Savior and everything would be fine with the universe. My mother said she would come to church. My mother actually said she would love to hear *Her Son, The Preacher*.

When I excitedly told the church leaders about my plans, they said my mother could only come to church if she wore a dress. You see, women could only wear dresses in a 1960's Baptist church. No Pants Allowed!

The church knew that my family was poor. My mother had only one dress to her name, and it had blue sequins all over it. My mother got married in that blue sequin dress. The blue sequin dress was mini-skirt short and even being a dress, would not have been acceptable for our *organized religion* church. You can come to church in hot pants or a tank top today, but now is now, and then was then. My mother made sure her kids had food and clothes before she bought anything extra. There was simply no money to buy an appropriate dress to hear *Her Son, The Preacher*.

As a result, my mother never heard her son preach. My mother never got saved, and the saddest part was that it didn't really bother me all that much until after she died in 1983. At the time of the *Blue Sequin Dress* incident, I did not think my mother would ever die. Mothers did not die. I did not yet know anyone whose mother had died. I believed I would always have time to *save her,* and then time just passed by.

After she died, I made a promise to my mother. I would never allow another *organized religion* or a member of any *organized religion* to ever send another mother to Hell because all they had to wear to church were pants or a *Blue Sequin Dress.* I do not believe in Hell anymore, and I would not allow anyone to think they were being sent to Hell by *organized religion!*

Although I did not even recognize it, my personal battle against Christian dogma actually began in my mid-teens. The battles started out as minor disagreements with my pastor, the deacons of the church, and the Sunday school teachers who taught me *dogma.* I sincerely believed these people were teaching me the Words of God, but it turned out they were teaching me the Words of Themselves; their own interpretations. What started out as confusing ideas because of my lack of true knowledge, became the dogma that grew into anger and distrust.

My anger and distrust were based on two simple premises. The first premise was that these dogmatic authorities' interpretations of certain verses I thought meant something good for me, ultimately, seemed to demonize me, rather than proving the love of Jesus and God. Their agenda was not for me to be free and happy in my Christian faith, but rather to be *bound and imprisoned* by my Christian faith. The second premise was that I was obligated to go along with *organized religion's* dogma because I did not know any better. Now, I *do* know better, and I will share my new understanding with anyone who wants to read about the death of many Christian dogmas.

Disorganized Christianity is my writing style, my words, my phrases, my emotions, my story, and not my editor's. I hired an editor to correct my grammar, not my soul.

I truly and humbly believe *Disorganized Christianity* will be an ember for the firestorm of corrected biblical information that will follow with its publication.

CHAPTER 2

Resurrection!

In the following Bible resurrection verses, I will be bringing into question the validity of the Bible's declaration of the resurrection of Jesus. I am also questioning: Why has Christianity, with its absolute unwavering dogmas about the resurrection, overlooked simple Bible verses that actually contradict this event and then with its incorrect traditions cast a shadow over the most important event in Christian faith?

Without an infallible biblical resurrection, it does not matter whether Jesus was born of a virgin. Without an infallible biblical resurrection, it does not matter whether Jesus lived a sinless life. Without an infallible biblical resurrection, Jesus' lineage does not matter. Without an infallible biblical resurrection, it does not matter whether Jesus was crucified on the cross. Without an infallible biblical resurrection, it does not matter whether Jesus was the Son of God.

1 Corinthians 15:12-19 *12 Now if Christ be preached that he rose from the dead, how say some among you that there is no resurrection of the dead? 13 But if there be no resurrection of the dead, then is Christ not risen; 14 And if Christ be not risen, then is our preaching vain, and your faith is* *also vain. 15 Yea, and we are found false witnesses of God, because we have testified of God that he raised up Christ, whom he raised not up, if so be that the dead rise not. 16 For if the dead rise not, then is not Christ raised; 17 And if Christ be not raised, your faith is vain, ye are yet in your sins. 18 Then they also who are fallen asleep in Christ are perished. 19 If in this life only we have hope in Christ, we are of all men most miserable.*

Without an infallible biblical resurrection, there is *no* basis for Christianity. So, why do Christians treat the resurrection so lightly?

The Bible actually gives a sign of prophesy that could identify Jesus or anyone as the true Son of man. **Matthew 12:38-40** *38 Then certain of the scribes and of the Pharisees answered, saying, Master, we would see a sign from thee. 39 But he answered and said unto them, An evil and adulterous generation seeketh after a sign, and there shall be no sign given to it, but the sign of the prophet, Jonah; 40 For as Jonah was three days and three nights in the belly of the great fish, so shall the Son of man be three days and three nights in the heart of the earth.*

In verse 39 the scribes and Pharisees asked Jesus (Master) for a sign and Jesus said, *"No!"* and then gives them a sign. The sign predicted that as Jonah was in the belly of the great fish for *three days and three nights,* so must Jesus after his crucifixion be in the heart of the earth *three days and three nights.*

Growing up, I was told Christianity was the only true religion because Jesus was the only Savior, Lord, Leader, Teacher or Prophet to be raised from the dead. Jesus rose from the dead so we could have the assurance we would be raised from the dead also.

2 Corinthians 4:14 *Knowing that he who raised up the Lord Jesus shall raise up us also by Jesus, and shall present us with you.* **I Corinthians 15:52** *In a moment, in the twinkling of an eye, at the last trump; for the trumpet shall sound, and the dead shall be raised incorruptible, and we shall be changed.*

Let's say that again!

The infallible Holy Bible gave a prophetic sign with a clear definition of who the Son of man and the Savior of the world would be. Christianity made this prophesy fit Jesus Christ, or did they? Christianity's faith, hope, and the authority of their resurrection dogma depends on this prophesy and its fulfillment.

Throughout time, other great religions never had a resurrected person or deity. Their leaders, figureheads, representatives, never even claimed to have been raised.

Buddhism: Siddhartha Gautama Buddha was born around 563 BC and died around 483 BC. Buddha had no writings of him ever being resurrected from the grave.

Hinduism: It is said Hinduism always existed. Although Hinduism does not have a founder, a key figurehead was Mahatma Gandhi. Mahatma Gandhi was born around 1869 and died around 1948. Mahatma Gandhi had no writings of him ever being resurrected from the grave.

Islam: Muhammad was born around 570 AD and died around 632 AD. Muhammad had no writings of him ever being resurrected from the grave.

Confucianism: Confucius was born around 551 BC and died around 479 BC. Confucius had no writings of him ever being resurrected from the grave.

To have a resurrected savior is significant in the scheme of a religion. A resurrected savior gives a sense of uniqueness. A resurrected savior gives a sense of superiority. A resurrected savior of course gives a sense of ultimate power over death. A resurrected savior gives a sense of divine order, from the beginning of time to the end of time as we understand it and then into eternity.

The prophesy of Jesus' New Testament resurrection is clearly stated in the book of Jonah in the Old Testament.

There is a story in the Old Testament about a very bad city called Ninevah. **Jonah 1:2** *Arise, go to Ninevah, that great city, and cry against it; for their wickedness is come up before me.*

God wanted Jonah to preach to the people in the city and get them to repent their wicked ways. Jonah basically told God, *"No thanks."* **Jonah 1:3** *But Jonah rose up to flee unto Tarshish from the presence of the Lord.*

Jonah then got on a ship that just happened to get caught in a storm God created. **Jonah 1:4** *But the Lord sent out a great wind into the sea, and there was a mighty tempest in the sea, so that the ship was in danger of being broken.*

Jonah told the ship's crew that the storm was his fault for not obeying God and then the ship's crew threw Jonah overboard. **Jonah 1:14-15** *14 Wherefore, they cried unto the Lord, we beseech thee, let us not perish for this man's life, and lay not upon us innocent blood; for thou, O Lord, hast done as it pleased thee. 15 So they took up Jonah, and cast him forth into the sea; and the sea ceased from its raging.*

With Jonah now floating in the sea, God had a great fish come to swallow him up. Our Sunday school story said it was a whale. The story goes on to say that Jonah stayed in the belly of the great fish for *three days and three nights,* fulfilling prophesy.

Jonah probably figured that God was going to leave him in the belly of the great fish forever. Jonah didn't know about God's plan and the *three days and three nights* timetable of Jesus' resurrection. On schedule, the great fish opened its mouth and vomited Jonah out onto dry land. **Jonah 2:10** *And the Lord spoke unto the fish, and it vomited out Jonah upon the dry land.*

After being vomited onto dry land, Jonah repented and went to Ninevah and cried out against the city. **Jonah 3:4** *And Jonah began to enter into the city a day's journey, and he cried, and said, Yet forty days, and Ninevah shall be overthrown.*

The city repented and God spared the city, **Jonah 3:10** *And God saw their works, that they turned from their evil way; and God repented of the evil that he had said that he would do unto them, and he did it not.*

Ninevah, a very bad city, had the ability to make God repent. I am not saying having God repent is a bad thing. I *am* saying that as absolute as God is made out to be, He sure did repent a lot and then turned away from the *evil* actions he was hell bent to fulfill. I am also asking whether God is capable or guilty of doing evil things? It says in verse 10 he is! Does that mean we can cause God to repent of *organized religion's* absolute condemnation of our souls, even if we do not obey the current Bible with man's mistranslations and misinterpreted rules?

This entire Old Testament story was to prophesy about the timetable of Jesus' resurrection. These two Bible verses are very important, so let's read them.

Old Testament Prophesy

Jonah 1:17 *Now the Lord had prepared a great fish to swallow up Jonah. And Jonah was in the belly of the fish three days and three nights.*

New Testament Prophesy

Matthew 12:40 *For as Jonah was three days and three nights in the belly of the great fish, so shall the Son of man be three days and three nights in the heart of the earth.*

Now, if Jesus was crucified and buried on Friday (Good Friday), stayed in the heart of the earth through Saturday, and then rose again on Sunday morning (Easter), the Bible prophesy of Jesus being the Son of man and Christianity's savior has a problem.

Matthew 16:21 *From that time forth began Jesus to show unto his disciples, how he must go unto Jerusalem, and suffer many things from the elders and chief priests and scribes, and be killed and be raised again the third day.*

Jesus told his disciples he would be raised again the third day. You would think Jesus knew on which day he was going to be raised from the dead. Jesus rose from the dead *on* the third day.

Luke 9:22 *Saying, The Son of man must suffer many things, and be rejected by the elders and chief priests and scribes, and be slain, and be raised the third day.* Jesus told his disciples he would be slain and be raised the third day. You would think Jesus knew on which day he was going to be raised from the dead. Jesus rose from the dead *on* the third day.

John 2:18-21 *18 Then answered the Jews, and said unto him, What sign showest thou unto us, seeing that thou doest these things? 19 Jesus answered, and said unto them, Destroy this temple, and in three days I will raise it up. 20 Then said the Jews, Forty and six years was this temple in building, and wilt thou raise it up in three days? 21 But he spoke of the temple of his body.*

Jesus not only said he would be raised *on* the third day, he said *he* would raise himself in three days. Jesus certainly would have known on which day he was going to be raised from the dead. And once again, Jesus rose from the dead *on* the third day.

Mark 8:31 *And he began to teach them, that the Son of man must suffer many things, and be rejected by the elders, and by the chief priests, and scribes, and be killed, and after three days rise again.*

In this case, Jesus told his disciples he would be killed and after three days rise again. You would think Jesus would know on which day he was going to be raised from the dead, but now we have Jesus raised from the dead after the third day.

Matthew 27:63 *Saying, Sir, we remember that the deceiver said, while he was yet alive, After three days I will rise again.*

The chief priests and Pharisees were talking to Pilate and said that they remembered the story told about Jesus and how he would be raised again *after* the third day. Again, we have Jesus being raised from the dead *after* the third day. Given just these few verses the "infallible" Bible has a very troublesome translation problem concerning how many days and nights Jesus actually spent in the *heart of the earth*.

Matthew 16:21, Luke 9:22, and John 2:18-21 read on the third day while Mark 8:31 and Matthew 27:63 read after three days. You might feel tempted to use the excuse that these are such short phrases and the books of the Bible were written at different times by different people, so it could just be a small mistake.

A major problem with that line of reasoning is that even Matthew — in the same book — cannot get the timing of the story straight.

With all of Christianity's prophesies and credibility on the line, the exact timing of whether Jesus rose from the dead , ON the third day or AFTER the third day is crucial. These verses represent the account of the resurrection, the single most important event in the Bible. I believe that the resurrection of Jesus is of much greater consequence than even his birth. Buddha, Gandhi, Muhammad and Confucius were all born, but none of them ever rose again. Only one major religious savior has claimed to be resurrected from the dead.

Does it matter when the resurrection happened and how it is celebrated? It should.

Matthew 28:1 *In the end of the Sabbath, as it began to dawn toward the first day of the week, came Mary Magdalene and the other Mary to see the sepulcher.*

As it began to dawn would lead us to believe that the visit by Mary Magdalene was at sunrise, *light out*, not dark. Christians celebrate Easter, the resurrection, with traditional sunrise services. Traditional, but not biblically true.

Mark 16:1-2 *1 And when the Sabbath was past, Mary Magdalene, and Mary, the mother of James, and Salome, had brought sweet spices, that they might come and anoint him. 2 And very early in the morning of the first day of the week, they came unto the sepulcher at the rising of the sun.* At the *rising of the sun* would lead us to believe that the visit by Mary Magdalene was at sunrise, *light out*, not dark. Christians celebrate Jesus' resurrection with traditional sunrise, *At the rising of the sun,* services. Traditional, but not biblically correct.

Luke 24:1 *Now upon the first day of the week, very early in the morning, they came unto the sepulcher, bringing the spices which they prepared, and certain others with them.*

Luke 24's version of *very early in the morning* could mean the visit by Mary Magdalene was at dawn or sunrise, *light out*, like the other versions, but I will offer the possibility it was very early in the morning and still dark. Why still dark?

John 20:1 *The first day of the week cometh Mary Magdalene early, when it was yet dark, unto the sepulcher, and seeth the stone taken from the sepulcher.* In John 20:1 it is early, but in Mark 16:1-2, it is very early. In my opinion "very early" is earlier than "early" and in the Mark 16:1-2 version of *"very early at the rising of the sun,"* it is *light out* and in the John 20:1 version of *early* it is *dark out*. John 20:1 *it was yet dark*. I am not interpreting it is *light* or *dark* in these Bible verses by manipulating any words. The

Bible translations are using the words *rising of the sun*, light and *it was yet dark*, dark.

When we look at all the verses closely, it is either *at the rising of the sun*, barely the beginning of the morning or *it was yet dark*, before the light of day. These *Mary Magdalene visiting the tomb* contradictions are no more unusual than those found in other Bible stories.

The resurrection problem is not *that* the visit by Mary Magdalene alternately happened at either light or dark — even though the timing is contradictory — but the revealing fact that Jesus *had already risen*, before either version of the Marys even got there.

If both Marys arrived in the dark or early at the rising of the sun, it follows that Jesus rose from the dead *in the dark!* And yet, the scriptures state that Jesus rose *before* the third day, not *on* the third day or even *after* the third day. In addition to the obvious ambiguity of the third day morning resurrection of the prophesy, we also do not have a "Sunday night." As matter of simple fact, Christians have never even *claimed* that Jesus was in the heart of the earth on Sunday night. Remember the prophesy states, "Three days and three nights."

Now, with their Sunday sunrise service verses in jeopardy, Christianity also may now not even have a third *day*.

I had read all of these verses dozens of times when I as a young Christian and never comprehended the significance that Jesus had already risen, *before* the third day. And then, one day the revelation that Jesus had already risen before Mary Magdalene's visit just became obvious, even though the fact had always been there.

Could there possibly be other facts for us to uncover? Let's see what we can find together!

The four gospels account for the *visit* of the Marys: in Matthew, *began to dawn;* Mark, *at the rising of the sun;* Luke, *very early in the morning,* and then John, *when it was yet dark.* However, it really doesn't matter *when* the visit took place. We read in **Matthew 28:5-6** *5 And the angel answered and said unto the women, Fear not; for I know that ye seek Jesus, who was crucified. 6 He is not here; for he is risen.* Jesus did not *have a sunrise service* resurrection! Jesus did not *have* a third day or a third night in the heart of the earth.

New Testament Prophesy

Matthew 12:40 *For as Jonah was three days and three nights in the belly of the great fish, so shall the Son of man be three days and three nights in the heart of the earth.*

My revelation is that Jesus was not in the heart of the earth for three days and three nights. The Bible declared this sequence of events as a prophesy to define the Son of man in Jonah 1 and Matthew 12. Now, let's count the days and nights; Friday night, Saturday day, Saturday night and then Sunday day. Even if we allow Friday *day* (which I am not willing to do), you can not in any way, shape or form end up with Sunday night!

But yet, *both* Friday day and Sunday night are *needed* in order to fulfill Christianity's prophesy and at this point even Sunday *day* is in question. We have a problem!

Friday night: buried
Saturday: day
Saturday: night
Sunday day: resurrection

Traditional, but not biblical.

If you had a Thursday night burial (which *is not* celebrated today) and a Sunday morning after day light resurrection (which *you do* celebrate today) you would have had an *on the third day* resurrection. But, you would still not have an *after* three days resurrection. Let's examine *that* option:

Thursday night: buried
Friday: day
Friday: night
Saturday: day
Saturday: night
Sunday day: resurrected

If you had a Friday night crucifixion (which you *do* celebrate today) *and* a Sunday night in the *heart of the earth* (which you *do not* celebrate today) and then a Monday resurrection (which you also *do not* celebrate today) you would have ended up with a *on the third day* resurrection. But, you would still not have an *after three days* resurrection:

Friday night: buried
Saturday: day
Saturday: night
Sunday: day
Sunday: night
Monday day: resurrected

None of these projected examples are close to being fulfilled for a *three days and three nights in the heart of the earth* prophesy. The Bible account of Jesus as being the Messiah does not have an *after three days and three nights in the heart of the earth,,* in any scenario.

Which begs the question of; which is it — *on the third day* or *after the third day or is it really Friday night, Saturday day and Saturday night*? Do we have yet another biblical contradiction or misinterpretation problem?

We might consider whether the accounting of the *three days and three nights* prophesy is actually crucial to biblical credibility or is it okay to be a little off?

But how can *organized religion* assure us that God's *infallible word* really is *infallible* when the resurrection timetable is not even correct? Similarly, if the Bible is the *infallible* Word of God and *organized religion* is not absolutely correct in its translation, then its authority must be seriously flawed or, at least be in question. I say that if *organized religion* represents God and God's absolute eternal judgment to send us *converted non-Christians* to *hell,* then *organized religion* had better make sure God's word is absolutely flawless and *infallible!*

I do not care whether *organized religion* agrees with my analysis. I am *not* here to change *their* minds. I am here to give intellectual and spiritual support to any *converted non-Christian*, who might have questions, and have found themselves condemned for doing so.

Disorganized Christianity offers a better and more solid common sense argument based on actual Bible verses than *organized religion* can use against us *converted non-Christians,* using the interpretation of their own translated Bible verses.

Jonah 1:17 *Now the Lord had prepared a great fish to swallow up Jonah. And Jonah was in the belly of the fish three days and three nights.* The Old Testament absolutely declares the prophesy of three days and three *nights in the belly of the great fish* for Jonah. Since no one celebrates Jonah and his great fish ride, there is no way to legitimize Jonah's *three days and three nights* adventure.

Matthew 12:40 *For as Jonah was three days and three nights in the belly of the great fish, so shall the Son of man be three days and three nights in the heart of the earth.* The New Testament absolutely declares the prophesy of *three days and three nights in the heart of the earth* for Jesus. If my calculations are correct and the *infallible* Bible proves Jesus was not in the heart of the earth *three days and three nights*, is Jonah and the great fish prophesy now just a cute story? And if my biblical calculations are correct, has Jesus' resurrection now been reduced also to just a cute story?

Because the *infallible* Bible has been successfully challenged and found to be incorrect on the resurrection timetable, will *organized religion* now have to declare the Jonah and Jesus prophesies as nothing more than cute stories?

If — with this new information in hand — this is your stand, what other prophetic messages might have been misinterpreted and could now be considered little more than just cute stories? It certainly brings into question a little more of the Bible's controlling authority. With each newly revealed contradiction and misinterpretation, it would appear that *organized religion* gives up a little more controlling and condemning authority.

Now that the declaration and explanation of the *three days and three nights* in the heart of the earth has been brought into question, I would like to clarify that I am not saying absolutely that the Bible *says* Friday, Saturday and Sunday. Of course, some committed Bible scholar, Orthodox Jewish Rabbi or just someone else reading with a new set of eyes and searching with a different heart might be able to take a particular Bible translation and prove that Jesus actually was buried on Thursday night at dusk and then resurrected on Sunday *after* sunrise. I have also read interpretations stating that Jesus was *really* buried on Wednesday night and had a Saturday morning after sunrise resurrection in keeping with the original Jewish Saturday Sabbath and not the Catholic and Protestant Sunday Sabbath. But even these interpretations would become more difficult to make chronologically accurate now that we have read and understand **John 20:1** ... *while it was yet dark,* before the third day!

The Bible does talk about an extra High Sabbath in the middle of the crucifixion week. This particular High Sabbath was in addition to the regular Sabbath during the week of the crucifixion. Technically speaking, if you take the Sabbath and High Sabbath and manipulate the fact that the crucifixion really did take place on Thursday, then you could possibly show three days and three nights with a Sunday after sunrise resurrection, on the third day. But then you still have to contend with John 20:1. The first day of the week cometh Mary Magdalene early, when it was yet dark, which again takes out the sunrise resurrection. *Disorganized Christianity* will keep a watchful eye and ear out for that one. Nice try and close though! I feel absolutely certain that new revelations and new challenges will quickly follow. In addition to John 20:1, the Bible still has to contend with the numerous and very clearly stated contradictions found in the on the third day and after the third day verses.

No matter how much *organized religion* might try to dismiss *Disorganized Christianity*, they will still have to rationalize John 20:1 where Jesus had already raised from the dead before the third day, regardless of whether it be Saturday or Sunday.

Christianity today observes a Friday *night* (at dusk) Good Friday, Saturday *day* and Saturday *night*, and Sunday *day* (after sunrise) Easter. If my alternative scenarios of the three days and three nights analysis are wrong, (and realize you have to prove that I am wrong first), *organized religion* is still incorrect for celebrating the resurrection the way it does. Traditional, but not biblical.

I do not know —and cannot even *begin* to explain nor even care to try to explain — how this *three days and three night's* contradiction or misinterpretation could have gone on for so long. This conflicting timetable has evidently been missed or ignored by almost everyone and corrected by no one.

I have read how a number of people have *noticed* and even questioned the *three days and three nights'* contradiction/misinterpretation, yet have not been willing to declare the importance of this glaring misrepresentation.

I would willingly agree that it would not matter whether something was wrong, if the error had no significance. But accuracy surrounding the resurrection of Jesus Christ, your Savior — arguably THE single most important pillar underlying Christianity — should be significant.

Disorganized Christianity is making the declaration that *organized religion's control and condemnation* of *converted non-Christians* stops today! The resurrection story is important and essentially vital to any Christian's faith. The glaring inconsistencies have to go if you intend to give your declaration of faith any credibility.

As you fact check *Disorganized Christianity* against other sources, you will find many explanations surrounding the *three days and three nights* prophesy. I only ask that you read the *entire* explanations. Some of the logic might actually make sense in a fragmented way. Facts will seem sensible at the *beginning* of an explanation. If the explanations only have to address *parts* of the story, they can be made to work. But when you get to the middle or towards the end of these explanations that is where Christianity will most likely throw in a *"blah, blah, blah and then blah"* statement to close the argument.

The statement *"blah, blah, blah and then blah"* is my expression used to describe any Christian's non-valid response to — or deliberate evasion of — a valid question. These statements can *start out* with sufficient credibility so the weak and inconclusive endings will become shrouded behind those strong beginnings and mediocre middles.

An example of such a *blah, blah, blah and then blah* explanation might sound something like this: "The unusual High Sabbath in the middle of the week, which was actually the first Sabbath of the week, but did not actually effect the second traditional Sabbath of the week, was recorded as a one time special occurrence that was discovered and recorded by a NASA computer and, therefore, the time continuum based on the flux capacitor readings could really have caused a skewed quantum molecular disturbance that made it appear that Jonah was really on a submarine in the ocean and not in the actual belly of a great fish. So, it really does not matter if it was *on three days and three nights* or *after three days and three nights* anyway."

Just thought I would try it. Did you feel baffled and confused?

One of the most frequently used rebuttals to the three days and three nights contradiction is that the meaning of the words three days and three nights is actually satisfied because when you say one day, it really means both night and day or when you say one day or one night, you are actually fulfilling a 24 hour timeline. This rebuttal explains if you say one day, it really means both night and day, therefore the Friday night really counts as one day (not fulfilled) and one night (fulfilled) and then you had Saturday, where the one day (was fulfilled) and the one night (was fulfilled) and then you had the Sunday day (which was fulfilled or maybe not) and the night (not fulfilled).

But how does Saturday actually count as one day and one night, but the Friday night and Sunday day do not have to hold up to the day and night standard?

Genesis 1:3-5 *3 And God said, Let there be light: and there was light. 4 And God saw the light, that it was good: and God divided the light from the darkness. 5 And God called the light Day, and the darkness he called Night. And the evening and the morning were the first day.*

According to the Creation story: God created the heavens and the earth in six days and six nights. In Genesis Chapter One we actually find six verses declaring that it takes an evening and a morning to make "a day."

Genesis 1:5 *And God called the light Day, and the darkness he called Night. And the evening and the morning were the first day.*

Genesis 1:8 *And God called the firmament Heaven. And the evening and the morning were the second day.*

Genesis 1:13 *And the evening and the morning were the third day.*

Genesis 1:19 *And the evening and the morning were the fourth day.*

Genesis 1:23 *And the evening and the morning were the fifth day.*

Genesis 1:31 *And God saw every thing that he had made, and, behold , it was very good. And the evening and the morning were the sixth day.*

The Bible clearly states just one evening or just one morning does not make one day. The Bible clearly states the evening and the morning are needed to make a day. That being the case, it would also take an evening and a morning each to satisfy the prophesy of three days and three nights in the heart of the earth.

You can play with words all you like, but if you go back to the Jews and their timelines of a 12-hour day and a 12-hour night separated by sunset and sunrise, you will find that they were very exact as to what constituted a day and what constituted night.

John 11:9 *Jesus answered, Are there not twelve hours in the day? If any man walk in the day, he stumbleth not, because he seeth the light of this world.*

It only seems logical that if there is a day and a night, and if Jesus says that there are twelve hours in a day, then there must be twelve hours in a night. Furthermore, if Jesus was the King of the Jews and the Jews were God's chosen people, and the Bible was written about the Jewish people and their Messiah, then it only seems fair and logical to use Jewish time lines to describe day and night and what three days and three nights really are meant to be. You would never hear a Messianic Jew argue that a sunset is not the start of a night and that sunrise is not the start of a day, nor that they could be the same time, even if they were trying to prove that Jesus' resurrection was on the third day or after the third day!

I once had a discussion with a very good friend of mine who believed that all three days and nights were fulfilled using the above interpretation of one day being both day and night. His mind was perfectly made up that he was correct and that I was not going to convince him otherwise. He proceeded to get a little upset, because I would not agree with him. I could see the rising frustration in his eyes and hear it in his voice. What he did not understand, even though I reassured him I was not trying to convince him he was wrong, was that I did not care what he believed. He is free to believe anything he wants. I just wanted him to understand that his existence was not diminished by his beliefs, and he did not have to prove that I was wrong.

We will accept your challenges, as long as we all play by a certain set of rules.

Yes, they are *my* rules. But I believe that most people will find them agreeable. If you do not like my rules, then stop reading *Disorganized Christianity,* After all, I stopped reading *your* Bible!

Romans 10:14 and 17 *14 How, then, shall they call on him in whom they have not believed? And how shall they believe in him whom they have not heard? And how shall they hear without a preacher? 17 So, then, faith cometh by hearing, and hearing by the word of God.*

This verse states that our faith comes from hearing the word of God; the Bible. I believe it is God's moral responsibility to be certain that the faith we are supposed to have — that we hear about in God's word — is the exact faith that God is going to judge us on.

MY RULES:

1) Thou shalt not use an interpretation, as fact, that you heard about in a lost historical writing that many brilliant scholars agree with, that says, "black is white and white is really the new shade of gray," *without*

naming the lost historical writing and providing the current location of the actual documents that are being interpreted. You must also name the brilliant scholars, their credentials and their motivation for agreeing to this new interpretation.

2) Thou shalt not say that in the original text, *this* word really means *that* and *that* word really means *this*, so *Disorganized Christianity* is "wrong," without declaring which *original text* you are quoting from and then providing the location of that *original text* being used to support your argument.

3) Thou shalt not say that *this* word really means *that* and *that* word really means *this*, "*because.*" My mother told me more than once that *because* is not an answer. I am going to honor my mother's wisdom in this matter. **Exodus 20:12** *12 Honor thy father and thy mother, that thy days may be long upon the land which the Lord thy God giveth thee.*

4) Thou shalt not say that, "God spoke to *you* last night and personally gave *you* a new translation or a new revelation." **Revelation 22:18** *For I testify unto every man that heareth the words of the prophesy of this book, If any man shall add unto these things, God shall add unto him the plagues that are written in this book; 19 And if any man shall take away from the words of the book of this prophesy, God shall take away his part from the tree of life, and out of the holy city, and from the things which are written in this book.*

5) Thou shalt not judge, lest ye be judged! To *mean spirited and intolerant* Christians who have read the Bible, that means that you may not judge somebody for what they do and then demand that everyone ignore what they could judge *you* for. I only explain this rule because *mean spirited and intolerant* Christians do not really seem to understand that *thou shalt not judge.*

All of these *"thou shalt nots"* remind me of the Bible. To offer a sense of "balance," let us try some *"thou shalt"* rules.

1) Thou shalt love one another in your interpretations, so that others might grow from them and be blessed by them, not be *controlled* or *condemned* by them. **Hebrews 10:24** *And let us consider one another to provoke unto love and to good works,*

2) Thou shalt interpret the Bible with God's honor and God's love for mankind at the heart of your interpretation and *not* succumb to imposing *your own agenda* in the name of God.

A CLOSER LOOK AT APOSTLES

Matthew 10:2-4 *2 Now the names of the twelve apostles are these: the first, Simon, who is called Peter, and Andrew, his brother; James, the son of Zebedee, and John, his brother; 3 Philip and Bartholomew; Thomas and Matthew, the tax collector; James, the son of Alphaeus, and Lebbaeus, whose surname was Thaddaeus; 4 Simon, the Canaanite, and Judas Iscariot, who also betrayed him.*

These twelve men were the original Apostles who followed Jesus around during his ministry, and he must have told them many wondrous things about the past, present, and future of why he came down to earth!

These 12 Apostles' names are found in three books of the Bible: Matthew 10:2-4, Mark 3:16-19, and Luke 6:13-16. In Acts 1:13 eleven Apostles are named minus Judas Iscariot. In Acts 1:26 we find that Matthias was chosen to replace Judas Iscariot by a casting of lots. The Apostle Paul was not the apostle that replaced Judas Iscariot. Saul of Tarsus, who later became Paul, was self-appointed as an Apostle. The Apostle Paul never actually met Jesus, and, in fact, spent most of his pre-apostle time persecuting and killing Christians.

The Apostle Paul is still a very controversial figure, mainly for two reasons. The Apostle Paul very rarely agreed with the eleven other chosen Apostles regarding the Jesus message, and he is best known for being the Apostle to the Gentiles.

Romans 11:13 *For I speak to you Gentiles, inasmuch as I am the apostle of the Gentiles, I magnify mine office.*

Get ready for a truly astounding revelation that was not given to me by the higher powers of the universe or God, but can be found — like many more hidden verses — in your scriptures, if you just read with a "new set of eyes and understand with a different heart." The Bible went to great lengths — including Jesus verbally, who actually commanded his Apostles — to exclude the Gentiles from the Jesus salvation message.

Matthew 10:5-6 *5 These twelve Jesus sent forth, and commanded them, saying, Go not into the way of the Gentiles, and into any city of the Samaritans enter not. 6 But go, rather, to the lost sheep of the house of Israel.*

In Jesus' own words, recorded in God's *infallible* word, he came for the Jews, not the rest of us. I guess that could place us at another crossroads of confusion in scripture where we proclaim "Well, not exactly," again!

John 3:16 *For God so loved the world, that he gave his only begotten Son, that whosoever believeth in him should not perish, but have everlasting life.*

Did Jesus change his mind? Or did God change His mind about only the house of Israel being worthy? Or did *organized religion's* interpretation or actual rewriting of God's infallible word conveniently include the masses to satisfy their own agenda? Which *infallible* Words of God eventually included anyone besides the Jews? Yes, I was confused. I never read such a thing, nor was my personal exclusion in the original Jesus message ever pointed out to me.

The names of the Apostles given in various Bible versions include a little controversy over a couple of the Apostles having different names, while still being the same person. For example, Nathaniel and Bartholomew are supposed to be the same person. Thaddeus, Jude, and a second Judas are allegedly the same person. These supposedly different names given to a couple of the original twelve Apostles are not earth shattering, but this detail is consistent with biblical translation problems.

The Bible does not give a clear and definitive answer for the number of years the Apostles and other disciples followed Jesus during his ministry. The number ranges from one year to three and a half years, depending again on who is interpreting Jesus' timeline for *miracles and preaching*.

If these twelve Apostles left their homes, families, and professions to follow and be taught by some preacher, doesn't it seem logical to think that they would have known that Jesus was going to be crucified, buried, and then rise again from the dead? At the time of the resurrection, they didn't. Simon Peter and another disciple went into the tomb of Jesus, and the Bible says that they still didn't know what was going on, nor what had actually happened.

John 20:9 *For as yet they knew not the scripture, that he must rise again from the dead.*

Twelve apostles and many disciples were with Jesus personally, night and day, for one year to three and a half years. These followers were being trained personally, by Jesus himself, to carry on a message of salvation for the Jews. According to the Bible, even after Jesus' crucifixion, burial, and resurrection, they were still unclear as to what the message was. Even today, we are still addressing — with all of these misinterpretations and different translations — unclear commandments and punishments in a Bible---God's verbal and written words, that are 4,000 to 6,000 years old.

In **Luke 24:6-11** *6 He is not here, but is risen! Remember how he spoke unto you when he was yet in Galilee, 7 Saying, The Son of man must be delivered into the hands of sinful men, and be crucified, and the third day rise again. 8 And they remembered his words, 9 And returned from the sepulcher, and told all these things unto the eleven, and to all the rest. 10 It was Mary Magdalene, and Joanna, and Mary, the mother of James, and other women that were with them, who told these things unto the apostles. 11 And their words seemed to them as idle tales, and they believed them not.*

Early in the morning when a group of Jesus' supporters came to the burial tomb, they were surprised to find the tomb empty. The two angels at Jesus' tomb had to remind them that Jesus did teach them about his death, burial, and resurrection. Those angels reminded everyone that Jesus had, in fact, taught them about his death, burial, and resurrection, and then they remembered. After they did remember Jesus' teachings, they were not very effective in getting other supporters to believe Jesus had risen from the grave.

Again, these are in most cases hand-picked followers of Jesus, and yet they did not even have a clue about why they were dedicating their lives and futures. I remember my mother asking me, "Didn't you hear what I said?" OK, I had a different agenda of having fun that hot summer day instead of mowing the lawn. Who's fault was that? Certainly not hers!

John 14:1-9 *1 Let not your heart be troubled; ye believe in God, believe also in me. 2 In my Father's house are many mansions; if it were not so, I would have told you. I go to prepare a place for you. 3 And if I go and prepare a place for you, I will come again, and receive you unto myself, that where I am, there ye may be also. 4 And where I go ye know, and the way ye know. 5 Thomas saith unto him, Lord, we know not where thou goest; and how can we know the way? 6 Jesus saith unto him, I am the way, the truth, and the life; no man cometh unto the Father, but by me. 7 If ye had known me, ye should have known my Father also; and from henceforth ye know him, and have seen him. 8 Philip saith unto him, Lord, show us the Father, and it sufficeth* *us. 9 Jesus saith unto him, Have I been such a long time with you, and yet hast thou not known me, Philip? He that hath seen me hath seen the Father; and how sayest thou then, Show us the Father?*

Jesus challenged and then reminded Thomas and Philip, who had been with Jesus the entire time of his ministry on earth, that they still did not know who he was.

Let's say that again!

For a period of one to three and a half years Jesus personally taught his chosen twelve Apostles and other disciples that he would be crucified, buried, and then rise again from the dead. When the time came to appreciate and revel in the glory of these resurrection events, Jesus' followers did not even remember — maybe they just never understood — the prophesy. Either way, my concern is that if Jesus could not verbally convince his own personally chosen twelve Apostles — over a period of possibly only a few years — of his crucifixion, burial, and resurrection from the dead, why should we be expected to believe the same story after it has been passed down verbally for centuries, from agenda to agenda, and, then, to an *organized religion* with ulterior motives?

CHAPTER 3

Questions?

Many people have asked me "How did you find all of these scriptures?" They said to me, "I have read the Bible all my life, and I didn't see these scriptures. I actually remember reading those passages, but I never saw that."

Well, I read those same passages for 19-plus years, and I did not see them either. I even preached from these same scriptures. One day, I just started reading with a new set of eyes and started searching with a different heart.

Acts 17:10-11 *10 And the brethren immediately sent away Paul and Silas by night unto Berea: who coming hither went into the synagogue of the Jews. 11 These were more noble than those at Thessalonica, in that they received the word with all readiness of mind, and searched the scriptures daily, whether those things were so.*

Well, one day I went home to find out *whether those things were so.*

Hopefully, you will also go home after reading *Disorganized Christianity* and read your Bible with a new set of eyes and search with a different heart. I started my new search with a very *angry* heart because I was going to show *those mean spirited and intolerant* Christians a thing or two! In time, my angry heart has changed to a very sad heart. Sad, that so many *mean spirited and intolerant* Christians have used and abused their understanding and misinterpretation of their scriptures — no matter which version they use — to *control and condemn* anyone who does not obey the Bible *their* way.

I wrote this book in the hope that *mean spirited and intolerant* Christians will never be able to succeed in *controlling or condemning* anyone, again. I harbor no delusions that *organized religion* will not belittle *Disorganized Christianity.* I believe *organized religion* will also attack me for the things I have done in the past which are *true* and also attack me for things in the past which are *not true.*

The Salem witch hunts were not really about hunting witches. The act of hunting witches was just another sordid chapter about people gaining spiritual power and silencing anyone who would dare to question and oppose them.

In 1 Samuel Chapter Three, we read about mediums and witches, and how even against God's commandment to cast them out of the land, the Israelite leaders ignored God and consulted mediums and witches anyway to gain extra knowledge. Much like the Israelite leaders, it seems that *organized religion* will do whatever it takes to get its own way when God will not grant their agenda!

If you can discredit the messenger, then it follows naturally that you can discredit the message. You may be able to discredit *me* as a person, but *Disorganized Christianity* shares a message that will not be discredited because doing so would also require *organized religion* to discredit the *source* of the evidence used: *their* Bible.

I am absolutely convinced there are more verses in the Bible that we have *all* overlooked. Some of these overlooked — or previously not even *recognized* — verses might hold the truth that will set all *converted non-Christians* free from *organized religion's* controlling dogma.

John 8:31-32 *31 Then said Jesus to those Jews who believed on him, If ye continue in my word, then are ye my disciples indeed; 32 And ye shall know the truth, and the truth shall make you free.*

Before we go looking for new hidden verses though, let's see what we actually *know* about what we *think* we already know. At the end of this chapter I have provided a few basic questions for you to ponder, and I have provided some blank space for you to write down your answers. I believe it is important that you write down your answers, as you come to understand the *questions*. If you do not write down your answers, and you just glance at the *questions* and then answer them in your mind, you could fall into the trap of translation or interpretation errors.

We humans have a remarkable ability to convince ourselves *as facts*, things we have not actually proven to ourselves to be factual. The problem is that we do not *want* to hold ourselves accountable to the real truth if that could possibly force us to have to change not only our thoughts and actions, but the entire foundation upon which we have based our concept of reality. Even today, we just want to understand enough, or memorize enough, to *prove our own position and then use that information to serve our own purpose.*

I believe that inadequate knowledge of facts and the pursuit of personal agendas form the basis for all *new* Bible translations and misinterpretations from the beginning of time. We get most of our new translations or new interpretations directly from God through the televangelist who spouts, "God spoke to me last night," and "God said I am going to give you special wisdom that only you deserve."

I remember how Oral Roberts, one great patriarch of the faith, in the mid-1980's claimed that God told him to raise $8,000,000 or God would call him home. In due course, the congregation raised the money. Oral Roberts also said a 900-foot Jesus told him to build the City of Faith Medical and Research Center. And they built the center. These two alleged God spoken revelations came to pass.

Does that mean these God spoken revelations really came from God? Is it wrong to challenge these God spoken revelations because they only included the *raise the money* part, but then God "forgot" to add in the spoken revelation of how to *manage the money*? The money is gone, and the purpose of the spoken revelations is not what the moneychangers sold the flock. Was it still God's true spoken revelation given that the entities left today are not even a shadow of what was originally promised? It is odd that we only hear about the *send the money* part, but never get a detailed follow-up on the results of the money being squandered without any accountability; except for being told that God knows why and it is not for us to question God's will.

If you're interested in learning more, www.believersweb.org/view.cfm?ID=556 has a very complete article on this subject, both good and bad.

I am not trying to just single out Oral Roberts. Oral Roberts simply happened to be one of the spiritual leaders most of us knew about and believed in during the 1970's, 80's and 90's.

If a new scriptural translation or new interpretation is revealed from a recently discovered clay pot in another part of the desert, or a recently discovered manuscript found underneath some other old manuscripts in an ancient library, or perhaps in the Vatican archives and then our preachers say, "Yes, you must believe whatever I understand this message from God to say," do we have to believe it is true?

Be careful with all of these new translations or new interpretations!

Consider **Revelation 22:18-19** *18 For I testify unto every man that heareth the words of the prophesy of this book, If any man shall add unto these things, God shall add unto him the plagues that are written in this book; 19 And if any man shall take away from the words of the book of this prophesy, God shall take away his part from the tree of life, and out of the holy city, and from the things which are written in this book.*

Some people argue that these verses refer to the entire Bible while other people argue that this book concerns only the book of Revelation. Whichever book it might be, leave it alone! *Organized religion* should stop adding to, and taking away from, the Bible. Why was the Catholic Church of England given a new translation? The Roman Church was already established in England. The Catholic Church of England has to be one of the best examples of all time of *proving your own position to then serve your own purpose.*

King Henry VIII was married to Catherine of Aragon but wanted to marry Anne Boleyn, a woman 20-plus years younger. The Pope did not want to grant King Henry VIII's requested annulment. Even in those days, King Henry VIII knew not to go directly against the church. Instead, King Henry VIII waited a while, separated from Catherine, married Anne and in 1533 — after he had changed church rules making himself the boss — had his first marriage annulled.

This is the "quick version" most of us understand as the beginning of the new Church of England. The example of King Henry VIII's proving his own position to then serve his own purpose is better explained by the following text.

I have tried to make *Disorganized Christianity* my own book, with my own thoughts and in my own words. In the new Church of England case however, I believe we need a historical view or interpretation of the events written by scholars.

Let's start by reading the rest of the Church of England story. I have searched the Internet and library bookshelves and found numerous accounts of the earliest days of the Catholic Church of England. I have tried to find the most understandable version of this historical event. God did not help me with my version choice anymore than I believe God helped other translators and interpreters of the many versions of the Bible out there. I do not have a political or monetary bias for the version I chose. I chose this version because it mirrored all the other accounts and did not make any of the players out to be any worse or better than they could already be determined to be, according to any other version. In "The Story of Christianity, An Illustrated History of 2000 years of the Christian Faith," David Bentley Hart writes, starting on page 200:

The Catholic Church In England

The Anglican Church was not born out of any great popular movement for reform in England; nor did it begin as a Protestant establishment. When King Henry VIII (1491-1547) had himself declared head of the Church in his dominions, he understood this to mean head of the Catholic Church in England. In breaking with the pope, he did not intend to adopt an Evangelical theology or Church discipline. He detested Martin Luther and took pride in his title 'Defender of the Faith', which the pope had granted him for writing an anti-Lutheran defence of Catholic sacramental theology entitled Assertio Septem Sacramentorum ('The Defence of the Seven Sacraments") in 1521.

Indeed, the hesitancy with which reform was embraced in England left its mark on the communion ever after; not only in its historical emphasis upon the need to preserve the 'Apostolic Succession' (the direct continuity of its bishops in a line of consecration going back to the Apostles), or in the existence

41

today of Anglican monastic orders, but in the regularity with which 'High Church" movements have arisen that have been theologically, liturgically, and devotionally committed to the position that the Anglican Church is a Catholic communion.

Henry would not have broken with Rome at all had he been able to procure an annulment of his marriage to Catherine of Aragon (1485-1536) – supposedly on biblical grounds –so that he might marry the younger Anne Boleyn (c. 1507-36) and so perhaps produce a male heir. The pope dared not grant such a request, however, since Catherine was the aunt of the holy Roman Emperor Charles V (1500-58). In 1531, after seven years of waiting, Henry separated from Catherine; a year and a half later, he married Anne; and five months after that, he had the new archbishop of Canterbury, Thomas Crammer (1489-1556) – Henry's own appointment in 1533 – officially declare the first marriage annulled.

The Monarch's Supremacy

Crammer (who had Lutheran leanings) counselled Henry to note that, in scripture, it is kings – and not popes – who are God's anointed rulers over all spheres, spiritual no less than temporal. This suited both Henry's taste for the new, 'French' monarchical absolutism, and the political designs of Thomas Cromwell (c. 1485-1540), the powerful head of the king's Privy Council, who in 1534 convinced Parliament to pass the 'Act of Supremacy', which declared the English monarch the sole head of the Church in England. Cromwell had few discernable convictions, but he favoured Reformation for reasons of state, and he was largely responsible for the dissolution of the English monasteries and seizure of their property by the crown. Henry, however, remained Catholic by conviction; he insisted upon a celibate priesthood, retained the sacramental theology of the Roman Church and steadfastly resisted 'Lutheran' reforms to the end.

So, King Henry VIII really didn't even care about the right religion. He just wanted a religion that would allow him to take a new wife and be declared the boss. After he got what he wanted, he just kept the parts of each translation that suited him. Crammer and Cromwell had no desires to find the right religion either. They just used religion to gain lands, money, and power.

You don't have to look very far among today's religions, denominations, and sects to find glass churches, stadium filled churches, television and radio empires, and Internet broadcasters preaching, "Send us your money so we can continue to spread the message of Jesus!"

Disingenuous money and power hungry preachers since the beginning of Christendom have *proven their own position as a means to serve their own purpose.* These preachers may not want to trade in a wife, but it sure seems like they want to trade for a lifestyle the rest of us are told we should not covet.

The next few chapters of *Disorganized Christianity* include a look at *Contradictions,* followed by the chapter I call *Translations and misinterpretations!* Some of what I am going to share next in this *Questions* chapter could very easily be placed in either of these following chapters. I choose to address this next subject in *Questions* because I am not claiming a contradiction or a mistranslation or a misinterpretation. I am claiming the blatant act of ignoring the very words in the Bible, in red letters, that Jesus Christ spoke about riches.

In some Bibles, every word the publishers believed Jesus actually spoke were highlighted in red letters. I am questioning how preachers can preach a message on the absolute acceptance — and in some cases their deserved riches from God — that completely go against the teachings of Jesus in the New Testament.

Crazy thought, I know, but if all these preachers are begging us to send them money, simply so they can continue the work of evangelizing the world and that every dollar counts towards the ultimate goal of saving every soul, why would these preachers want to spend our money to live an extravagant lifestyle instead of spending our money to save souls?

Mark 16:15 *And he said unto them, Go ye into all the world, and preach the gospel to every creature.*

The Bible tells the elders to serve God willingly and not for filthy lucre or as lords over God's inheritance, but as examples for their flocks to follow.

1 Peter 5:1-3 *1 The elders who are among you I exhort, who am also an elder, and a witness of the suffering of Christ, and also a partaker of the glory that shall be revealed: 2 Feed the flock of God which is among you, taking the oversight of it, not by constraint but willingly; not for filthy lucre but of a ready mind; 3 Neither as being lords over God's inheritance, but being examples to the flock.*

These verses provide a simple statement on how to be an elder, local preacher, or televangelist. Are these self-centered, narrow-minded preachers embodying the correct example? Alright television preachers, let's prove your true convictions: God or things? If the Bible and you tell us not to covet:

Exodus 20:17 *Thou shalt not covet thy neighbor's house; thou shalt not covet thy neighbor's wife, nor his manservant, nor his maidservant, nor his ox, nor his ass, nor anything that is thy neighbor's* and you preachers are living in a world the vast majority of your flock can only fantasize (covet) about, are you preachers really being true to God? Are you preachers being that good example?

What if one of your flock sees your extravagant lifestyle and goes out to get that thing you have? What if one of your flock goes out and commits a crime to obtain that thing you have? What if one of your flock destroys his marriage and family because he has an uncontrollable passion to obtain that thing you have? Is that flock member's sin your fault? Was that flock member just weak? After all, you preachers cannot be held responsible for every one in your flock; the same flock that provides you money to own that thing you have — can you?

These next verses are very important in explaining my sadness at how these preachers who live high and mighty and then come to us and try to *control and condemn us on this earth and then declare our damnation in the hereafter* while all the time begging for money to pay for Jesus' ministry and their material things. These verses do not talk about mansions and limousines and jet planes but, like most Bible stories, talk in much simpler terms. I believe the flock will understand the message even if their preachers don't.

You preachers teach us that we should not be a stumbling block to our brother:

Romans 14:13-21 *13 Let us not, therefore, judge one another any more; but judge this, rather: that no man put a stumbling block or an occasion to fall in his brother's way. 14 I know, and am persuaded by the Lord Jesus, that there is nothing unclean of itself; but to him that esteemeth anything to be unclean, to him it is unclean. 15 But if thy brother be grieved with thy food, now walkest thou not in love. Destroy not him with thy food, for whom Christ died. 16 Let not then your good be evil spoken of; 17 For the kingdom of God is not food and drink, but righteousness, and peace, and joy in the Holy Spirit. 18 For he that in these things serveth Christ is acceptable to God, and approved of men. 19 Let us, therefore, follow after the things which make for peace, and things with which one may edify another. 20 For food destroy not* *the work of God. All things indeed are pure; but it is evil for that man who eateth with offense. 21 It is good neither to eat meat, nor to drink wine, nor anything by which thy brother stumbleth, or is offended, or is made weak.* Are you preachers at all guilty of being the same stumbling block you preach to us we should not be to others?

I am absolutely certain you preachers are not going to like those verses and will probably spend most of your pulpit time defending the lifestyle you think God *gave* you. Go ahead and keep your lifestyle. Your God is going to judge you. Your flock may even now judge you. However, I am not going to judge you. Your lifestyle of *things* is none of my business, just as our lifestyle is none of your business.

I do not care if you are looking at your 70 years down here on earth instead of your eternity in heaven! When the people that make up your flocks made their choices in *things* and then they cannot afford to pay their own tithes and offerings to you and then you rant at them not to make those choices because they are *cheating God*, are you at fault? Do you take any responsibility? Aren't your flock's choices the very same choices you have taught them by your own actions, to choose? Aren't these the same material *thing* choices you really have your faith in?

There is a relatively new phenomenon called Prosperity Preaching currently circulating in churches. I absolutely know from the bottom of my heart and soul that those *things* are your choice because I have heard you say: "I am entitled to those *things*, and God has blessed me with those *things*, so why not?" I have also heard you say that if I send you a bunch of money, God will bless me with a lot more money, and I can have those *things* God really wants me to have, too!

We do have an odd contradiction in both words and actions between the Old Testament and the New Testament teachings concerning riches.

There are many stories in the Old Testament that consistently identify God's love and blessings for man when God rewards him with riches. The temptation of Job by Satan is the most famous story of God giving a man riches and blessings and then Satan tempting God to test Job's love of God after those *things* had been taken away.

Job 1:9-11 *9 Then Satan answered the Lord, and said, Doth not Job fear God for nothing? 10 Hast not thou made an hedge about him, and about his house, and about all that he hath on every side? Thou hast blessed the work of his hands, and his substance is increased in the land. 11 But put forth thine hand now, and touch all that he hath, and he will curse thee to thy face.*

These Old Testament verses are what you preachers use to try to prove that your riches and *things* are God given and that you deserve them. But the Old Testament is about the law and the law no longer binds us since Jesus came to be our sacrifice, correct? So, what does Jesus say about your riches and *things*?

I am saying: "You cannot preach just what you want from the Old Testament —which is where you get most of your condemnation verses and mystic prophesy verses where your God says 'I can have all the money I want' — to prove your own position, and then jump to the New Testament and say, "I pray in Jesus' name" a couple of times and proceed to declare that you are preaching the Gospel of Jesus, simply to then serve your own purpose!

You can have it your way and you can use the Old Testament verses and New Testament verses intermingled to get what you want. But, because we *converted non-Christians* are aware that the New Testament verses on riches you want to ignore are in complete contradiction with your specially selected Old Testament verses on riches, we simply do not believe you are correct anymore. We are just not willing to believe in your sincerity nor be compelled to give you our money simply by the number of tears you shed anymore. We are no longer going to believe you really have lost souls and our best interest at heart. We now recognize and believe you just want your own *things*.

Are you preachers preaching Old Testament law or New Testament grace? Are you preachers preaching that we live under the Old Testament rules of law with punishment and atonement for our sins through animal blood sacrifice, or are we under New Testament rules of commandments, punishment and then atonement for our sins through Jesus' blood sacrifice? Are you declaring yourselves as Old Testament preachers bound by the Torah and the Old Testament laws or as New Testament preachers bound by the grace of God through Jesus Christ your Savior? If you preachers choose the New Testament version of Christianity and Jesus, then how about we take a look at what Jesus said about your riches and *things*.

The New Testament has a different stand on riches being identified with God's love and blessings. New Testament verses do not tell you that you will be blessed with money and material *things* if you preach the word. In fact, it tells you quite the opposite. Remember, the New Testament does say that if you serve God, *Don't do it for filthy lucre.* I guess "filthy" could be in the eye of the beholder. But with all the riches and glory you have accumulated through doing God's work of preaching the gospel of Jesus Christ, please give us the New Testament verses that tell you it is all right to have these many material earthly *things*. I don't believe you can!

In his own words Jesus told his original twelve disciples in **Matthew 10:10 1** and **9-10** *1 And when he had called unto him his twelve disciples, he gave them power against unclean spirits, to cast them out, and to heal all manner of sickness and all manner of disease. 9 Provide neither gold nor silver, nor copper in your purses, 10 Nor a bag for your journey, neither two coats, neither shoes, nor yet a staff; for the workman is worthy of his food.*

Jesus told his disciples to go out and preach God's word and to depend on God. Jesus told them to take nothing extra, not even for comfort or security. No money, no bag, no extra coat, no shoes, no staff, just their faith that God would take care of them! This new Prosperity Preaching style by a bunch of preachers and televangelists goes completely against what the Bible says about riches. I will offer you several New Testament verses that actually state that Prosperity Preachers are not biblical. Simply because you listen to someone preach from the Bible, does not mean that what you heard is biblical.

2 Timothy 4:3-4 *3 For the time will come when they will not endure sound doctrine but, after their own lusts, shall they heap to themselves teachers, having itching ears; 4 And they shall turn away their ears from the truth, and shall be turned unto fables.*

Just because some preachers preach from the Bible does not mean they are automatically Biblical!

Matthew 7:15 and **20** *15 Beware of false prophets, who come to you in sheep's clothing, but inwardly they are ravenous wolves. 20 Wherefore, by their fruits ye shall know them.* Also, **Matthew 7:21-23** *21 Not every one that saith unto me, Lord, Lord, shall enter into the kingdom of heaven, but he that doeth the will of my Father, who is in heaven. 22 Many will say to me in that day, Lord, Lord, have we not prophesied in thy name? And in thy name have cast out demons? And in thy name done many wonderful works? 23 And then will I profess unto them, I never knew you; depart from me, ye that work iniquity.*

These new Prosperity Preachers are using these same verses, but they are trying to tell you about your sins, not their sin! If what they preach is not what the Bible says, then they are false prophets.

In 1 Timothy Chapter 6 we can read that God is very explicit on the matter of ministers not getting caught up in the Prosperity of their Preaching. The entire chapter is devoted to the ministers of Jesus' message to be content in trusting God for the basic necessities of life while serving God and expecting their riches to come later in heaven.

Jesus tells them that their reward comes after serving him on earth, not while serving him on earth. This is your chapter. This is your Bible. This is your God's commandment to your preachers. I don't care whether you have a jet and a mansion and a limousine, but it seems your God does. Laugh at me. Scorn me. Threaten to punch me. I don't care if you are mad at me, but are you really afraid of God yet? Your God is watching and recording your every move (purchase): **Proverbs 1:7** *The fear of the Lord is the beginning of knowledge, but fools despise wisdom and instruction.*

I have tried to keep most of the verses I am quoting short and precise. There is always a little more understanding about a verse if you read the verses around it and keep the verse within the meaning the author intended. I am going to write out the entire chapter of 1 Timothy Chapter 6. I am trying to make the point that God has a specific way he wants his ministers to act when it comes to riches, and he spells it out very clearly in this chapter. I have not made any special revelations, interpretations or declarations concerning what the Bible says about Prosperity Preachers. I will simply let the Bible speak for itself. After you read 1 Timothy Chapter 6, you can then decide whether you want the Prosperity Preachers to bless you their way after you send them your money, or you can decide to let God bless you, His way through Jesus, without having to pay money for that blessing.

1 Timothy 6:1-21 *1 Let as many servants as are under the yoke count their own masters worthy of all honor, that the name of God and his doctrine be not blasphemed. 2 And they that have believing masters, let them not despise them because they are brethren but, rather, do them service because they are faithful and beloved, partakers of the benefit. These things teach and exhort. 3 If any man teach otherwise, and consent not to wholesome words, even the words of our Lord Jesus Christ, and to the doctrine which is according to godliness, 4 He is proud, knowing nothing, but doting about questions and disputes of words, of which cometh envy, strife, railings, evil suspicions, 5 Perverse disputings of men of corrupt minds, and destitute of the truth, supposing that gain is godliness, from such withdraw thyself. 6 But godliness with contentment is great gain; 7 For we brought nothing* *into this world, and it is certain we can carry nothing out. 8 And having food and raiment let us be therewith content. 9 But they that will be rich fall into temptation and a snare, and into many foolish and hurtful lusts, which drown men in destruction and perdition. 10 For the love of money is the root of all evil, which, while some coveted after, they have erred from the faith, and pierced themselves through with many sorrows. 11 But thou, O man of God, flee these things, and follow after righteousness, godliness, faith, love, patience, meekness. 12 Fight the good fight of faith, lay hold on eternal life, unto which thou art also called and hast professed a good profession before many witnesses. 13 I command thee in the sight of God, who maketh all things alive, and before Christ Jesus, who before Pontius Pilate witnessed a good confession, 14 That thou keep this commandment without spot, unrebukable, until the appearing of our Lord Jesus Christ; 15 Which in his times he shall show, who is the blessed and only Potentate, the King of kings, and Lord of lords; 16 Who only hath immortality, dwelling in the light which no man can approach unto; whom no man hath seen, nor can see; to whom be honor and power everlasting. Amen. 17 Charge them that are rich in this age, that they be not high-minded, nor trust in uncertain riches but in the living God, who giveth us richly all things to enjoy; 18 That they do good, that they be rich in good works, ready to distribute, willing to share, 19 Laying up in store for themselves a good foundation against the time to come, that they may lay hold on eternal life. 20 O Timothy, keep that which is committed to thy trust, avoiding profane and vain babblings, and oppositions of knowledge falsely so called, 21 Which some, professing, have erred concerning the faith. Grace be with thee. Amen*

Let's say that again.

The first instruction in verse 1 is to not let God's word be blasphemed. (*Webster's New Collegiate Dictionary, Copyright 1981 by G. & C. Merriam Co.*) here are some definitions of blaspheme: 1, to speak of or address with irreverence; 2, to utter blasphemy. I believe that trying to make God's word say what you want it to mean is blasphemy. Take it or leave it.

Verse 2 says that the flock should not despise the preachers who are trying to preach God's word.

Verse 3 talks about the preachers who start their own Bible commentary.

Verse 4 identifies these preachers as proud, knowing nothing, doting about questions and disputes of words. I must interject my personal statement concerning verse 4: *proving their own position to then serve their own purpose.* Continuing in verse 4, the Bible says with these false teachings comes envy, strife, railings, and evil suspicions.

Verse 5 is the Prosperity Preachers doomsday verse. Verse 5 tells the flock to withdraw and separate themselves from anyone who preaches that gain is godliness. This is not my verse, translation, or misinterpretation.

Verse 6 states that Godliness with contentment is great gain. Well, I suppose the definition of contentment could be the Prosperity Preachers' avenue to blaspheme, or could it? Does the Bible define what contentment should be or is contentment also in the eye of the beholder? If you stop reading 1 Timothy Chapter 6 at this point, you may be subject to the Prosperity Preachers' own revelations about contentment. But if you read verse 8, contentment is very clearly defined by God. My suggestion is to keep reading and keep pointing out that your preachers are either insincere or incorrect.

Verse 8 says, And having food and raiment let us be therewith content. God did not promise you a mansion, a jet, a limousine, or an unlimited credit card. God actually promised you only your basic necessities. God said you were to have faith in God just to provide what He felt you needed. God commanded in **1 Timothy 6:8** *And having food and raiment let us be therewith content.* Read your Bible! Read the verses in your Bible and do not misinterpret God's true meaning of your rewards on this Earth. I cannot even attempt to interpret verse 8 as suggesting that Prosperity Preachers are somehow entitled to personal jets!

Going back to verse 7, we can read: For we brought nothing into this world, and it is certain we can carry nothing out. If you preachers believe in your Bible and understand that you cannot take your *things* with you when you die, why accumulate more *things* for yourselves, when there are souls to save?

Verse 9: But they that will be rich fall into temptation and a snare, and into many foolish and hurtful lusts, which drown men in destruction and perdition. This verse is very prophetic and actually is being fulfilled today if you search the Internet for "Preacher Scandals."

Verse 10: For the love of money is the root of all evil, which, while some coveted after, they have erred from the faith, and pierced themselves through with many sorrows. This verse has been so widely used against the flock. I am saying and I do agree it could be useful for the flock, but the verse's actual intent was directed at the ministers of the flock, not the flock itself.

Verse 11: But thou, O man of God, flee these *things*. This verse directly states "flee these *things*." It is no coincidence that I have used the word *things* to describe the filthy lucre the Prosperity Preachers so covet.

Verse 14: That thou keep this commandment without spot, unrebuk-able, until the appearing of our Lord Jesus Christ. With the many Internet preacher scandals we read about and all the local preacher scandals many of us *converted non-Christians* have suffered through, I do not think this verse is going to work well for these preachers.

Verse 17: trust in the living God, who giveth us richly all *things* to enjoy. I would guess that the Prosperity Preachers could cut and paste this verse to justify getting those rich *things*!

Verse 18: That they do good, that they be rich in good works, ready to distribute, willing to share. Some Prosperity Preachers validate their *things* because they give back to the flock. How "much" is good works? If my flock allows me to have a $10,000,000 salary and a lot of extra perks, and I share $1,000,000 with the flock, which also happens to be tax deductible for me, does that qualify as rich in good works? Sounds like a lot, perhaps, but isn't that 10% your tithe anyway?

Galatians 6:7-8 *7 Be not deceived, God is not mocked, for whatever a man soweth, that shall he also reap. 8 For he that soweth to his flesh shall of the flesh reap corruption; but he that soweth to the Spirit shall of the Spirit reap life everlasting.* Maybe $1,000,000 of "rich in good works" is just not quite enough.

You Prosperity Preachers could face another problem in validating your money and *things* if you argue, "That was then and now is now and situations are different. Are you seriously suggesting that "God did not have the correct plan for the future? Are you actually suggesting that God could not have seen the future and the special financial needs of television, radio and the Internet? It sounds like you are trying to convince us — albeit through a misguided strategy — that your God had a very shortsighted view of the future! I think you have a very shortsighted belief that your God knew the correct way to save souls.

Mark 16:15 *And he said unto them, Go ye into all the world, and preach the gospel to every creature.* The Bible says, "Go ye into all the world." The Bible does not say, "Stay in the studio and collect money so you can broadcast to all the world." You may argue that television and radio and Internet outreach for souls can reach bigger numbers and you may have a point, but what does God teach us about large numbers over smaller numbers or even one?

Matthew 18:12-14 *12 How think ye? If a man have a hundred sheep, and one of them be gone astray, doth he not leave the ninety and nine, and goeth into the mountains, and seeketh that which is gone astray? 13 And if so be that ye find it, verily I say unto you, he rejoiceth more over that sheep than* *over the ninety and nine which went not astray. 14 Even so it is not the will of your Father, who is in heaven, that one of these little ones should perish.*

Your Bible states that God wasn't concerned with the larger numbers. Your Bible says that God was concerned and had a passion for the individual lost sheep or lost soul.

John 13:34 *A new commandment I give unto you, that ye love one another; as I have loved you, that ye also love one another.* I believed that the correct way — the Bible's way; God's word's way — was one-on-one preaching and loving one another. This strategy may be a slow strategy, but biblically it is a very strong and powerfully long lasting and loving strategy.

Matthew 10:1 *And when he had called unto him his twelve disciples, he gave them power against unclean spirits, to cast them out, and to heal all manner of sickness and all manner of disease.* Since you local preachers and televangelists declare that you are "called to the ministry by God," you could certainly be described as modern-day Christian disciples by definition.

Since you seem to believe — by merit of whatever verses you manipulate to prove that you deserve the money and *things* granted to you because of your service to God — in your haste to enjoy the fruits of your labor, did you forget the labor part? Did you forget to even read the job description at the beginning of Matthew 10:1? Or was this verse just for the original twelve disciples, but not for you?

I have not seen any of you exercise power against unclean spirits, to cast them out, and to heal all manner of sickness and all manner of disease. I suppose I could leave the *power against unclean spirits to the* exorcists, but what about healing all *manner of sickness* and all *manner of disease*? It says *all* manner of sickness and *all* manner of disease.

There are numerous special faith healers around, but the Bible reads that all of you modern day disciples should be able to perform these healings. Jesus bestowed on his New Testament disciples and apostles these healing powers, so they could demonstrate the power of Jesus. Why did the legitimate healing practices stop with modern day New Testament disciples? We could certainly use those healing powers to demonstrate Jesus' power today! Sadly, according to the *special* select few faith healers working today, the everyday Christian disciple's ability to heal sickness is not valid. Did God only call them to perform these miracles. Am I calling these special faith healers of today frauds? Yes!

Okay then, don't heal me. Don't heal my friend's arthritic hip. Don't heal my other friend's lung cancer. We probably brought these health issues on ourselves anyway. Instead, you *chosen* faith healers go ahead and keep visiting the Children's Burn Center closest to your mansion and heal those children who had nothing to do with their conditions. Have you faith healers ever burned your finger or had a really bad sunburn? It is sad you choose to sit in your mansions and not heal the very children that God commanded you to love. And now you want to get mad at me?

Am I testing you? No! That would be the ultimate exercise in futility because you could not pass that test, even if all your money and *things* depended on it. And maybe it should! Only Jesus could give you that power, and by written Bible standards, you do not represent that Jesus. If you did represent that Jesus, why have you not asked God to be with you to help you perform those burn victim miracles? You profess to want to save everyone from the fiery flames of hell in the future, yet you will not save these children from the fiery torment of their present? Let me assure you that I am not trying to be jovial here. This is a challenge I absolutely know you cannot — and will not — accept because you know you will fail.

John 3:2 *The same came to Jesus by night, and said unto him, Rabbi, we know that thou art a teacher come from God; for no man can do these miracles that thou doest, except God be with him.*

What a true following you faith healers would have if you actually televised a real healing! Heal a child's severely burnt skin right before the camera, rather than just curing somebody's bad back.

John 6:2 *And a great multitude followed him, because they saw his miracles which he did on those that were diseased.*

You faith healers can no longer stand there with your bare faces exposed to the world and proceed to rationalize that it might not be God's will for these children's pain to be healed, simply to cover up your own ineptness.

Acts 6:8 *And Stephen, full of faith and power, did great wonders and miracles among the people.* **Acts 8:6-8** *6 And the people with one accord gave heed unto those things which Philip spoke, hearing and seeing the miracles which he did; 7 For unclean spirits, crying with a loud voice, came out of many that were possesed with them; and many taken with palsies, and that were lame, were healed. 8 And there was great joy in the city.*

This verse says that Philip did drive out unclean spirits. All right, then our modern day preachers and faith healers can do that too, or it kind of looks like they can do that. We have never really seen an "unclean spirit," so we really don't know whether or not it was driven out for certain, but Philip also made the lame to be healed and palsies to be healed. Our modern day preachers and faith healers come up rather short on that one. Some of you faith healers do have a staff of invalids that show up every once in a while to get healed though. Close, I guess, but not close enough!

Stephen and Philip were not the big name disciples or Apostles of Jesus, but the great Apostle Paul even got into the healing arena.

Acts 19:11-12 *11 And God wrought special miracles by the hands of Paul, 12 So that from his body were brought unto the sick handkerchiefs or aprons, and the diseases departed from them, and the evil spirits went out of them.* I believe if a modern day follower of Jesus had the faith and power of

Stephen and Philip and Paul, Jesus would help them do those same miracles of healing diseases today. But where are you? Is there no one to answer the call of Jesus? Show yourself! You preachers and faith healers do not even fulfill your labor, as defined by Jesus in Matthew 10:1, but you presume to tell us you are worthy of our money for your *things*. By the way, when exactly did the specialty of faith healing become a distinct and separate discipline for God's select disciples, and where in the Bible did God create the division between you faith healers and all the rest of Christendom?

Many preachers command, "Do as I say, not as I do."

Matthew 6:19-21 *19 Lay not up for yourselves treasures upon earth, where moth and rust doth corrupt, and where thieves break through and steal, 20 But lay up for yourselves treasures in heaven, where neither moth nor rust doth corrupt, and where thieves do not break through or steal; 21 For where your treasure is, there will your heart be also.*

Unacceptable! You preachers cannot claim that you are so great and deserving that God told you in a private message that you can have both heaven and *things*!

Matthew 6:24 *No man can serve two masters; for either he will hate the one, and love the other; or else he will hold to the one, and despise the other.*

All right, here comes the big one. Here comes the rest of the verse, 24: Ye cannot serve God and mammon (money)(things). This one is your verse. I mean God's verse. It's not my verse.

Revelation 20:12 *And I saw the dead, small and great, stand before God, and the books were opened; and another book was opened, which is the book of life. And the dead were judged out of those things which were written in those books, according to their works.*

According to your Bible, you preachers will get to stand in front of your God and try to convince Him you did not ever see or hear or read that verse. Not anymore!

Mark 16:15 *And he said unto them, Go ye into all the world, and preach the gospel to every creature.*

These are Jesus' own personal words! I wonder how many creatures to whom you are commanded to preach the Jesus message are not actually hearing the word of God and therefore miss out on the salvation you claim is so close at hand, simply because a lot of the tithes and offerings given to you are going to your lifestyle and not to the mission field?

Understand that I am not declaring all preachers to be guilty of this hypocrisy. I have known and still know several preachers who truly love God, Jesus, and their flock. These loving, faithful preachers do not finance an extravagant lifestyle out of their flock's wallet or purse. Are you entitled preachers angry, yet? I was very angry with you for a while. You will get over your anger once you find the true love of Jesus and his real mission for your life.

It is time we start holding ourselves accountable to what we know, and more importantly, what we don't really know. I am now asking you again to write down your answers to the following questions. If you are not willing to follow the Questions Exercise and write down your answers, I am concerned that you still do not recognize and comprehend what I am trying to share with you.

After reading *Disorganized Christianity* to the end, I hope you come back and write down your answers. You may not know the answers, and that is a sad commentary on what we believe we know. But discovering that we only know part of the answer is the real problem we face today. How can we hope to know the whole answer if we do not know the whole problem?

We walk through life and believe in a Bible we do not even know. We walk through life, sometimes condemning others based on a Bible we do not even know. We walk through life and depend on a salvation provided by a Bible we do not even know.

I now invite you to take a few moments to complete the Questions Exercise. You may be surprised by what is revealed!

QUESTIONS EXERCISE

WHERE IS THE LORD'S PRAYER FOUND IN THE BIBLE?

_____

WHERE ARE THE 10 COMMANDMENTS
FOUND IN THE BIBLE?

_____

WHAT ARE THE 10 COMMANDMENTS?

1. _____
2. _____
3. _____
4. _____
5. _____
6. _____
7. _____
8. _____
9. _____
10. _____

WHAT IS THE GREATEST COMMANDMENT?

_____

HOW MANY WISE MEN WERE PRESENT AT JESUS' BIRTH IN THE STABLE?

_____

WHO WERE THE ORIGINAL 12 APOSTLES?

1. _____
2. _____
3. _____
4. _____
5. _____
6. _____
7. _____
8. _____
9. _____
10. _____
11. _____
12. _____

WHO REPLACED THE APOSTLE THAT BETRAYED JESUS?

_____

WHAT IS THE DIFFERENCE BETWEEN AN APOSTLE AND A DISCIPLE?

_____

EXTRA CREDIT:

WHY IS THE SABBATH ON SUNDAY WHEN THE BIBLE SAYS IT IS SATURDAY?

_____

_____

WHEN WAS THE BIBLE DIVIDED INTO CHAPTERS AND VERSES?

_____

WHO WAS THE FIRST OF GOD'S CREATIONS TO SIN IN THE GARDEN OF EDEN?

_____

IN WHAT YEAR DID MADALYN O'HAIR GET PRAYER TAKEN OUT OF SCHOOLS?

_____

No! I am not going to give you the answers. This class is _"New Eyes and Different Heart 101."_ Use your own Bible, or the Internet. The answers to _all_ these questions and _all_ the new questions _you_ might find, can be found in your Bible or on the Internet.

CHAPTER 4

Contradictions!

I have tried my very best to avoid contradictions in *Disorganized Christianity*. I believe you will *not find* any contradictions in *Disorganized Christianity*. Am I issuing a challenge?

No, it is not a challenge. The hunt for *any* contradictions and misinterpretations will start immediately without my formally issuing a challenge.

My expectation is that when someone reads *Disorganized Christianity* and disagrees with my examples or interpretation of verses, they will immediately try to ridicule or dismiss *Disorganized Christianity* as a meaningless book, in order for their Bible version to withstand this perceived onslaught of hate and misinformation.

I am not trying to destroy *your* Bible version. You can keep *your* Bible, and you can keep any translation and any version of the Bible you want. It is none of my business what you want to believe. I am only trying to stop *organized religion* from engaging in any further attempts to *control and then to mandate our condemnation on this earth, and to stop the declaration of our damnation in the hereafter* that has been so perfectly executed against anyone who disagrees with them.

I am not trying to destroy *your* Bible, or *your* hope, or *your* joy, or *your* blessings or *your* eternal salvation. I am trying — with all my being and with all my power of recollection and discernment over the last 45 years — to keep translations and misinterpretations of *your* Bible version from destroying *my* hope, *my* joy, *my* blessings, and *my* eternal salvation. Along with the self-serving protection of my own rights, I am trying to aid and arm with the necessary information, any *converted non-Christian* who wants to be free of *organized religion's* control of them.

Please keep *your* Bible and whatever translation and interpretation you think will give you assurance of an everlasting life. Just do not try to shove your choice down *our* throats!

If you *can* find a valid contradiction or misinterpretation (or two) in *Disorganized Christianity* please remember — and I am declaring this right now to everyone — "*I* can make a mistake, while interpreting a book read and analyzed by billions of other people also searching for the truth."

I am not God; he is not allowed mistakes; *I* am just me!

1 Corinthians 2:7 *But we speak the wisdom of God in a mystery, even the hidden wisdom, which God ordained before the ages unto our glory.*

Also read **2 Timothy 3:16** *All scripture is given by inspiration of God, and is profitable for doctrine, for reproof, for correction, for instruction in righteousness.*

And read **1 Corinthians 14:33** *For God is not the author of confusion but of peace, as in all churches of the saints.*

Organized religion claims that God the Almighty wrote their book. With eternal damnation and a fiery hell now waiting for all of us *converted non-Christians,* we simply demand that — according to the Bible's allowed translations — God is not allowed any contradictions, misinterpretations or mistakes. *All scripture is given by inspiration of God.* Again, just in case you were not paying attention, *organized religion* is *not* allowed any contradictions, misinterpretations or mistakes when it comes to God declaring our damnation.

The frequently offered excuse that *All scripture was given by inspiration of God,* but then a bunch of other guys messed it up is not valid. Why would the all-knowing and all-loving God give *my* inspired scripture to a bunch of guys He knew ahead of time would mess it up and then — as God — claim to have the right to condemn *me* to hell because I did not follow *the same rules* God did not feel were important enough to ensure were kept in complete accuracy? Why not pick some different and more trustworthy guys? Why not give the entire message to someone like Moses? I will tell you more about Moses and the Ten Commandments later.

How can all these contradictions and misinterpretations just happen? How could God allow these contradictions and misinterpretations to just happen? Some readers might be thinking that *Disorganized Christianity* was written on the false premise that there might be a few questionable verse mistakes, but that there really is nothing to base any credibility of contradictions on.

Okay! Let's just see how strong the false premise theory is when others use *Disorganized Christianity* to silence the Bible's control and condemnation of us on this earth and then silence the damnation of our souls in the hereafter!

Since my first day at Sunday school, God has been portrayed as my Father and to all Christians is held up as our Father. In many Bible verses God is portrayed as our Father and even our loving Father.

Consider The Lord's Prayer, **Luke 11:2** *And he said unto them, When ye pray, say, Our Father, who art in heaven, Hallowed be thy name. Thy kingdom come. Thy will be done, as in heaven, so in earth.*

In **Romans 1:7** *To all that be in Rome, beloved of God, called to be saints: Grace to you and peace from God our Father, and the Lord Jesus Christ.*

In **2 Thessalonians 2:16** *Now our Lord Jesus Christ himself, and God, even our Father, who hath loved us, and hath given us everlasting consolation and good hope through grace.*

God likens heaven to little children.

Matthew 18:1-3 *1 At the same time came the disciples unto Jesus, saying, Who is the greatest in the kingdom of heaven? 2 And Jesus called a little child unto him, and set him in the midst of them, 3 And said, Verily I say unto you, Except ye be converted, and become as little children, ye shall not enter into the kingdom of heaven.*

The Bible tells us in many verses how God — as our Father — loves us and actually demands that we, *the children,* be protected. Jesus also gave a warning to anyone that would harm children:

Matthew 18:6 *But whosoever shall offend one of these little ones who believe in me, it were better for him that a millstone were hanged about his neck, and that he were drowned in the depth of the sea.*

I never went to Catholic mass, and I am certain I never will. There are many so-called Fathers or priests who conveniently "forgot" that particular verse or just didn't think it applied to them, yet they readily remember the actual verses that condemn the actions of others, along with the verses that require money to be paid and little prayers to gain forgiveness.

Forgiveness comes from *God,* not so called Fathers or priests. *Webster's New Collegiate Dictionary* defines a parable as: *"a short fictitious story that illustrates a moral attitude or a religious principle."* Parables are usually written in the Bible as mysterious stories.

Matthew 13:35 *That it might be fulfilled which was spoken by the prophet, saying, I will open my mouth in parables; I will utter things which have been kept secret from the foundation of the world.*

The parable is then left for anyone, and I mean *anyone*, to tell *us* the meaning of that parable.

The following parable written by *me,* only illustrates that there are too many versions of the *rules* and there are way too many new dads eager to interpret and change the rules.

PARABLE OF THE TWO DADS

Let us say, you were *The* Dad and you had several children. You decided to go away, but you were still *The* Dad, and you still wanted to be in control. In order to stay in control while you were gone, you *told* Mom ten rules the kids had to obey or they would be punished when you got home. Now, believing your children were very smart and given the fact that you didn't have any parchment handy to write down these ten rules, you instead *told* Mom the ten rules that were to be memorized.

So *The* Dad leaves and doesn't say *when* he is coming back, but only *that* he will come back, so watch for his return. *The* Dad does not have a job, does not bring home the groceries, and does not actually pay the rent. *The* Dad isn't there for the birthdays or the proms and actually doesn't even verbally strengthen his children's self-worth problems, broken-heart problems, and that "special problem" one of them ends up having, which wasn't covered by the original ten rules.

The children ask, "Where is Daddy?"

The Mom says, "He's coming home soon, so be ready, but no, he cannot help with the self-worth problems, the broken-heart problems and that special problem one of you has that wasn't covered in the original ten rules, *right now*. But, remember what he said about the ten rules."

After months and years pass, no one can even remember the ten rules. Mom has a new Daddy who buys the groceries, pays the rent, tends to the self-worth problems, the broken-heart problems, and even that special problem one of the children has that wasn't covered in the original ten rules.

Now, since the new Dad is the one taking on all the responsibilities, he changes and adds to The Dad's ten rules. The children — having been cared for, provided for and loved — willingly agree to the changes in the ten rules, which they can't remember anyway.

The sad part is that a new Dad comes into the picture and changes everything. At this point, the children do not have a chance in hell of obeying the original ten rules they are "going to be punished for breaking," because they have been changed.

The saddest part is that the *old* Dad, who can see the new Dad and what he is doing, surely must not care. He surely is too busy, because otherwise why wouldn't *he* come back to fix the self-worth problems, the broken heart problems and that special problem one of them has, which wasn't covered by the original ten rules.

The old Dad could come back, and this time with a more reliable communication system in hand, write down the old original ten rules because he knows they are better and kick the new Dad's butt out of the house.

What is the point of this parable?

I personally had three dads while I was growing up. Each dad had a different set of rules, values, rewards, and punishments. The Bible tells us to honor our mothers, fathers, and dads:

Exodus 20:12 *Honor thy father and thy mother, that thy days may be long upon and which the Lord thy God giveth thee.* The Bible tells us we should also revere our fathers:

Hebrews 12:9 *Furthermore, we have had fathers of our flesh who corrected us, and we gave them reverence. Shall we not much rather be in subjection unto the Father of spirits, and live?* We are instructed to honor and revere our earthly fathers.

There was a group of men in biblical times known as the Pharisees.

Matthew 23:2 *Saying, The scribes and the Pharisees sit in Moses' seat.*

These Pharisees positioned themselves in *Moses' seat* or — in today's terms — as Pastors, televangelists and other church leaders. Pharisees would make themselves appear greater than they really were. Pharisees lived the teachings of the Bible mostly to enhance their lives through *proving their position to then serve their own purpose,* by adding to and taking away from the scriptures. The Pharisees wanted to be praised and honored and revered in their time. The Bible describes these men in Matthew 23:1-12 and detailed some rules to address them. One of the major condemnations of the Pharisees comes from **Matthew 23:9** *And call no man your father upon the earth; for one is your Father, who is in heaven.* I understand the Bible tells us not to call any church leader, nor anyone who would *sit in Moses' seat,* "Father." I never went to Catholic mass to confess to a "Father," and I am sure I never will.

If we did not have all these contradictions and misinterpretations in the Bible, I feel absolutely certain we would also not have — according to David Barrett and the editors of the *World Christian Encyclopedia* — 19 major world religions which are subdivided into a total of 270 large religious groups and many smaller ones.

Approximately 34,000 separate Christian groups have been identified in the world. "Over half of them are independent churches that are not interested in linking with the big denominations" (religioustolerance.org).

With 34,000 organized groups each having their own interpretations of the Bible and each group knowing their ten rules are the best, that is a whole lot of "new Dads" coming around to tell us what to do! Please note that I am not validating the information found on the religioustolerance. org website. In my search for information, I found the website and was intrigued by its seemingly unbiased approach to sharing religious information. I feel quite sure other Internet sites you look at will have different numbers, but every site will ultimately make it very clear that "There are a lot of new Dads out there."

Any reader can claim that my desire and my expectation of God to accurately give me the rules by which He is ultimately going to judge me by is unreasonable. All I am going to point out about that is this: "It is alright for you to drift through life with your complacency, your misinterpretations and hope what you want to believe is true and then hope it gets you into heaven. But if you want to *prove your own position and then use it to serve your own purpose* or follow someone else who has *proven their own position and then used it to serve their own purpose*, well, then you can go to hell."

There really is no hell, but I believe this gets my point across.

If God had chosen Moses to ensure the accuracy of the entire Bible, then you could keep the *All scripture is given by inspiration of God* part because God actually spoke to Moses through a burning bush.

Exodus 3:4 *And when the Lord saw that he turned aside to see, God called unto him out of the midst of the bush, and said, Moses, Moses.* If God chose Moses to ensure the accuracy of the entire Bible, then you would also have had an accurately written version of the Bible message that *Disorganized Christianity* would have no desire or need to challenge.

God actually wrote the Ten Commandments with His own finger on two stone tables (tablets).

Exodus 31:18 *And he gave unto Moses, when he had ceased speaking with him upon Mount Sinai, Two tables of stone, written with the finger of God.*

Exodus 24:12 *And the Lord said unto Moses, Come up to me into the mount, and be there; and I will give thee tables of stone, and a law, and commandments which I have written, that thou mayest teach them.*

Moses was supposed to teach *these* Ten Commandments to his people:

Exodus 20:3-17 *3 Thou shalt have no other Gods before me. 4 Thou shalt not make unto thee any carved image, or any likeness of anything that is in heaven above, or that is in the earth beneath, or that is in the water under the earth; 5 Thou shalt not bowdown thyself to them, nor serve them; for I, the Lord thy God, am a jealous God, visiting the iniquity of the fathers upon the children unto the third and fourth generation of them that hate me; 6 And showing mercy unto thousands of them that love me, and keep my commandments. 7 Thou shalt not take the name of the Lord thy God in vain; for the Lord will not hold him guiltless that taketh his name in vain. 8 Remember the Sabbath day, to keep it holy. 9 Six days shalt thou labor and do all thy work; 10 But the seventh day is the Sabbath of the Lord thy God; in it thou shalt not do any work, thou, nor thy son, nor thy daughter, thy manservant, nor thy maidservant, nor thy cattle, nor thy stranger that is within thy gates; 11 For in six days the Lord made heaven and earth, the sea, and all that in them is, and rested the seventh day; wherefore, the Lord blessed the Sabbath day, and hallowed it. 12 Honor thy father and thy mother, that thy days may be long upon the land which the Lord thy God giveth thee. 13 Thou shalt not kill. 14 Thou shalt not commit adultery. 15 Thou shalt not steal. 16 Thou shalt not bear false witness against thy neighbor. 17 Thou shalt not covet thy neighbor's house; thou shalt not covet thy neighbor's wife, nor* *his manservant, nor his maidservant, nor his ox, nor his ass, nor anything that is thy neighbor's.*

Okay, I concede. I give up my argument and now believe God *did* know how to do it right. God proved this with the Ten Commandments. God did not merely *inspire* them, He literally wrote them. God personally delivered them. God verbally told Moses to teach them. And we do have those original Ten Commandments displayed all over the place. You can find them in courthouses, in legislature offices, on monuments, in public buildings, and even on the United States of America's Supreme Court walls.

If you stay up late at night and look for religious programs' fundraisers you can even find little crosses that have tiny peep holes in the body of the cross where the original ten commandments have been written.

The book of Exodus clearly shows us that God knew how to do it right. But since God knew how to do it right, couldn't God have given us the *entire* Bible the *Moses way*? I am not asking anyone whether or not it was *practical* for God to hand write and personally deliver the entire Bible from Genesis to Revelation. However, God is *God!* God was there from the beginning.

Genesis 1:1 *In the beginning God created the heaven and the earth.*

God does not have to operate under time constraints. Is the Earth 6,000 years old or is the Earth six billion years old? Either of those choices — or even somewhere in between — allows for God to have had plenty of time to personally write and ensure the delivery of an *infallible* Bible. In short, God could have had it *His* way and not man's way.

2 Peter 3:8 *But, beloved, be not ignorant of this one thing, that one day is with the Lord as a thousand years, and a thousand years as one day.*

The Bible clearly says that one day is like a thousand years and a thousand years is like one day to God. Given all of the scriptural confusion in churches and around the world today, would it be too much to ask to have God take either one day or a thousand years to personally deliver the entire Bible the *Moses way?*

Is anyone going to try to tell us that God did not have the time or the ability to personally write the entire Bible? Is anyone going to try to convince us God did not *need* to personally write the entire Bible? Is anyone seriously trying to tell us it was all right for God to just simply *inspire* the words, verses, and chapters of the Bible to the kind of men He would soon come to repent that he even *created?* Because God became so angry with these men and their sinful lives that He then proceeded to *kill* all these trusted men!

2 Timothy 3:16 *All scripture is given by inspiration of God, and is profitable for doctrine, for reproof, for correction, for instruction in righteousness.*

Keep in mind that we are still in Genesis and not very far removed from the original creation of Adam and Eve, and God already has a problem with man.

Genesis 6:5-7 *5 And God saw that the wickedness of man was great in the earth, and that every imagination of the thoughts of his heart was only evil continually. 6 And it repented the Lord that he had made man on the earth, and it grieved him at his heart. 7 And the Lord said, I will destroy man whom I have created from the face of the earth; both man, and beast, and the creeping thing, and the fowls of the air; for it repenteth me that I have made them.*

Let's say that again!

God created man and over time He entrusted the holy Word(s) of God to these men's memories, but in a very short time these men became so sinful and bad they turned from the Word(s) of the Law that God gave them and then — because of their sins — God killed everything on the earth. God stated that He was going to kill every living creature on the face of the earth. Well, not exactly!

Genesis 6:6-7 *6 And it repented the Lord that he had made man on the earth, and it grieved him at his heart. 7 And the Lord said, I will destroy man whom I have created from the face of the earth; both man, and beast, and the creeping thing, and the fowls of the air; for it repenteth me that I have made them.*

Genesis 6:17 *And, behold, I, even I, do bring a flood of waters upon the earth, to destroy all flesh, wherein is the breath of life, from under heaven, and everything that is in the earth shall die.*

Well, not exactly!

God really didn't mean everything. God said everything a couple of times, but He didn't really mean everything the second time either. The words in my Bible I used to rely on, and the words in my Bible *organized religion* used to control me with say, "Everything."

Genesis 6:8 *But Noah found grace in the eyes of the Lord.* And **Genesis 6:18** *But with thee I will establish my covenant; and thou shalt come into the ark, thou, and thy sons, and thy wife, and thy sons' wives with thee.*

While the Bible says everything, the Bible didn't really mean everything. I am not translating, interpreting, or contradicting the Bible. I am reading the exact words of the Bible.

Genesis 6:6-7 *6 And it repented the Lord that he had made man on the earth, and it grieved him at his heart. 7 And the Lord said, I will destroy man whom I have created from the face of the earth; both man, and beast, and the creeping thing, and the fowls of the air; for it repenteth me that I have made them.*

Later in Genesis 6 God provides himself with another escape. God doesn't exactly mean everything was bad, because He clearly says that Noah and his family were all right.

Genesis 6:17 *And, behold, I, even I, do bring a flood of waters upon the earth, to destroy all flesh, wherein is the breath of life, from under heaven; and everything that is in the earth shall die. Verses 7 and 17 read: everything.*

Genesis 6:18-19 *18 But with thee will I establish my covenant; and thou shalt come into the ark, thou, and thy sons, and thy wife, and thy sons' wives with thee. 19 And of every living thing of all flesh, two of every sort shalt thou bring into the ark, to keep them alive with thee; they shall be male and female.*

God was executing the total destruction of man and all living creatures. Verse 17 says Destroy all flesh. Except, not exactly. It seems that God had determined that Noah and his sons and their wives were worthy to survive. But given that, how was Noah supposed to know which of the male and female beasts and creeping thing and fowls of the air were worthy of survival? God not only said man was bad, but the beasts and the creeping thing and the fowls of the air grieved God's heart that God even made them, so why put them back on the earth?

I will tell you why I believe God should not have put Noah back on the earth in the chapter *Noah and the Ark.*

I am not calling God a liar. I am calling the translators that translated God's word inept. When God said, "Everything," did He really mean everything in verses 7 and 17 as the Bible states, or did He actually mean everything *except* for Noah and his family in verse 8 and verse 18?

"Well, not exactly!" is a frequently used statement throughout *Disorganized Christianity.* Again, I am not calling God a liar or saying that God got confused or that God was lazy in the words He used. I am saying, "Words do have meanings and words do have consequences, and if the Bible wants to use words to control and condemn us, then they had better be the correct words." With the dubious group of translators used to ensure that God's word remains accurate, that seems to be easier said than done.

If *organized religion* cannot even guarantee that their translators are able to absolutely declare God's personal words to be true and correct —and they incorrectly use and confuse a simple word such as "everything" — then do not expect us to put much credence in your specially manipulated controlling and condemning verses.

Controlling and condemning verses are those special verses the people of *organized religion* take upon themselves to interpret in such a way as to maintain their control over our actions, and subsequently our declared condemnation if we don't obey them.

My concern is that while these entrusted men were learning the Word(s) of God so they could pass them on to us for our eternal salvation, they were actually disobeying those very Word(s) of God to such an extent that God grew angry enough to kill them. Just how concerned with accuracy do you think these entrusted men were about faithfully preserving the very Word(s) of God they were breaking? You do realize that Christianity is actually depending on those wicked men's integrity for its eternal salvation?

I don't merely mean the first words of the Bible: *In the beginning God created the heaven and the earth*, or the snake part or the marriage part or the Cain and Abel part or the genealogies, but the *law* part they were evidently breaking on a daily basis.

In our modern everyday lives, it is simply not reasonable to assume that *I* am going to remind *you* of the laws *we are* not supposed to break, while *I* am actually breaking them. Who would believe that? Only a hypocrite or a self-serving person would try to pull off a stunt like that, and just how much credibility and trust would you — or anyone — be willing to give that kind of person?

These are the law parts of the Old Testament used today to try to *control and condemn us on this earth and then to declare our damnation in the hereafter.* The *problem* I have with present day selective translations and misinterpretations is that while these men of God were breaking most of the laws God was trying to teach them, how can I *possibly* have any faith that these same men *accurately transferred* those rules to Noah and his sons before God killed *all flesh* on the planet?

Noah and his sons represented the only conduit left on the planet to further the Word(s) of God. It seems unrealistic for me to believe I shouldn't worry about an accurate transfer of these Word(s) of God. Do you sincerely expect anyone to believe that God still had enough control over these men to represent the truth while He was simultaneously preparing to kill them? Try to convince us of that piece of logic once again and maintain a straight face! And are you then going to try to convince us that we have to passively stand by and accept *our* eternal damnation as a result of the contradictions and misinterpretations that resulted from the remnants of these men?

What about these men?

From the time of Adam and Eve to the global flood of Noah — which was the result of God's final repentive attitude toward men — and the fact the Bible was *verbally* given to man spanning multiple generations, how can we be certain that either Noah *or* his sons Ham, Japheth or Shem knew *all* of the scriptures and teachings that had gone before? Are you trying to convince us these four men knew — by memory — *every word* of God's law? Nowhere does the Bible state that God took the time to tell Noah and his three sons ALL of the Words of God before the global flood. And yet, that transfer of knowledge would be very important and essential to further God's words and the law.

Now it can be said that the Law of Moses hadn't been written yet, and I would agree. If the Law of Moses wasn't the law yet, what *was* the law? Was the law of Noah's time actually written down or merely conveyed by word of mouth and then later translated by whoever had the most power and influence at that time? Sounds a lot like today.

The global Flood of Noah was not punishment for Adam's alleged sin in the Garden of Eden; Adam's banishment from God was his punishment. The Old Testament expressly declared that the banishment from the Garden of Eden and the total destructive flood of Noah was for breaking a law. God's law was passed on from God to His chosen men and then throughout the people.

After the global flood, the responsibility for carrying on the traditions and Word(s) of the Lord had to be entrusted to *only* Noah and his three sons because women certainly were not afforded any authority to communicate the Word of God in those days. Women are not even allowed to speak in church today.

1 Corinthians 14 34-35: *34 Let your women keep silence in the churches; for it is not permitted unto them to speak, but they are commanded to be under obedience, as also saith the law. 35 And if they will learn anything, let them ask their husbands at home; for it is a shame for women to speak in church.*

I am personally not against women preachers. If you believe you have a message to offer, then by all means preach it. But is it *really* God's message or just your own feminist driven ego that drives you to disobey God by preaching to us, "Do not break the law!" God said women can't preach in church, and *you* say women can preach in church.

1 Timothy 2:11-14 *11 Let the woman learn in silence with all subjection. 12 But I permit not a woman to teach, nor to usurp authority over the man, but to be in silence. 13 For Adam was first formed, then Eve. 14 And Adam was not deceived, but the woman, being deceived, was in the transgression.*

How do you *women preachers and women televangelists* justify these verses biblically? They really do not appear to have *any* wiggle room. Again, Not My Verses! I actually have listened to some very smart and instructive women during my growing up years, primarily in Baptist churches. The main rationalization offered for the presence of these women teachers, was that there were not enough men in the congregation willing to teach.

The Bible says that the Word(s) of God were given and passed on verbally, daily from God. You could say the Word(s) of God were spoken or inspired to men who then verbally passed these words along for generations *and then* after the flood you can believe the Word(s) of God were spoken or inspired to *another* bunch of men who actually wrote these words down on parchment.

When I make the statement that most certainly the translators of God's word mistranslated the very words they were tasked with memorizing and writing down, and then certain Christians get angry with us for having concerns, must I remind you that God had those very concerns Himself, before He even gave those very words.

Deuteronomy 4:9-10 *9 Only take heed to thyself, and keep thy soul diligently, lest thou forget the things which thine eyes have seen, and lest they depart from thy heart all the days of thy life; but teach them to thy sons, and thy sons' sons; 10 Specially the day that thou stoodest before the Lord thy God in Horeb, when the Lord said unto me, Gather me the people together, and I will make them hear my words, that they may learn to fear me all the days that they shall live upon the earth, and that they may teach their children.*

God even spoke of the possibility that Word(s) of God given to these chosen men could depart from their memory. Since God had to tell these chosen men not to forget His own words, could it not have happened? I believe it could — and actually did — happen.

I am sharing these verses again because it is so important to *Disorganized Christianity.*

Exodus 31:18 *And he gave unto Moses, when he had ceased speaking with him upon Mount Sinai, Two tables of stone, written with the finger of God.*

Exodus 24:12 *And the Lord said unto Moses, Come up to me into the mount, and be there; and I will give thee tables of stone, and a law, and commandments which I have written, that thou mayest teach them.*

I have had Christians tell me God did not really use His own finger to actually write the Ten Commandments. These Christians said it was *blah, blah, blah and then blah* about figures of speech and symbolism.

So I asked them, "OK, then which other stories in the Bible were figures of speech or just symbolism? Were the 'symbolism passages' marked in the Bible so we *converted non-Christians* would know which verses they were or were we just supposed to take Christianity's word on the *symbolism* verses?"

I then asked them "If the Bible states that God wrote the Ten Commandments with God's own finger and you now say that God did *not* really use God's own finger, I have to then ask w*ho actually* gave us the finger, that wrote the Ten Commandments?"

Of course they would get mad at me for mocking *their* Bible. In truth, I really was not mocking *their* Bible. I was just stating the facts from *their* Bible.

Exodus 31:18 *And he gave unto Moses, when he had ceased speaking with him upon Mount Sinai, Two tables of stone, written with the finger of God.*

Sometimes you may just have to read the Bible twice to get the message. Were the Ten Commandments the *only* verses important enough to have God's full attention? We certainly would not be reading *Disorganized Christianity* or the *Pearl of Great Price* or the *Koran* or the *Watchtower* or the *Book of Mormon* or any other book on religion if God gave God's full attention to the *entire* Bible. God could have. God *should* have. God owes it to us. God said it. God just didn't prove it!

1 Corinthians 14:33 *For God is not the author of confusion but of peace, as in all churches of the saints.*

If God *did* prove that He was not the author of confusion by giving all the churches of the saints the true, correct, and unmistakable Word(s) of God, we would have had enough clarity to not need the past Crusades. The Crusades were started by righteous men of God who took it upon themselves to "help" God convert *everyone* to *their* brand of Christianity. Sounds a little familiar and a *lot* like current state of events to me. I am not going to get into the monetary motivation of the Crusades.

In my earliest Christian years — as a teenager and as a young adult defending my Christian faith — I was taught and I would repeat to others: "God has His reasons and we are not to question God!" Every time we could not, or did not, want to venture a guess or give an answer that would cause us to lose biblical credibility, we as Christians would simply say, "God has reasons, and we are not to question God!"

Disorganized Christianity actually gives you the biblical verses of people who questioned God and not only got away with questioning Him, but then changed God's mind and then He repented on some "evil" actions.

Yes, the Bible says that God repented of His own "evil" actions. Unbelievable, isn't it, that the *all-knowing from the beginning of time* God would not have everything sufficiently under control to not let a few people change His mind and drive Him to repentance. Simply changing your mind is trivial. Being genuinely repentant carries with it a responsibility of admitting that you were wrong in either thoughts or actions and with this admission you must follow through with correction.

While writing *Disorganized Christianity*, I have engaged in extensive conversations with family, friends, clients, and strangers about what I was doing. Many responded by saying "Oh yeah, the Bible is full of contradictions. That's why I don't believe in the Bible or go to church anymore." I then asked them to share with me some Bible contradictions. Almost no one could actually identify a Bible contradiction by verse.

Instead they would say "The actual contradictions are not important anyway." It seems odd that these contradictions were important enough to turn them away from the Bible and the church, but not important enough to actually identify. I believe it is essential that we should know these contradictions and understand them.

Webster's New Collegiate Dictionary: Contradiction 1. "the act of contradicting," 2. "an expression or proposition containing contradictory parts," 3. "a. logical incongruity. b. opposition of factors inherent in a system or situation."

Now, let's consider my extended definition: "When two or more Bible verses do not match."

First type of contradiction: There are certain verses in the Bible which, when matched with other verses, seem to create a contradiction but they really don't. I believe these are merely the result of someone changing their mind over a period of time or describing different situations. To those trying to find biblical contradictions, these examples are easy prey. These contradictions should not hold much validity or really concern anyone.

For example, in **Numbers 6:5** long hair is acceptable: *All the days of the vow of his separation there shall no razor come upon his head; until the days be fulfilled, in the which he separateth himself unto the Lord, he shall be holy, and shall let the locks of the hair of his head grow.* This verse was about the conditions you had to follow if you wanted to take the vow of a Nazirite.

In **1 Corinthians 11:14** long hair is *not* alright: *Doth not even nature itself teach you that, if a man have long hair, it is a shame unto him.* In the 1960's and 70's this verse was used against hippies and teenagers with hair longer than a bowl cut.

In **Dueteronomy 20:14** robbery is commanded: Dueteronomy 20 is actually a chapter on the law of *warfare*. This chapter instructs the Israelites that after they go to battle and win the fight that they shall keep the spoils. *But the women, and the little ones, and the cattle, and all that is in the city, even all the spoil thereof, shalt thou take unto thyself; and thou shalt eat the spoil of thine enemies, which the Lord thy God hath given* . Is it not robbery if you have killed the previous owners first?

In **Exodus 20:15** robbery is *not* commanded: *Thou shalt not steal.* This is one of those original Ten Commandments.

In **Exodus 25:18** make images: *And thou shalt make two cherubim of gold, of beaten work shalt thou make them, in the two ends of the mercy seat.* This verse talks about decorating the Ark of the Covenant with images of golden cherubims.

In **Exodus 20:4** make *no* images: *Thou shalt not make unto thee any carved image, or any likeness of anything that is in heaven above, or that is in the earth beneath, or that is in the water under the earth;.* This is another one of those Ten Commandments.

Second type of contradiction: There are some verses in the Bible which, when matched with other verses, just have different numbers, different times, different places, or different names used for the same people. These verses in the overall credibility of the Bible need not cause any more concern than to serve as examples of the sloppiness of God's inspired translators really not doing their job.

In **Genesis 11:12** the Father of Shelah is stated to be Arpachs: *And Arpachs had lived five and thirty years, and begot Shelah.*

Meanwhile, in **Luke 3:35-36** the Father of Shelah is Cainan and subsequently Arpachs: *35 ... who was the son of Shelah, 36 Who was the son of Cainan, who was the son of Arpachshad.* One person removed, and then his name is misspelled!

The following table shows some more misplaced names across biblical verses:

	Genesis 11:11-18 FATHER – SON		Luke 3:35-46 FATHER - SON
1	Shem – Arpachs	5	Reu – Peleg
2	Arpachs – Shelah	4	Peleg – Eber
3	Shelah – Eber	3	Eber – Shelah
4	Eber – Peleg	2	Shelah – Cainan
5	Peleg – Reu	extra guy	Cainan – Arpachshad
		1	Arpachshad - Shem

Some genealogies in different books of the Bible use reversed sequencing so I numbered the sequence.

Exodus 3:1 and **Exodus 4:18** Jethro was the father-in-law of Moses; *3:1 Now Moses kept the flock of Jethro, his father-in-law, the priest of Midian; and he led the flock to the west side of the desert, and came to the mountain of God, even to Horab. 4:18 And Moses went and returned to Jethro, his father-in-law, and said unto him, Let me go, I pray thee, and return unto my bretheren who are in Egypt, and see whether they are yet alive. And Jethro said to Moses, Go in peace.*

Moses was a very important and dominant figure in the Old Testament. Let us keep in mind that we are not talking about someone's fourth cousin on their great grandmother's brother's son's side of the family. **Judges 4:11** and **Numbers 10:29** Hobab was the father-in-law of Moses; *11 Now Heber, the Kenite, who was of the children of Hobab, the father-in-law of Moses, had separated from the Kenites, and pitched his tent as far as the oak of Zaanaim, which is by Kedesh. 29 And Moses said unto Hobab, the son of Raguel the Midianite, Moses' father-in-law, We are journeying unto the place of which the Lord said, I will give it to you; come thou with us, and we will do thee good;*

for the Lord hath spoken good concerning Israel. How could the translators so obviously misidentify his father-in-law?

Third type of contradiction: There are certain verses in the Bible where it becomes absolutely *essential*, even mandatory, that one verse matches another verse. When verses of absolute obedience are mandated, they *must* be consistent. When verses of eternal condemnation are spewed, they *have to be* consistent and clear.

In the remainder of *Disorganized Christianity* I will give you many more examples of this third type of contradiction and their destructive effects.

It is essential that the Bible be very clear and consistent in its translation and with the interpretation of one word over another. Consider, for a moment, that an entire denomination or faith can be created simply because a couple of verses are in conflict when they are actually supposed to be talking about the same thing.

For example, one verse might say *many* and another verse says *all*. *Many* and *all* are two entirely different words with two entirely different meanings!

If you think that I am being silly and am trying to insult your intelligence by emphasizing that *many* and *all* are two different words with two different meanings and you already absolutely know that *all* means *all* and *many* means *many*, then imagine my own bewilderment when I discovered that the Bible doesn't understand *many* and *all* to be two different words with two different meanings. This is a prime example of a major contradiction in one of the most important doctrinal beliefs for Christians. The doctrinal belief in question is that *ALL* humans have sinned.

Romans 5:19 *For as by one man's disobedience many were made sinners, so by the obedience of one shall many be made righteous.*

This verse implies that because Adam sinned, *many* were made sinners and because of the obedience of one, Jesus, *shall many be made righteous.*

1 Corinthians 15:22 *For as in Adam all die, even so in Christ shall all be made alive;* The first half of this verse reads in Adam *all die.* The second half of this same verse reads in Christ *all shall be made alive. Many* and *all* are *not* the same words and do *not* have the same meanings.

All means *All.*

All means *All, All* the time. *All* does *not* mean *Many* or *Almost All.* Yet, in the interpretation of the Bible, where in Christianity's dogma does *All* mean *All* and when does *All* mean *Many* or *Almost All*?

Here we are clearly looking at another opportunity for those with an agenda to *prove their own position, and to then use it to serve their own purpose.*

Now, I have barely addressed the *All* and *Many* issue in this chapter, but I will go into further detail in the chapter *Translations and misinterpretations!* because I feel it is very important to clarify *organized religion's* abuse of this misinterpretation.

Just so you do not feel like I accidentally found and isolated a single verse that might prove a contradictory use of *many* and *all* or that I manipulated the verse to say what I want the verse to say, please read the following verses:

Again, **Romans 5:19** *For as by one man's disobedience many were made sinners, so by the obedience of one shall many be made righteous.* This verse reads that because Adam sinned many were made sinners.

Romans 3:23 *For all have sinned and come short of the glory of God.*

Another verse records it as *all* who have sinned. This *many* and *all* contradiction occurs not only in the same Bible, not only in the same New Testament; it is in the same *book*, Romans.

Romans 6:23 *For the wages of sin is death, but the gift of God is eternal life through Jesus Christ, our Lord.*

"Many were made sinners" is quite different from all have sinned and all die. If many were made sinners and the wages of sin is death, then that allows for the fact that not all men are sinners and there would not be wages of death for anyone who was more than the many. I am not presuming to know how many constitutes "more" than "many." It could be one or it could be a billion. But, even just one non-made sinner proves my point.

Many are not *All*! Is there now suddenly no need for a savior for the rest of Adam's lineage who were not made sinners? Again, *many* means less than *all*, so there must be someone or a bunch of someones left who do not need the obedience of one, Jesus.

There is a monumental difference between the phrase *many will die* and the phrase *all will die*. Did Jesus die on the cross for *many* sinners or *all* sinners? Was God's eternal punishment delivered because *many* sinned or *all* sinned or just *one* sinned? Do *all* of God's creatures need Jesus or do just *many* of God's creatures need Jesus?

If you think I am picking apart certain words in certain verses, you are exactly right. For one, they are *God's* words and second, they are God's verses; definitely not yours and not mine. But these *are* the words and verses that the Bible uses to *control and condemn us on this earth and then declare our damnation in the hereafter.*

Not any more!

Mark 3:28-29 talks about the unpardonable sin: *28 Verily I say unto you, All sins shall be forgiven unto the sons of men, and blasphemies with* *which they shall blaspheme; 29 But he that shall blaspheme against the Holy Spirit hath never forgiveness, but is in danger of eternal damnation.*

This Bible verse clearly reads that the unpardonable sin, *hath never forgiveness.* This Bible verse does *not* read that the unpardonable sin *maybe, never hath forgiveness.* This Bible verse does *not* read that the unpardonable sin, *hath never forgiveness* until you accept Jesus again as Savior, nor that the unpardonable sin *hath never forgiveness* until you do something to change *never.* Someone may try to assert that what the Bible *really* means is *blah, blah, blah and then blah* about this unpardonable sin.

I am saying that "I just read what the Bible really says about the unpardonable sin." Sounds like God *did have* an unpardonable sin. Well, not exactly!

THE BIBLE SAYS, "HATH NEVER FORGIVENESS!"

1 John 1:7 and **9** on no unpardonable sin: *7 But if we walk in the light, as he is in the light, we have fellowship one with another, and the blood of Jesus Christ, his Son, cleanseth us from all sin. 9 If we confess our sins, he is faithful and just to forgive us our sins, and to cleanse us from all unrighteousness.*

Jesus supposedly died for not only *my* sins and *your* sins, but also the sins of the whole world. **1 John 2:2** *And he is the propitiation for our sins, and not for ours only, but also for the sins of the whole world.*

THE BIBLE SAYS, "*CLEANSETH FROM ALL SIN AND ALL UNRIGHTEOUSNESS.*"

DID JESUS DIE FOR ALL SINS OR JUST MANY SINS?

The Apostle Paul, arguably one of the greatest and best known Apostles of Jesus, I am sure was hoping God did not have an unpardonable sin.

Acts 9:4-5 *4 And he fell to the earth, and heard a voice saying unto him, Saul, Saul, why persecutest thou me? 5 And he said, Who art thou, Lord? And the Lord said, I am Jesus, whom thou persecutest; it is hard for thee to kick against the goads.* This Bible verse reads that a man named Saul persecuted Jesus.

1 Timothy 1:12-16 *12 And I thank Christ Jesus, our Lord, who hath enabled me, in that he counted me faithful, putting me into the ministry, 13 Who was before a blasphemer, and a persecutor, and injurious; but I obtained mercy, because I did it ignorantly in unbelief. 14 And the grace of our Lord was exceedingly abundant with faith and love which is in Christ Jesus. 15 This is a faithful saying, and worthy of all acceptation, that Christ Jesus came into the world to save sinners, of whom I am chief. 16 nevertheless, for this cause I obtained mercy, that in me first Jesus Christ might show forth all long-suffering, for a pattern to them who should hereafter believe on him to life everlasting.*

Paul the Apostle was originally named Saul of Tarsus.

Acts 9:11 *And the Lord said unto him, Arise, and go into the street which is called Straight, and inquire in the house of Judas for one called Saul of Tarsus; for, behold, he prayeth...* Saul changed his name to Paul in **Acts 13:9** *Then Saul (who also is called Paul), filled with the Holy Spirit, set his eyes on him.* Saul had persecuted and *blasphemed Jesus Christ* as recorded in Acts 9:4-5 and 1 Timothy 1:12-16, respectively.

Mark 3:28-29 *28 Verily I say unto you, All sins shall be forgiven unto the sons of men, and blasphemies with which they shall blaspheme; 29 But he that shall blaspheme against the Holy Spirit hath never forgiveness, but is in danger of eternal damnation.*

Mark 3:28-29 actually reads that blaspheming *the Holy Spirit* is the unpardonable sin, not blaspheming Jesus. But, Jesus and the Holy Spirit are one and the same.

In **1 John 5:7** *For there are three that bear record in Heaven, the Father, the Word, and the Holy Spirit; and these three are one.*

We have the Father and the Holy Spirit but who is the *Word*? This scripture is another core validation verse for Christians to declare the Trinity: God the Father, Jesus the Son, and the Holy Spirit; yet Jesus has always been accepted as being the *Word*.

If Bible scholars want to try to say that I am twisting verses and names around just so I can prove the Apostle Paul blasphemed Jesus and the Holy Spirit by identifying Jesus as the *Word*, please be careful! It does not really matter to me whether or not Jesus is the *Word*. But, I absolutely guarantee that it is critical for *organized religion* to believe that Jesus is the *Word*.

John 1:1-2 *1 In the beginning was the Word, and the Word was with God, and the Word was God. 2 The same was in the beginning with God.*

John 1:14 *And the Word was made flesh, and dwelt among us (and we beheld his glory, the glory as of the only begotten of the Father,) full of grace and truth.*

Remember that John 3:16 declares that Jesus was the only begotten Son of God.

If Jesus the *Word* and the Holy Spirit are the same, then Saul — who became Paul — blaspheming against Jesus would be equal to blaspheming against the Holy Spirit. Paul realized that this blaspheming was against Jesus and the Holy Spirit because as noted above in 1 Timothy 1:12 Paul admitted his blaspheming against Jesus, and then in **1 Timothy 1:16**, Paul said Jesus *forgave* him of this blasphemy: *Nevertheless, for this cause I obtained mercy, that in me first Jesus Christ might show forth all long-suffering, for a pattern to them who should hereafter believe on him to life everlasting.*

After that Paul went on to become arguably one of the greatest Apostles and writers of the Bible.

Sounds like God *did not have* an unpardonable sin. Here we go again!

In **Matthew 1:16** Joseph, Mary's husband's father was Jacob: *16 And Jacob begot Joseph, the husband of Mary, of whom was born Jesus, who is called Christ.*

Meanwhile, in **Luke 3:23** Joseph, Mary's husband's father was Heli: *23 And Jesus himself began to be about thirty years of age, being (as was supposed) the son of Joseph, who was the son of Heli:*

Another genealogical table for your consideration:

Matthew 1:15-16		Luke 3:35-46	
SON - FATHER		SON – FATHER	
1	Jesus - Joseph	5	Jesus –Joseph
2	Joseph - Jacob	4	Joseph – *Heli*
3	Jacob -Mattan	3	Heli – Matthat
4	Matthan - Eleazr	2	Matthat – Levi
5	Eleazar - Eliud	1	Levi – Melchi

Most genealogies are terribly wrong, and I do not usually care whether they are correct. However, I feel that this genealogy is very important. We are talking about Christ's grandfather and it is two positions away from accuracy.

There are a lot of explanations as to why this obvious contradiction occurred. One thought is to dismiss the contradiction because the bloodline for Joseph is not really important since he was not Jesus' actual father anyway. Thus, let's leave Joseph's genealogy out.

Another contradiction fix is to state that the bloodline was really of Mary, the mother of Jesus. The genealogy did not say Mary's father, it said Joseph's father. So why even mention Joseph? Stop trying to correct the mistake after the fact; it isn't going to fix the contradiction! Again, I am not concerned or interested in the excuses for why a translator got the Jesus genealogy wrong. I am concerned about why it was even allowed to be in the Bible in the first place and then found to be wrong. A lot of genealogies differ. However, I strongly believe Christ's genealogy should not differ!

ON THE THIRD DAY... AFTER THE THIRD DAY

In **Matthew 16:21**, on the third day: *raised again the third day.*

In **Luke 9:22,** on the third day: *be raised the third day.*

In **Mark 8:31**, after the third day: *and after three days rise again.*

In **Matthew 27:63**, after the third day: *After three days I will rise again.*

I am not going to write out the entire verses concerning *on the third day and after the third day* in this chapter because I have previously addressed this contradiction in the chapter *Resurrection*!

However, I *do* believe that there is really no excuse for there to be any contradictions of any verses if the Bible is, in fact, *infallible*: **2 Timothy 3:16** *All scripture is given by inspiration of God, and is profitable for doctrine, for reproof, for correction, for instruction in righteousness.*

This verse clearly states *all scripture*, not just the scripture we want to be correct or the scripture God made sure was translated correctly. The Bible verse reads *all scripture*. Is this a situation where *all* means *all* or where *all* means *many scriptures are given by inspiration of God?* I am just asking whether or not the Bible intends for *all* to mean *all* or *all* to mean *many*.

I used the *New Scofield Reference Bible, Authorized King James Version* (copyrighted 1967) for the translation of *all* my verses. Some people to whom I gave a pre-published copy of *Disorganized Christianity* wished I had used a different version or *their* favorite version because it gives a better flavor to what the original text meant to say. Respectfully, I listened. In my heart of hearts I thought "That is exactly my point. We choose the version that gives us the best translation to *prove our own position, to then serve our own purpose.*"

I am not declaring the *Scofield Version of the King James Version* to be the best translation. The *Scofield Version of the King James Version* was not chosen because it was the best translation for me in 1967. Back then, I actually did not even know or understand that there were other versions of the Bible. This was simply the version of the Bible my pastor told me to buy for myself from the church bookstore, in order to prepare my sermons.

I can't — and don't want to — tell you which version on today's church bookstore shelf is better or worse. What I *do* believe, today, is that there are far too many Bible versions out there.

1 Corinthians 14:33 *For God is not the author of confusion but of peace, as in all churches of the saints.*

What confused me for a very long time as a young Christian were the evangelists who traveled the church circuits in the 60's and 70's preaching their version of the Bible with the most exaggerated prophecies and revelations. These personal morsels of allegedly God-given information were the basis for their popularity and led to lost souls being saved, while the preachers' own personal power and fame were being elevated. Today, similar evangelists are on the television and the Internet and their fame can grow even faster. Most of these modern televangelists have one thing in common: God speaks to them personally all the time. Televangelists openly declare: "God spoke to me last night and told me this verse really means that and that verse really means this."

Those same televangelists then say: "If you look in the original text or the original language, then you would understand this means that and that means this. When the Word of God uses this word for blah, blah, blah and then blah and you look at the original text or the original language, this blah could mean that blah, but because it is preceded by this blah, blah, then it really means blah, blah and blah, but if it was preceded by that blah, blah, then it could only mean blah, blah, blah, and therefore, I am right and you should send me your money so we can continue our online ministry and save the world from the previously revealed blah, blah."

If God *really* told you preachers and televangelists anything, why didn't God also tell you how to clean up the Word of God? As we have learned in *Disorganized Christianity* so far, the Word of God certainly could use some clarification!

I'll remind you that I am just writing down the words exactly as *someone else* translated them into the *New Scofield Reference Bible, Authorized King James Version* (copyrighted 1967). I am not *interpreting* any words or verses.

If there really is an original written text in some museum or in the Vatican or in some obscure library, then why don't you preachers in the name of Christian clarification get a group of the best of you together and translate the Bible accurately? It should be fairly easy, simply using the "insider information" about the Bible God so generously gives you every week!

What is it that makes *organized religion* believe that each time the Bible has been retranslated, that every instigator like King Henry VIII didn't have an ego problem or a personal agenda to protect? Is it so hard to believe that the Word of God is not as accurate as you preach? Do you still really believe that I am trying to *destroy* the Bible?

I am just trying to show that others have mistranslated the Bible for years to further their own egos and their own personal agendas. If you sincerely want to be certain that the message of God that will lead you to heaven is actually biblically accurate, whether it includes Jesus or not, you must stop and give what I am sharing in *Disorganized Christianity* some serious consideration.

When these local preachers and televangelists claim that the meaning of this word or that phrase really means something different in the "original text," are they saying there really *is* an actual bunch of parchment somewhere we can look at to really understand what one particular word or phrase really means in the context of the original writing? If there is such a document — or collection of documents — that includes everything God wants us to live, die, and be judged by, then why not actively challenge the thousands of mistranslations and misinterpretations that have arisen over time?

This confusion and ambiguity has created *thousands* of religions and for preachers and mankind in particular something needs to be done to fix this biblical confusion: **I Corinthians 14:33** *For God is not the author of confusion but of peace, as in all churches of the saints.*

Are we to believe that a few men with no egos or hidden agendas for power took a bunch of parchments with a lot of writing on them, gathered from many different locations over a period of thousands of years and then put together a Bible that is supposed to inform the world of God's ultimate plan for man?

You could claim "My pastor told me God wrote the Bible and then planted only the words God wanted to have in the Bible into the brains of a bunch of guys in a dream or in a conscious state of complete obedience. God then hid all the writings in a cave. Then, when it was time to create the Bible as we know it today, he told a *few* different guys to translate everything from languages that were no longer used into a modern language, to give us exactly what he wanted us to know in the Bible."

It sounds more unbelievable the more you try to explain it!

Modern-day televangelists often claim that in the original text or original language *this* word and *that* word really means something else. Are they saying it is *their* new definition of the actual word that means something else because God spoke to them and explained it from an original text that no one seems able to actually produce?

You may have noticed that I keep using the modern televangelist as the example of the abuse of contradictions and misinterpretations. In fact, you can use any preacher or individual since the beginning of time up until today to prove such abuse of contradictions and misinterpretations to *prove his own position to then serve his own purpose.*

I feel certain that if you could find 24 of the best male preachers or men of God alive today and gathered them in a room for a year with the actual original parchment text of the Bible, (if you could actually locate it!) those guys would *still* not translate the Bible correctly. Each of them would have so much pride and ego at stake that it would take an act of God *(sorry about that!)* for each of them to admit maybe they were wrong and someone else was right. For the sake of a correct translation of God's word, as directed by God, for the purpose of saving humanity and clearing up all the reasons to have so many divisions, they could not do it. And they *would* not do it. I know this for a fact, because it hasn't been done or even attempted.

Jimmy Swaggart, the hellfire and brimstone preacher, rose to become one of the premier preachers of his day. Jimmy Swaggart is an example of just one man trying to change what we all had been taught the Bible said about sin. When Jimmy Swaggart got caught in sin— because he was bigger than life and from his standpoint bigger than God — he rewrote (to condone his own actions) the very Bible verses he had been using to condemn others.

It is well documented that in 1986 Jimmy Swaggart went after and destroyed an Assembly of God minister named Marvin Gorman and subsequently Jim Bakker of the Praise the Lord television empire. (see: *deceptionbytes.com/jimmy-and-frances-swaggert-a-study-in-duplicity/*) Jimmy Swaggart accused each man of suffering a "moral failure." Jimmy Swaggart had previously been instrumental in determining fallen preachers' punishments for "moral failure," if they had been caught. These two men did not attempt to prove their innocence in a public forum.

In 1988 Jimmy Swaggart got caught up in some "moral failure" allegations of his own, and after he could no longer deny them, he went on national television to ask for forgiveness. He cried some alligator tears and begged his wife and family and congregation to pray for his healing in what has been labeled the "*I have sinned*" speech.

The national presbytery of the Assemblies of God, a denomination of Christianity, gave him a punishment consisting of "*typical Assemblies of God discipline for preachers who admit to moral failures.*" I wonder how many sinful preachers they had previously dealt with to arrive at a "*typical Assemblies of God discipline for preachers who admit to moral failures?*"

Was sexual immorality such a rampant issue with preachers within the Assemblies of God denomination during the 1970's and 80's that they actually had to clarify how bad it was by creating a predetermined "*typical discipline?*"

Whatever happened to, "*Don't sin?*" **Exodus 20:14** *Thou shalt not commit adultery.* Jimmy Swaggart got his "*typical Assemblies of God discipline for preachers who admit to moral failures*" punishment the first time he *got caught* sinning.

Then, in 1991, Jimmy Swaggert got caught up in another incidence of "moral failure," but *this* time before any organizations could chastise him, he told his congregation at the Family Worship Center that, "The Lord told me it's flat none of your business."
(*see community.seattletimes.nwsource.com/archive/?date=19911017&slug=1311458*)

There goes God again, personally talking to Christianity's finest preachers. God never personally talked to me, especially about sinning being acceptable. Has God ever told *you* or anyone you know that it was all right to sin? I thought that sin was precisely what condemned the entire world, to an eternal hell.

We can read in **1 John 3:6-9** 6 *Whosoever abideth in him sinneth not; whosoever sinneth hath not seen him, neither known him. 7 Little children, let no man deceive you; he that doeth righteousness is righteous, even as he is righteous. 8 He that committeth sin is of the devil; for the devil sinneth from the beginning. For this purpose the Son of God was manifested, that he might destroy the works of the devil. 9 Whosoever is born of God doth not commit sin; for his seed remaineth in him. And he cannot sin, because he is born of God.*

Jimmy Swaggart has actually written a Bible commentary book on how to interpret God's word. Sounds like a translation nightmare waiting to let anyone *prove their own position, to then serve their own purpose.*

So Jimmy, save your hellfire and brimstone for the people that still want to follow you, but let *us* be free from your *control and our condemnation on this earth and your declaration of our damnation in the hereafter.* For those who still want to follow you and give you their money, remember that it is written in **Matthew 7:15** *Beware of false prophets, who come to you in sheep's clothing, but inwardly they are ravenous wolves. 16 Ye shall know them by their fruits. Do men gather grapes of thorns, or figs of thistles? 17 Even so, every good tree bringeth forth good fruit, but a corrupt tree bringeth forth bad fruit. 19 Every tree that bringeth not forth good fruit is hewn down, and cast into the fire. 20 Wherefore, by their fruits ye shall know them.* Jimmy, you can get mad at me, but you know that *you* preached that one! I heard it from your own voice.

This Jimmy Swaggart segment of *Disorganized Christianity* is offered to prove beyond a shadow of a doubt that in the 20th and 21st century televangelists who allegedly get their daily messages directly from God and then preach *their version* of the Bible is a flawed concept. I am not trying to singularly condemn Jimmy Swaggart. Jimmy Swaggart did that to himself not once, but twice — on record. Jimmy was the best, and many of us followed him and believed him when he told us not to sin or God would punish us.

Jimmy Swaggart was very adamant and very mean in his sermons against sin and the punishment that would surely result. I also believe Jimmy Swaggart was mean towards sin because he *really believed* that he was preaching against sin *for you and me*. After he himself sinned and got caught again, he did not settle for his own *old* preaching, but decided that a *new* approach would suit him better. He told those in authority over him, his own congregation, "The Lord told me it's flat none of your business" when *he* sinned. And now? Now he wants us to accept his new Bible study guide for *us* to follow. Not Today! I feel absolutely sure that Jimmy Swaggart would have been one of the 24 men chosen to translate God's original word if it had been done, back then.

Jimmy has a special Bible version he peddles. This new translation is the King James text, with his own commentary on how to better understand God. Now that sounds like something we *converted non-Christians* do not need! A new translation from yet another egotistical, agenda-driven preacher wanting to show us the way and what God and Jesus *really* meant. Sounds like another new Daddy to me.

Do you sincerely believe that if you *could* get the original written text of the Bible and then gather one Assembly of God preacher, one Southern Baptist preacher, one Roman Catholic priest, one Jehovah's Witness witness, one Mormon (Church of Jesus Christ of The Latter-day Saints) bishop, and one guy who says, "I Believe In God. I just don't know who *he* is, or *she* is, or *they* are or we are" all in one room, that you could have *any chance* of coming up with a credible way to heaven?

Matthew 7:14 *Because narrow is the gate, and hard is the way, which leadeth unto life, and few there be that find it.*

I will concede that if the actual original written text were to be found in a completed form and retranslated today, mankind would have a better chance for an accurate translation. Everyone involved in the actual translation, including every Christian, every *converted non-Christian,* every member of all *organized Christian* religions and every "never have been a Christian" would have a watchful set of new eyes and a different heart awaiting the outcome. No one person or little power group would be able to force his or her own interpretation to prove his or her own position to then serve his or her own purpose, this time.

I really do not know when or where or even *if* — assuming, for a moment, that the genuine entire original written biblical text existed and was made available — a group of men, probably not unlike the group mentioned above, could actually get together to translate God's word. Even *if* they had different titles, Pharisees, Sadducees, Apostles, Disciples, King or scribe, I am quite sure they would still have had some of the same objections to each other's personal God-given interpretation.

The Nicene Creed that helped define the Bible for the Catholic Church as we know it did not come from a supernatural, God-inspired revelation. Regardless of when or whether Constantine *really* became the first Christian Emperor of Rome, he was not really interested in Christianity. When Constantine ordered the clarification of Jesus as the Son of God at the Council of Nicea in 325 AD, he did have a variety of experts: 300 Bishops. Constantine wanted to overcome objections that hindered religious unity, so he needed to reinterpret an older Arian dogma that stated Jesus was *not* the Son of God. The Council of Nicea declared that Jesus was: *We believe in One Lord, Jesus Christ, the only Son of God.* You can find the entire Nicene Creed on many Internet sites. Yes, even the all-powerful and divine words from God have different words and thus different meanings. For your consideration:

NICENE CREED 325 AD

We believe in one God,
the Father, the Almighty,
maker of heaven and earth,
and of all that is, seen and unseen.

We believe in one Lord, Jesus Christ,
the only Son of God,
eternally begotten of the Father,
God from God, Light from Light,
true God from true God,
begotten, not made, one in Being with the Father.
Through him all things were made.
For us men and for our salvation,
he came down from heaven:
by the power of the Holy Spirit
he was born of the Virgin Mary, and became man.
For our sake he was crucified under Pontius Pilate;
he suffered, died, and was buried.
On the third day he rose again
in fulfillment of the Scriptures;
he ascended into heaven
and is seated at the right hand of the Father.
He will come again in glory to judge
the living and the dead,
and his kingdom will have no end.

We believe in the Holy Spirit,
the Lord, the giver of life,
who proceeds from the Father and the Son.
With the Father and the Son he
is worshipped and glorified.
He has spoken through the Prophets.

We believe in one holy catholic
and apostolic Church.
We acknowledge one baptism
for the forgiveness of sins.
We look for the resurrection of the dead,
and the life of the world to come.

Amen.

The Nicene Creed served the purpose of reinterpreting a previously held *organized religious* dogma and gave us a new *organized religious* dogma. God didn't have *anything* to do with the new dogma, *man* did. Man even changed the so-called God inspired Nicene Creed of 325 AD dogma to the Constantinople Creed in 381 AD and then changed it back to the original Nicene Creed of 325 AD dogma at the Council of Ephesus in 431.

Was God confused when He inspired all these guys to mandate the true creed or what? Wait a minute! Maybe God didn't have *anything to do* with the Nicene, Constantinople, and Ephesus Creeds that define the *organized religions* of today!

When objections arise, you get compromise. With compromise comes confusion. With confusion comes a different version of **2 Timothy 3:16** *All scripture is given by inspiration of God, and is profitable for doctrine, for reproof, for correction, for instruction in righteousness.*

With all the translations and interpretations of the Bible we have today, how can any humble, truth-seeking individual or group honestly say, "Our version is the true Bible?"

My own Bottom Line is this: If the underlying basis of Bible information is flawed, how can the conclusions made by the Bible be anything but flawed? I will show you — using nothing but the *King James Version* throughout *Disorganized Christianity* — that the Bible conclusions are flawed because the Bible information at its basis is flawed.

CHAPTER 5

Translations
and misinterpretations!

Wwhat some people may label as "contradictions" in the Bible could potentially be little more than misinterpretations of the many translations that are available. Before we get to any really important misinterpretations, let's look at a fun misinterpretation; a personal favorite of my own that will not hurt anyone nor change the course of anyone's religious beliefs. This riddle was shared with me years ago, and I have used it quite often.

Who was the first person to smoke in the Bible? Answer: Rebekah.

Genesis 24:64: *And Rebekah lifted up her eyes, and when she saw Isaac, she lighted off the camel.*

If you do not know the history of words or phrases, you might not fully understand or appreciate any interpretation. "Rebekah lighted or lit off the camel." Camels were used for transportation in this story. A camel is also a very popular brand of cigarette. If you don't smoke, you may not understand or appreciate the hazy humor of *lighting off the camel* cigarette.

It is generally accepted that interpretations of the Bible are done in two ways: historical interpretations and literal interpretations.

I will give an example of a *historical interpretation* and a *literal interpretation* of an old Sunday School Bible story that was actually told as *fact* in our church in the 1960's. This *factual* story has since been debunked and established as being false due to the availability we now have to go to the Internet to fact check stories for correct information. In the 1960's, 70's, and 80's we did not have the Internet, so we were stuck with doctrine that might be true or not, purely based on what we were taught by our preachers. If we had wanted to research any stories for their validity, we had to go to the library. But back then we tended to not research such facts in our Bible stories simply because our preachers told us they were true, and we believed our preachers would never lie to us.

This story is found in three of the four gospels written in the New Testament:

Matthew 19:24, Mark 10:25, and Luke 18:25.

Jesus was talking to his disciples about a rich young ruler and how this rich young ruler had kept all of the commandments but was still in danger of going to hell. In the Old Testament — as well as currently in the 20th and 21st century — riches were viewed by popular religions as a sign of God's blessing and being poor was viewed as having *displeased* God in some way. However, this message of equating blessings with being rich was contrary to Old Testament teachings as detailed in this story and throughout the New Testament.

In **Matthew 19:24** *And again I say unto you, It is easier for a camel to go through the eye of a needle, than for a rich man to enter into the kingdom of God.*

In **Mark 10:25** *It is easier for a camel to go through the eye of a needle, than for a rich man to enter into the kingdom of God.*

In **Luke 18:25** *For it is easier for a camel to go through a needle's eye, than for a rich man to enter into the kingdom of God!*

The story of the rich young ruler is particularly important when you take into account why the disciples were so amazed at Jesus' remarks about riches and heaven. The disciples had been taught from their youth through Old Testament teachings that being given riches was a sign that a person was *loved and favored* by God. Aramaic, the language that the original stories were *probably* written in, presents another interpretation challenge. We need to use some common sense to choose the most logical interpretation of this story and not just go for the most glorious storyline that will sell the most tickets to church.

We were told as young Christians that the story of the camel going through the eye of a needle was a perfect example of something hard to do by yourself, but with God's help it *could* be possible. We were told that with God's help anything was possible.

Using a *historical interpretation*, we were told that there was an actual gate in Jerusalem that was intentionally made very small. This small gate was designed to provide security for the city against a possible attack by night visitors. If anyone wanted to enter the city at night, they had to dismount their camels, unload them and then have their camels crawl through the gate literally named *the eye of the needle.*

Two quick interpretations I have heard of this entertaining story are: (1) that anyone attempting to enter the city would have to completely bare themselves of all their possessions and all their camel might be carrying, thereby exposing any weapons that could be used in an attack, and (2) That anyone trying to enter the city, (Heaven), must unburden themselves of all worldly possessions (sin), and come to God with nothing except their faith and belief in Jesus.

Using a *literal interpretation,* we were told that it would be absolutely impossible for a full-grown camel to pass through the eye of a sewing needle without God's help.

In **Matthew 19:16-26** *16 And, behold, one came and said unto him, Good Master, what good things shall I do, that I may have eternal life? 17 And he said unto him, Why callest thou me good? There is none good but one, that is, God; but if thou wilt enter into life, keep the commandments. 18 He saith unto him, Which? Jesus said, Thou shalt do no murder, Thou shalt not commit adultery, Thou shalt not steal, Thou shalt not bear false witness, 19 Honor thy father and thy mother; and, Thou shalt love thy neighbor as thyself. 20 The young man saith unto him, All these things have I kept from my youth up. What lack I yet? 21 Jesus said unto him, If thou wilt be perfect, go and sell what you hast, and give to the poor, and thou shalt have treasure in heaven; and come and follow me. 22 But when the young man heard that saying, he went away sorrowful; for he had great possessions. 23 Then said Jesus unto his disciples, Verily I say unto you that a rich man shall with difficulty enter into the kingdom of heaven. 24 And again I say unto you, It is easier for a camel to go through the eye of a needle, than for a rich man to enter into the kingdom of God. 25 When his disciples heard it, they were exceedingly amazed, saying, Who, then, can be saved? 26 But Jesus beheld them, and said unto them, With men this is impossible, but with God all things are possible.*

I had originally researched the *camel and the eye of the needle* story to discover exactly where in Jerusalem the gate called the *eye of the needle* was located. I did *not* find even one record in which there was evidence of an actual gate called *the eye of the needle.* I found in many articles a declaration that there is *no record* of any current gate called *the eye of the needle* and that there is no record of any biblical gate called *the eye of the needle.* As young Christians we were told there *was* a gate in Jerusalem called the *eye of the needle.*

Well, not exactly! Besides the concern that there never has been a gate called the *eye of the needle,* another concern I have with regard to the *camel and the eye of the needle* story is with the possibly incorrect interpretation of the word *camel.* All Internet sites that try to explain where the original writings for the Bible came from agree that the original writings of the Bible were not written in English.

Perhaps this is obvious reasoning, but let's go backwards in literary time to consider the languages being used during biblical times and see whether this could make a difference in the story of the *camel and the eye of the needle.*

If you do an Internet search for *Bible* or *original writings of the Bible* you will get a sufficient number of websites with thoughts and theories to keep you busy until the end of time. Most websites assert that original Bible parchments were written in the biblical times language, Aramaic, and then the Bible was first translated into Greek and subsequently into Latin.

If God was entrusting men to hear, memorize, teach, and then write down His record, it only seems logical to have men write these words of God in the language of their own tongue. But over time, as we have seen in *Disorganized Christianity* so far, we have experienced examples of mistranslations and misinterpretations from God's original word when translated into other languages. The writers of God's word could barely keep the facts straight using the words of the *one* language they actually knew: Aramaic.

The Aramaic word used for "camel" in the *camel and the eye of the needle* story is *gamla.* Gamla has at least *three* different Aramaic definitions. The three different definitions are camel, rope, and beam. I am going to give the verse Matthew 9:24 again using each of the three definitions for gamla and see if you can see a possible concern over the use of the word *camel.*

Matthew 19:24 *And again I say unto you, It is easier for a camel to go through the eye of a needle, than for a rich man to enter into the kingdom of God.*

Matthew 19:24 *And again I say unto you, It is easier for a rope to go through the eye of a needle, than for a rich man to enter into the kingdom of God.*

Matthew 19:24 *And again I say unto you, It is easier for a beam to go through the eye of a needle, than for a rich man to enter into the kingdom of God.*

The use of the word *camel* seems to be the most descriptive and interesting pairing of the two objects: gamla and needle. The majority of the Internet sites tend to stick with the camel and the needle choice. Of the three words, the word camel does convey the impression of the most impossible task, which is what the story is trying to illustrate.

The use of the word *rope* seems to be the most logical of the three definitions. The Bible story trying to explain an impossible task could still be honored using the word rope, but it is not as colorful as a camel. When we sew with a needle we usually think of a needle and thread, not a needle and rope. I absolutely could not thread a needle with a rope. The integrity of the story though, could still be preserved using the definition: *rope*.

The use of the word *beam* does not seem to have any application to the story.

I do not actually care which definition of *gamla* the translators used. I believe my point has been made that there are opportunities for any translator to choose *the word* they want to make their translation fit their purpose. My challenge to the story of the *camel and the eye of the needle* does hinge on the fact that there *is no such gate.* My concern is that our preachers were taught by someone and then passed along a story about some non-existent gate in Jerusalem simply to glorify a Bible story that renounced "riches."

In this case I am not arguing that our preachers gave us a false story on purpose. I am suggesting that our preachers *have* made other mistakes that we, *converted non-Christians*, are now trying to correct. Should we now fact check every Bible story we are being told as true by our preachers and televangelists? Yes, I believe we should!

You are *commanded* to fact check everything you read in the Bible, by God. Do not take my word for it, read *your* Bible.

Acts 17:10-11 *10 And the brethren immediately sent away Paul and Silas by night unto Berea: who coming hither went into the synagogue of the Jews. 11 These were more noble than those at Thessalonica, in that they received the word with all readiness of mind, and searched the scriptures daily, whether those things were so.*

It is now time for *you* to go home and see *whether those things were so*.

I have obtained eight different Bible versions, each of which has been translated in its own way. I am going to share in full detail eight different verse translations from those eight different Bible versions. Remember that these different texts — written or interpreted by different men — are still supposed to be God's *infallible* word and the basis on which we will be judged to either Heaven or Hell!

Using these eight different translations we *will* get several different interpretations of the same verses!

All Eight Of God's Bible Translations Should Be The Same!

I am going to take a few verses, selected by me, that have been used extensively in *Disorganized Christianity* to prove that the same Bible that started it all, somewhere, could easily have different interpretations from translation to translation. When the translations are all presented, it will be easy to see why some people will get one meaning from one translation and some entirely different meaning from another translation. With these translation differences comes the confusion over what I believe God wanted to say in His *word*.

II Timothy 3:16 *All scripture is given by inspiration of God, and is profitable for doctrine, for reproof, for correction, for instruction in righteousness.*

I Corinthians 14:33 *For God is not the author of confusion but of peace, as in all churches of the saints.*

The eight translations I have chosen to examine are as follows:

Bible in Basic English
New International Readers Version
American Standard Version
New American Standard Bible
English Standard Version
New Living Translation
Wycliff Bible
Young's Literal Translation

I will record *my* version of the Bible text using the *New Scofield Reference* Bible, *Authorized King James Version* (copyrighted 1967) and then compare the next eight texts. The first two verses we will examine are about Jonah and the great fish. The first verse is found in the Old Testament and the second verse is found in the New Testament. In these verses we are examining the Old Testament story of Jonah being in the belly of the great fish for three days and three nights.

New Scofield, King James Version:

Jonah 1:17 *Now the Lord had prepared a great fish to swallow up Jonah. And Jonah was in the belly of the fish three days and three nights.*

Bible in Basic English: *And the Lord made ready a great fish to take Jonah into its mouth; and Jonah was inside the fish for three days and three nights.*

New International Reader's Version: *But the LORD sent a huge fish to swallow Jonah. And Jonah was inside the fish for three days and three nights.* (The great fish is now a "huge" fish).

American Standard Version: *And Jehovah prepared a great fish to swallow up Jonah; and Jonah was in the belly of the fish three days and three nights.*

New American Standard Bible: *And the Lord appointed a great fish to swallow Jonah, and Jonah was in the stomach of the fish three days and three nights.*

English Standard Version: *And the Lord appointed a great fish to swallow up Jonah. And Jonah was in the belly of the fish three days and three nights.*

New Living Translation: *Now the Lord had arranged for a great fish to swallow Jonah. And Jonah was inside the fish for three days and three nights.*

Wycliff Bible: *And the lord made ready a great fish, that he should swallow Jonah; and Jonah was in the womb of the fish three days and three nights.*

Although the word belly is used in most versions, we have now added a stomach and a womb.

This is another perfect example of an opportunity for someone to begin a new interpretation of the story: being in the womb is likened to the beginning of life from God that God could have for the repentant city of Ninevah, and the womb was also a better place for Jonah than in the great fishes' belly, because in the womb Jonah would not have been subject to the gastric digestion process of the stomach and — after all — we were all once in the womb for nine months before we were born, so three days could certainly be possible. That said, I have not yet figured out how swallowing something could make it end up in the womb. I do understand that this interpretation by me is kind of far-fetched and hard to swallow…

A simple translation of this simple verse was maintained by most translations. A few translations had *minor* changes, but why even have a minor translation change if we are looking at God's inspired word? Leave it alone! I do not believe that translators were put on this planet to *change* the words of God.

Did the new translators trying to sell their new revelations feel that if they did not change at least *something* in the Bible — even if it were something small and insignificant — that they would be perceived as mere copycats?

Young's Literal Translation: *And Jehovah appointeth a great fish to swallow up Jonah, and Jonah was in the bowels of the fish for three days and three nights.*

Belly, stomach, womb, and now bowels. Each have a different literal and interpretational meaning. Any preacher could go off on a rant that would certainly entertain their audience and certainly get a higher television or radio rating. Higher ratings could of course lead to more donations and glory thanks to this special insight and of course the fact that God was giving this particular preacher a better revelation of the scriptures than anyone else.

In these next verses we will be examining the New Testament story of Jonah being in the belly of the great fish for three days and three nights and the prophesy of Jesus being in the heart of the earth for three days and three nights.

New Scofield, King James Version:

Matthew 12:40 *For as Jonah was three days and three nights in the belly of the great fish, so shall the Son of man be three days and three nights in the heart of the earth.*

Bible in Basic English: *For as Jonah was three days and three nights in the stomach of the great fish, so will the Son of man be three days and three nights in the heart of the earth.*

New International Reader's Version: *Jonah was in the stomach of a huge fish for three days and three nights. Something like that will happen to the Son of Man. He will spend three days and three nights in the grave.* "Something like that will happen!"

American Standard Version: *... for as Jonah was three days and three nights in the belly of the whale; so shall the Son of man be three days and three nights in the heart of the earth.* There is that *whale.*

New American Standard Bible: *... for just as Jonah was three days and three nights in the belly of the sea monster, so will the Son of Man be three days and three nights in the heart of the earth.* Now we have a *"sea monster."*

English Standard Version: *For just as Jonah was three days and three nights in the belly of the great fish, so will the Son of Man be three days and three nights in the heart of the earth.*

New Living Translation: *For as Jonah was in the belly of the great fish for three days and three nights, so will the Son of Man be in the heart of the earth for three days and three nights.*

Wycliff Bible: *For as Jonas was in the womb of a whale three days and three nights, so man's Son shall be in the heart of the earth three days and three nights.* Now they spelled Jonah as Jonas, and we have another womb and whale.

Young's Literal Translation: ... for, as Jonah was in the belly of the fish three days and three nights, so shall the Son of Man be in the heart of the earth three days and three nights.

So we have bellies, wombs and bowels. We have great fishes and whales and sea monsters. We have misspelled character names. All of these different translations are coming from a book that should have *no* mistranslations or misinterpretations.

I simply ask that if this is *truly* the word of God and *organized religion* wants to use these words of God to *prove its own position and then use it to serve its own purpose* and *control us and condemn us on this earth and declare our damnation in the hereafter* why does it allow the text to be changed so much? Even the little changes from a great fish to a whale to a sea monster absolutely prove that you are not holding your translators accountable to a very high standard or possibly to any standard *at all*.

Why should we have to listen to your verses about our eternal judgment to hell and then give you *any* credibility to judge us when you can't even take God's word and hold all these translations to a consistent truth about *a great fish*? You may argue that it is "just three different names for a great fish," but if that is true, then consider the following passage from Genesis.

Genesis 2:19-20 *19 And out of the ground the Lord God formed every beast of the field, and every fowl of the air; and brought them unto Adam to see what he would call them: and whatever Adam called every living creature, that was the name thereof. 20 And Adam gave names to all the cattle, and to the fowl of the air, and to every beast of the field; but for Adam there was not found an help fit for him.*

Adam named all the living creatures. So if Adam called whatever swallowed Jonah a great fish and God mandated that whatever Adam called each living creature would henceforth be its name, then why did the translators not hear or understand God when He inspired the Jonah story to them? Did Adam name the fish: tiny fish, regular fish, medium fish, large fish, larger fish, fat fish, skinny fish, and then great fish? I am just curious as to how technical Adam got? Was the great fish a Gray Whale or an *Eschrichtius robustus*? Does it really matter whether the great fish was not actually a "*great fish*" but in fact a whale? It should. In reality, a whale is a mammal, not a fish.

Let us consider that whales are large aquatic *mammals* that breathe air through blowhole(s) into lungs (unlike fish that breathe using gills). Whales swim by moving their muscular tails (flukes) up and down. Fish swim by moving their tails from side to side; see www.enchantedlearning. com for reference.

Maybe God didn't know the difference between a great fish and a whale or maybe neither the old nor new translators knew the difference between a great fish and a whale. If *organized religion* cannot even get such simple things as a great fish and a whale *exactly* and *consistently* translated, then why should we give *them* any credibility with our eternal damnation? You preachers have several verses that you continuously condemn us with, but at this point why should we believe that you actually know what you are talking about?

When you get the whales and the great fishes sorted out, then let's have a talk!

Next, we will examine the biblical account following Jesus' resurrection that describes how graves of dead people were opened and the resurrected bodies went into the holy city to visit people. There is more on this subject in the chapter *Raised from the dead and then went visiting!*

Genuine living "Dead People!"

New Scofield, King James Version:

Matthew 27:53 *And came out of the graves after his resurrection, and went into the holy city, and appeared to many.*

Bible in Basic English: *And coming out of their resting-places, after he had come again from the dead, they went into the holy town and were seen by a number of people.*

New International Reader's Version: *They came out of the tombs. After Jesus was raised to life, they went into the holy city. There they appeared to many people.*

American Standard Version: ... and coming forth out of the tombs after his resurrection they entered into the holy city and appeared unto many.

New American Standard Bible: *... and coming out of the tombs after his resurrection they entered the holy city and appeared to many.*

English Standard Version: *...and coming out of the tombs after his resurrection they went into the holy city and appeared to many.*

New Living Translation: *They left the cemetery after Jesus' resurrection, went into the holy city of Jerusalem, and appeared to many people.*

Wycliff Bible: *And they went out of their burials, and after his resurrection they came into the holy city, and appeared to many.*

Young's Literal Translation: *... and having come forth out of the tombs after his rising, they went into the holy city, and appeared to many.*

I chose the translation of this particular passage not to prove that there is a great difference in each version, but simply to document that *dead people did rise from the dead and then did go visiting.* All nine versions declare: *dead people did go visiting after Jesus' resurrection.*

We will next examine the biblical account of angels and giants.

Here are some verses on Giants!

New Scofield, King James Version:

Genesis 6:4 *There were giants in the earth in those days; and also after that, when the sons of God came in unto the daughters of men, and they bore children to them, the same, became mighty men who were of old, men of renown.*

Bible in Basic English: *There were men of great strength and size on the earth in those days; and after that, when the sons of God had connection with the daughters of men, they gave birth to children: these were the great men of old days, the men of great name.*

New International Reader's Version*: The Nephilim were on the earth in those days. That was when the sons of God went to the daughters of men and had children by them. The Nephilim were the heroes of long ago. They were famous men. Nephilim were also on the earth later on.*

American Standard Version: *The Nephilim were in the earth in those days, and also after that, when the sons of God came unto the daughters of men, and they bare children to them: the same were the mighty men that were of old, the men of renown.*

New American Standard Bible: *The Nephilim were on the earth in those days, and also afterward, when the sons of God came in to the daughters of men, and they bore children to them. Those were the mighty men who were of old, men of renown.*

English Standard Version: *The Nephilim were on the earth in those days, and also afterward, when the sons of God came in to the daughters of men, and they bore children to them. These were the mighty men who were of old, men of renown.*

New Living Translation: In those days, and for some time after, giant Nephilites lived on the earth, for whenever the sons of God had intercourse with women, they gave birth to children who became the heroes and famous warriors of ancient times.

Wycliff Bible: Soothly giants were on the earth in those days, forsooth after that the sons of God entered (in) to the daughters of men, and those daughters begat; these were mighty of the world and famous men.

Young's Literal Translation: The fallen ones were in the earth in those days, and even afterwards when the sons of God come in unto daughters of men, and they have borne to them—they (are) the heroes, who, from of old, (are) the men of name.

Again, I chose this set of translations not so much to prove that there is significant difference in each version but more to document that there were fallen angels (sons of God) and these fallen angels mated with the daughters of men and created babies. These babies then became giants, the great men of the times. But there is a big time error in this scenario. You can find this error in the chapter *Angels and giants and creeping thing, oh my!*

All nine versions declare that fallen angels and the daughters of men bred giants.

1 Corinthians 15:22 *For as in Adam all die, even so in Christ shall all be made alive.* The first half of this verse reads that in Adam *all die.* The second half of this verse reads that in Christ *all shall be made alive.*

For me, one of the most frustrating aspects of *organized religion* is how preachers ordain themselves with the authority to say what one half of any verse means and then, without adhering to the same interpretation, define what the second statement in the same verse means to *prove their own position to serve their own purpose.* Let me explain.

My interpretation of this verse is that in Adam we *all die*. *My* interpretation of the second half of this verse is that in Jesus we *shall all live*. The first half of this verse states that everyone will die because of Adam. There are no conditions or reasons offered and we do not need to do anything else while on this planet to merit this death.

The second half of this verse states that *everyone* shall be made alive in Christ. There are no conditions or reasons and we do not need to do anything else while on this planet to merit this *life*. I am not adding any special God inspired knowledge nor cross referencing other verses. This verse simply reads that in Adam *we all die*, period. This verse simply reads that in Christ *we all live*, period.

However, *organized religion* interprets this verse differently. The first half of this verse states that *everyone* will die because of Adam's original sin. There *are no* further conditions or reasons, and we do not need to do anything else while on this planet to merit this death. This is identical to the interpretation I have.

The second half of this verse states *everyone* shall be made alive in Christ because he died on the cross for our sins that were passed down to us by Adam, (first half of the verse). *Organized religion's* interpretations imply that in this verse there *are* further conditions while on this planet to merit this life.

How can you reasonably — using the same words and word structure in the same sentence — come up with *two different interpretations* of the same words. These added conditions of how we shall live and accept Jesus have no foundation *in this verse*. *Organized religion* operates under a dogma that *All* men and *All* women are sinners and they will *all* die and go to hell just because they were born with the condemnation of Adam's sin. *All* men and *All* women do not have to do anything else to receive this eternal death condemnation; they simply just need to be born. This verse does *not* say that the Bible has to prove *why* they should die. The Bible merely states in this verse they will *all die.*

Organized religion operates under a second dogma that conditions gaining eternal life upon accepting Jesus as your personal Savior. Clearly, this condition for salvation through having a belief in Jesus is not found in *this* verse.

Hang on to your emotions for this next one!

There is *not* one absolute stand-alone verse in the Bible that *actually* tells anyone what exactly they are required to believe in, with respect to Jesus, in order to be saved. The actual conditions for salvation can be found in *many* verses, but depending on which particular *organized religion* building you happen to go to, preachers will then pick and choose *their* own acceptable terms.

Of course, you may want to challenge me on this statement, but before you get started, please take a moment to explain to yourself why — in the protestant grouping of *organized religions* we have today — do you have Baptists, Methodists, Episcopalians, Presbyterians, Lutherans, Assembly of God's, Nazarenes, Church of Christ's and I'll leave you to name the rest of the denominations. The common thread is that they *all* profess to believe in Jesus Christ the Lord and Savior of all mankind and yet all of these groups do not or will not believe the same dogma. I am not the one who confused them! Their translators confused them. Don't get mad at *me*; get mad at Bible translators!

So let us examine some *Salvation verses.* All of the following verses tell you what you have to do to be saved; to get into heaven or not be sent to hell. There are no additional conditions or mandates outlined before these verses nor after these verses to explain in detail what each verse *really* should "mean." These verses simply attempt to imply one way to get to heaven.

John 3:16 *For God so loved the world, that he gave his only begotten Son, that whosoever believeth in him should not perish, but have everlasting life.*

Okay, believe what? Believe that he was a real man? Believe he was God sent down to Earth as a man? Believe he is the Messiah? Believe he is the Savior? Believe he died on a cross? Believe he rose again from the dead? Using this verse, what precisely are we to believe? Maybe we can now add or subtract whatever conditions we want to, in order to secure our salvation?

Oh, wait! That is what *organized religion* has already done!

Matthew 18:3 *And said, Verily I say unto you, Except ye be converted, and become as little children, ye shall not enter into the kingdom of heaven.*

Okay, be "converted" from what to what? How do you become converted if you do not know what exactly you are being converted *to* or *from?*

Mark 16:16 *He that believeth and is baptized shall be saved; but he that believeth not shall be damned.*

Again, believe what? Note that now we have the condition of "baptism" added. This particular verse does not say either believe *or* be baptized, but both. At this time I do not want to get into the discussion of whether you need to be baptized by sprinkling, anointing, immersion or even by proxy. This major confusion and misinterpretation of baptism thanks to past translators' inaccuracy presents yet another point of difference between various *organized religions* that have declared their different truths as they interpret it, and subsequently used that trust as a controlling mechanism.

Acts 2:21 *And it shall come to pass that whosoever shall call on the name of the Lord shall be saved.*

Call what on his name? The verses surrounding this passage offer no suggestions at all as to what it means to call on the name of the Lord. This is an open-ended nightmare of misinterpretation just waiting to be exploited.

Acts 16:31 *And they said, Believe on the Lord Jesus Christ, and thou shalt be saved, and thy house.*

I am continually asking the question of *"believe what,"* because the Bible keeps telling me to *believe.* My question is really quite simple: to *believe* what, exactly? According to this verse, if I "believe on the Lord Jesus Christ" will my house or family also be saved? Can I believe enough for them, so *they* can get to heaven even if they don't believe or is this verse suggesting that if *I* believe, *they* will believe?

Once again, the Internet is filled with stories of millions of baby-boomers and millennials leaving "their house and family." Remember: according to the Pew Research Center, 106 *million* Christians are expected to leave their religion between 2010 and 2050.

Romans 10:9 *That if thou shalt confess with thy mouth the Lord Jesus, and shalt believe in thine heart that God raised him from the dead, thou shalt be saved.*

Okay, so now we have to believe that Jesus was raised from the dead, in order to be saved. I suppose at least that is *something* to believe in, even if we do not really know whether this raising from the dead happened *on the third day* or *after the third day* or before the third day according to different *infallible* verses in the Bible.

Matthew 10:22 *And ye shall be hated of all men for my name's sake, but he that endureth to the end shall be saved.*

This verse talks about being hated by all men and that if Christians endure this hate then they will be saved. So would that also mean that if *after* Christians are saved, they decide to no longer endure this hate then they can be UN-saved? Does this verse tell us that because Christians did not have the strength to endure this hate, they were never *really saved* to begin with?

Matthew 24:13 *But he that shall endure unto the end, the same shall be saved.*

Although I was never told to endure nor ever told anyone else to endure, this must be an important part of the salvation puzzle because it is mentioned twice. I ask again, must Christians "endure" in order to be saved? What must Christians endure? No special preacher thoughts or interpretations!

When the Bible reads the word saved, does it mean "saved" or does it mean *saved?* No, I am not being funny or argumentative. I have merely presented verses that tell Christians what they must do to be *saved.* Some of these verses are very explicit in the conditions that must be met to ensure salvation and other verses are open to interpretation. If the word in the verse says "saved," does it mean salvation from eternal hell, saved, or some other definition of personally being physically saved while on this planet?

And herein lies the basic point of this chapter: The word *saved* seems to be left up to anyone to interpret in the manner of what he or she wants it to mean.

If you read the entire context of these last two verses, Matthew 10:22 and Matthew 24:13, you would have a valid argument for the understanding that this word *saved* does not mean salvation into heaven, but simply being saved through the trials Christians have to endure during the last days before Christ comes a second time.

My point here is not to argue that this word *saved* in these two verses means actually *saved* as in salvation into heaven or just saved through earthly trials. My point is that the same five letters that spell the word *saved* are used interchangeably to mean *saved* as in salvation from hell and *saved* as in surviving.

In the days before the written word and before people could readily challenge the words they were told, it would be very easy to preach to someone that he or she had to endure whatever trials the preacher declared, in order to be *saved* from hell.

Then a new word is interjected into the salvation verses we all know and love. That word is "remission."

Webster's New Collegiate Dictionary, definition of remission: "remission 1. the act or process of remitting. Remitting 1. to release from the guilt of or penalty of."

Mark 1:4 *John did baptize in the wilderness, and preach the baptism of repentance for the remission of sins.*

Here we have an additional condition of *baptism of repentance* for the remission of our sins.

Acts 10:43 *To him give all the prophets witness, that through his name whosoever believeth in him shall receive remission of sins.*

Okay, one more time: believe in *what* through his name and where is the baptism part in this verse? Should we just take for granted that baptism is implied? Have you ever seen a chocolate cake recipe in a cookbook and then the author decided that since the title of the recipe is "chocolate cake" that he or she can leave chocolate out of the list of ingredients because it may sound redundant and we should "just know" that chocolate is an implied ingredient?

Hebrews 9:22 *And almost all things are by the law purged with blood, and without shedding of blood is no remission.*

I know that this verse does not exactly speak to the remission of *sins*. But, it is quite clear in **Romans 3:25** *Whom God hath set forth to be a propitiation through faith in his blood, to declare his righteousness for the remission of sins that are past, through the forbearance of God;*

To add to the confusion, the first part of **Hebrews 9:22** states that *almost all things are by the law purged with blood.* Okay, exactly *which* things aren't purged with blood and can I find them listed somewhere, or do I have to be dependant on some *organized religion* to tell me what the other *"almost things"* are?

Matthew 26:26-28 *26 And as they were eating, Jesus took bread, and blessed it, and broke it, and gave it to the disciples, and said, Take, eat; this is my body. 27 And he took the cup, and gave thanks, and gave it to them, saying, Drink ye all of it; 28 For this is my blood of the new testament, which is shed for many for the remission of sins.* Shed for *ALL* or *MANY*?

Some *organized religions* believe that the *cup* and the *bread* symbolizing Jesus' blood and body have to be taken *monthly*, in order for a person to be saved. Some o*rganized religions* believe that the *cup* and the *bread* have to be taken monthly to prove that you are not living in sin and as a result of complying you can stay in the good graces of that *organized religion.* Some *organized religions* believe that the *cup* has to contain actual wine and the *bread* has to be unleavened; no yeast used in the baking. Some *organized religions* believe that the *cup* can be grape juice and the *bread* can be any cracker on sale at your local market. It is odd, but I cannot find any specific conditions for the cup and bread for the remission of my sins from this verse.

Ephesians 2:8-9 *8 For by grace are ye saved through faith; and that not of yourselves, it is the gift of God- 9 Not of works, lest any man should boast.*

If this gift from God came from our faith only and we cannot claim any works to receive this gift, then it seems rather confusing when you read the *next* verse about this *works and faith* discrepancy.

James 2:20 *But wilt thou know, O vain man, that faith without works is dead?*

It is confusing enough just to read the Bible on our own and try to make sense of it all without also having an *organized religion* put tasks in front of you and place monetary demands on our faith. Which is the correct *infallible* Bible interpretation?

We have an example of one man just believing that Jesus was innocent and he was then saved, by Jesus himself.

Luke 23:33, 39-43 *33 And when they were come to the place which is called Calvary, there they crucified him, and the malefactors, one on the right hand, and the other on the left. 39 And one of the malefactors who was hanged railed at him, saying, If thou be the Christ, save thyself and us. 40 But the other, answering, rebuked him, saying, Dost not thou fear God, seeing thou art in the same condemnation? 41 And we, indeed, justly; for we receive the due reward of our deeds. But this man hath done nothing amiss. 42 And he said unto Jesus, Lord, remember me when thou comest into thy kingdom. 43 And Jesus said unto him, Verily I say unto thee, Today shalt thou be with me in paradise.*

The thief on the cross simply believed that Jesus was innocent and asked to be remembered when Jesus got to his kingdom. Jesus told the malefactor he was saved and would be with Jesus that day in paradise. This singular moment — with the whole world eventually watching, at least through these Bible passages — appears to have been the perfect time for Jesus to define his conditions for salvation. Jesus had enough of his mind and compassionate spirit about him to ask God to forgive the crowd and the one malefactor on another cross. Why not tell *all* of us what we need to do to receive eternal salvation and an eternity with God and Jesus in heaven? Perfect timing for salvation's clear message to be established or was the moment lost forever?

After considering these few Bible verses on salvation and faith and baptism and repentance and remission of sins and believing and enduring, my simple question remains: "In order to be *saved*, do I have to fulfill the conditions of *all* of these verses or just the verses I *want* to, because they all say that if I just do at least what that single verse says, I will be *saved*?"

If you or I *can* choose our own verses to believe, why do we need *organized religion* to choose our verses *for* us? Seriously, *organized religion* cannot even agree on which verses to believe for itself. How can it credibly tell us which verses are the "correct" verses for us?

Let's go back to the verse **1 Corinthians 15:22** *For as in Adam all die, even so in Christ shall all be made alive.*

This verse reads, *"Even so in Christ shall all be made alive."* This verse does not say *"Even so in Christ shall all be made alive"* on the *condition* that you accept Jesus as your personal Savior. This verse does not say, *"Even so in Christ shall all be made alive;"* on the *condition* you get baptized. This verse does not say, *"Even so in Christ shall all be made alive;"* on the *condition* you sell all of your possessions and give the money to the poor, like the rich young ruler.

Those were Jesus' words and no *organized religion* interpretation should be necessary. I never sold all of my possessions and gave the money to the poor in order to be *saved*. As I remember, I *was* the poor.

Accepting Jesus as your personal Savior is also not mandated in this verse in order to be *made alive*. Being baptized is not mandated in this verse to be *made alive*. Selling your possessions and giving the money to the poor is not mandated in this verse to be *made alive*. It may sound like I am repeating myself, but I have tried to state this thought in as many distinct ways as I can so it will be clear to us *converted non-Christians* that *organized religion* mandates its own conditions with *no biblical basis* in fact and that we are not bound by their conditions of salvation. I am not trying to convince any *organized religion* member of my interpretations because I believe they do not want to understand the concept.

If any *organized religion* member wanted to understand and accept any of these concepts, I think they would have become *converted non-Christians* long before me and the advent of *Disorganized Christianity. Organized religion* also cannot imply that this verse states that there are *other* verses that tell us how to be *made alive.* This verse does not *mandate* that anything else be done to be *made alive,* and it does not imply it. Plain and simple!

If 1 Corinthians 15:22 reads that man gets a universal and complete condemnation to death from God because of Adam and we have to accept this universal and complete condemnation to death, so be it. But, if that is true and absolute, then this verse should also give man a universal and complete reconciliation to life because of Jesus. To *organized religion* I say: this is your verse translation or interpretation, not mine!

CHAPTER 6

Numbers.

Numbers have such a strong, powerful and meaningful place in our existence. Most of the time we don't see the real mystery of numbers, the hidden wisdom of numbers or just the unbelievable beauty and order of numbers.

1 Corinthians 14:40: *Let all things be done decently and in order.* Well, there certainly is order in these numbers:

$$0 \times 9 + 1 = 1$$
$$1 \times 9 + 2 = 11$$
$$12 \times 9 + 3 = 111$$
$$123 \times 9 + 4 = 1111$$
$$1234 \times 9 + 5 = 11111$$
$$12345 \times 9 + 6 = 111111$$
$$123456 \times 9 + 7 = 1111111$$
$$1234567 \times 9 + 8 = 11111111$$
$$12345678 \times 9 + 9 = 111111111$$
$$123456789 \times 9 + 10 = 1111111111$$

$$9 \times 9 + 7 = 88$$
$$98 \times 9 + 6 = 888$$
$$987 \times 9 + 5 = 8888$$
$$9876 \times 9 + 4 = 88888$$
$$98765 \times 9 + 3 = 888888$$
$$987654 \times 9 + 2 = 8888888$$
$$9876543 \times 9 + 1 = 88888888$$
$$98765432 \times 9 + 0 = 888888888$$

$$1 \times 1 = 1$$
$$11 \times 11 = 121$$
$$111 \times 111 = 12321$$
$$1111 \times 1111 = 1234321$$
$$11111 \times 11111 = 123454321$$
$$111111 \times 111111 = 12345654321$$
$$1111111 \times 1111111 = 1234567654321$$
$$11111111 \times 11111111 = 123456787654321$$
$$111111111 \times 111111111 = 12345678987654321$$

$$1 \times 8 + 1 = 9$$
$$12 \times 8 + 2 = 98$$
$$123 \times 8 + 3 = 987$$
$$1234 \times 8 + 4 = 9876$$
$$12345 \times 8 + 5 = 98765$$
$$123456 \times 8 + 6 = 987654$$
$$1234567 \times 8 + 7 = 9876543$$
$$12345678 \times 8 + 8 = 98765432$$
$$123456789 \times 8 + 9 = 987654321$$

When I was a teenager looking at Christianity and the Bible from a child's perspective, everything was new and interesting. At 14 — in the 1960's — I did not understand what a virgin birth was.

Matthew 1:23 *Behold, the virgin shall be with child, and shall bring forth a son, and they shall call his name Immanuel, which, being interpreted, is God with us.*

I did believe in the virgin birth of Jesus because I was told that it was something special.

My stepfather drank an occasional beer. Being poor, I bet he really would have liked Jesus to show him how to turn water into wine!

John 4:46 *So Jesus came again into Cana, of Galilee, where he made the water wine.*

Numbers and unusual events (a virgin birth and turning water to wine) do fill the Bible with wonderment.

My stepfather and mother always made sure my brothers and sisters and I had good food to eat and that we always had enough. My mother would make lima bean soup on Monday and then she would add a ham hock or two on Tuesday and then she would add stewed tomatoes on Wednesday. She could make a little go a long way, and I do miss my mother's cooking.

In a long shot comparison, Jesus took five loaves of bread and two fishes and fed 5,000 men and still had leftovers.

Mark 6:41-44 *41 And when he had taken the five loaves and the two fishes, he looked up to heaven, and blessed, and broke the loaves, and gave them to his disciples to set before them; and the two fishes divided he among them all.*

I do not know if they cooked the fish before eating it. The Bible didn't say whether they cooked the fish. Maybe they served sushi style?

42 And they did all eat, and were filled. 43 And they took up twelve baskets full of the fragments, and of the fish. 44 And they that did eat of the loaves were about five thousand men.

Twelve baskets of leftovers is a lot of fragments. Numbers in the Bible are critical to understanding the magnitude of any miracle or everyday happenings.

In my early Christian years there were many exciting stories and prophecies. I can remember, even then, with all the stuff there was to learn and to be curious about that the number 666 was the most fascinating at the time.

If Jesus was the hero, then whoever this 666 guy was, he was the villain! According to the Bible this 666 guy is the anti-Christ. In the end times the anti-Christ is supposed to come into power and rule the world by offering mankind a false peace that some say will last for three and-a-half years and in the next three and-a-half years he will bring war and destruction.

Adolf Hitler was supposed to be the anti-Christ. Several Popes were named the anti-Christ. John F. Kennedy, George Bush, and Barack Obama have all been labeled as the anti-Christ by various groups. Even today, Christians and non-Christians remain fascinated by this 666 guy. But just who is he and do we have other clues besides the Bible that might shed some light on his origin and true purpose?

Let's look at **Revelation 13:17-18** *17 And that no man might buy or sell, except he that had the mark, or the name of the beast, or the number of his name. 18 Here is wisdom. Let him that hath understanding count the number of the beast, for it is the number of a man; and his number is six hundred three score and six.*

A score is equal to 20. Three score equals 60. The number of the anti-Christ is thus 666. The driving factor in this verse is; *no man might buy or sell.*

In the 1970's the food industry was introduced to a new pricing and labeling phenomenon called the Universal Product Code (UPC) barcode. This series of black stripes on a little sticker — subsequently printed directly onto the grocery product or packaging — caught the imagination of conspiracy Christians. Revelation 13:17 stated *And that no man might buy or sell, except he had that mark,* so they tried to figure what series of stripes would equal 666.

Local church preachers, old-time traveling evangelists, and modern day televangelists have had a well-documented history of telling tall tales and comparing quirky phenomena as a means to bolster their personas. The taller the tale, the bigger their persona and thus their paycheck.

Comparisons of tree branches and leaf formations that could be likened to Jesus and his crucifixion on the cross (another tree) would be expounded to excite the congregation and have them listen in a trance-like state of awe. The comparison of a fish being swallowed by a whale or sea monster and then escaping from the "great fish's belly" along with Jonah's miraculous escape from a "great fish's" belly caught everyone's imagination.

I remember one example given a long time ago, before it became everyday knowledge, of the Trinity (e.g. the Father, the Son and the Holy Ghost) being declared as three separate entities, yet still being one. This particular declaration was explained by using the example of water being liquid, solid ice, and steam, but still being simply water. The example is still being used today, but imagine the impact of its explanation in the 1960's and before. It was more than enough to set the table for the fire and brimstone message to follow!

I have included in this chapter a tall tale and some phenomena that may grab your attention and leave you wondering in awe, but there is no fire and brimstone message to follow.

NUMERALS

In our modern day decimal counting system these are the first ten basic numerals:

0,1,2,3,4,5,6,7,8,9. These numerals can be used to represent any numbered amount we want. We use 1 as the number one; 19 as the number nineteen; 478 as the number four hundred seventy eight, and so on.

Add up the first ten basic whole numerals in our modern day counting system, only once per numeral: 0+1+2+3+4+5+6+7+8+9 and the sum equals the number 45.

THE PHENOMENA
ROMAN NUMERALS

In the Roman numeral counting system these are the first six basic letters: I, V, X, L, C, D. Again, these letters can be used to represent any numbered amount we want. We use I as the number one; XIX as the number nineteen; CDLXXVIII as the number four hundred seventy eight. Add up the first six basic letters in the Roman numeral counting system only once per letter:

$$I + V + X + L + C + D = 666$$
$$1 + 5 + 10 + 50 + 100 + 500 = 666$$

These are not *my* personal new translations or misinterpreted numbers. These numbers have been around a lot longer than I have, for everyone to see.

One day I just noticed the correlation of the first six characters of the Roman numeral system and 666; with a new set of eyes. Absolutely fascinating!

The Apostle Paul was preaching and teaching God's word and the Jesus message to groups of people wherever he could find them. The audience marveled at the *wisdom* of the Apostle Paul and wondered how he could know so much.

As the Apostle Paul was preaching and teaching one day, he attempted to explain the New Testament record found in **1 Corinthians 2:7** *But we speak the wisdom of God in a mystery, even the hidden wisdom, which God ordained before the ages unto our glory.*

The *wisdom* that the Apostle Paul was preaching was not from him, but from God.

1 Corinthians 2:1-7 *1 And I, brethren, when I came to you, came not with excellency of speech or of wisdom, declaring unto you to testimony of God. 2 For I determined not to know any thing among you, except Jesus Christ, and him crucified. 3 And I was with you in weakness, and in fear, and in much trembling. 4 And my speech and my preaching were not with enticing words of man's wisdom, but in demonstration of the Spirit and of power; 5 That your faith should not stand in the wisdom of men, but in the power of God. 6 However, we speak wisdom among them that are perfect; yet not the wisdom of this age, nor of the princes of this age, that come to nothing; 7 But we speak the wisdom of God in a mystery, even the hidden wisdom, which God ordained before the ages unto our glory.*

We can see that the Apostle Paul went to great lengths to clarify that the message was not from *him*, but from God and that God had prewritten the Jesus message *before the ages.*

Let's say that again!

The Apostle Paul was declaring that the *Bible message* was ordained by God before the world was even formed, *the ages.* The Apostle Paul was also declaring that the *Jesus message* was ordained by God before the world was even formed, *the ages.*

Jesus, himself, even spoke of the message of God being written before the foundations of the world:

Matthew 13:35 *That it might be fulfilled which was spoken by the prophet, saying, I will open my mouth in parables; I will utter things which have been kept secret from the foundation of the world.*

So who wrote the Bible? Was it God *before the ages,* before the beginning of time as the Apostle Paul stated in 1 Corinthians 2:7 or was it rewritten and translated by the Catholic Church after the fact? Is God making a statement from *before the ages* (or the beginning of time) about Rome and the Catholic Church?

It seems odd that the Roman Catholic Church would identify the anti-Christ, the number of a man 666, using such a definitive display of their numerology base or did they just miss the coincidence? Now, you might argue that the Catholic Church does not have the power and would not influence anything like that.

If that is your thought process, I find myself having to ask, "What planet do you call home?" Years ago when I first discovered the Roman Numerals and the 666 correlation, I immediately went to the Internet and searched over 50 Roman Numeral sites and could not find a single other stated correlation between Roman Numerals and 666. Today — many years later — there are still only a couple websites I have found with a reference to the Roman Numerals and the 666 correlation. I am not claiming that I am the only one who knows of the Roman Numerals and the 666 correlation, but I had not seen *any* evidence of the match until very recently!

I did not include this chapter of *Disorganized Christianity* to reveal major never before seen Bible verses or to offer new meanings to old thoughts and dogmas, but merely to show that even the smallest pieces of evidence can be right in front of our eyes and minds; all we have to be willing to do, is just look and think.

Do not be too surprised about *Disorganized Christianity's new revelation* of the Roman Numerals, I,V,X,L,C,D, and the anti-Christ, 666. After all, we completely missed this correlation for over 2,000 years!

Also, do not be too surprised with some of the other *new revelations* you will find as we move forward through *Disorganized Christianity.* As you will soon discover, we have also missed some *true verses* and their meanings in the Bible for over 2,000 years.

CHAPTER 7

Raised from the dead and
then went visiting!

During my younger years our church used to have a visitation night. Our church congregation would meet on Thursday nights to go visit our friends and neighbors and try to convince them to come to church on Sunday.

It is not so unusual to see people of God trying to spread their message of faith and hope. The Mormons and Jehovah's Witnesses are seen in pairs visiting their neighborhoods almost on a daily basis. We are actually commanded to spread the Word of God by Jesus himself:

Mark 16:15 *And he said unto them, Go ye into all the world, and preach the gospel to every creature.*

In Luke 16:19 there is a story that is supposed to be true. This particular true Bible story is surrounded by parables.

Parables are basically stories in the Bible that are *not true* happenings, but are still tales that have *hidden* mysteries for us to learn.

Mark 4:11 *And he said unto them, Unto you it is given to know the mystery of the kingdom of God: but unto them that are without, all these things are done in parables:*

Jesus spoke in parables and his disciples asked him why.

Matthew 13:10 *And the disciples came, and said unto him, Why speakest thou unto them in parables?*

Jesus told his disciples in **Matthew 13:13** *Therefore speak I to them in parables: because they seeing see not; and hearing they hear not, neither do they understand.*

In the Bible we find parables about having *the faith of a mustard seed*: Mark 4:30-32; and *the fig tree*: Matthew 24:32-35; and *the ten virgins*: Matthew 25:1-13; and *the sower's soil*: Mark 4:3-8.

When his disciples asked Jesus what the kingdom of God was like he replied *"It is like a grain of mustard seed."*

The parable of the mustard seed basically implies that the grain of the mustard seed is the least of all the seeds in the earth, but it grows so big the fowls can lodge under the shadow of it.

Mark 4:30-32 *30 And he said, To what shall we liken the kingdom of God? Or with what comparison shall we compare it? 31 It is like a grain of mustard seed, which, when it is sown in the earth, is less than all the seeds that are in the earth; 32 But, when it is sown, it groweth up, and becometh greater than all herbs, and shooteth out great branches, so that the fowls of the air may lodge under the shadow of it.*

I have personally heard over a dozen sermons on the *hidden* mystery of this parable. One *clear* mystery understanding is, "If you have the faith of a mustard seed, your faith like the mustard seed will start very small and grow very great." I am not completely sure what the *hidden* mystery of this parable might be.

It was understood and accepted by all the Christians I knew that parables were distinguished by the fact that they *do not* use real characters' names. The story of the rich man and Lazarus (a named character) in Luke 16 does not follow this rule, and therefore is accepted by Christianity as being a *true story*.

To make my next point, it really does not matter whether the parable of the rich man and Lazarus is a story or a real account of an actual guy named Lazarus who died. Again, though, it is really frustrating to have to figure out *which* Bible stories are true and which stories are "just stories." Moreover, when we cannot figure out which is which, it provides another choice opportunity for *organized religion to prove its position and to then use that position to serve its own purpose.*

In this case, there is really no earth shattering new denominational changing truth to present nor dogma to announce. My point can be made regardless of whether this story is a parable or this story is true. It is a story in the Bible, and it has its purpose, and I have my concerns. The story recorded by Luke 16:19-31 is simply that there was a rich man who lived well and a beggar named Lazarus, and they both died.

Luke 16:19-25 *19 There was a certain rich man, who was clothed in purple and fine linen, and fared sumptuously every day. 20 And there was a certain beggar, named Lazarus, who was laid at his gate, full of sores, 21 And desiring to be fed with the crumbs which fell from the rich man's table; moreover, the dogs came and licked his sores. 22 And it came to pass that the beggar died, and was carried by the angels into Abraham's bosom; the rich man also died, and was buried; 23 And in Hades he lifted up his eyes, being in torments, and seeth Abraham afar off, and Lazarus in his bosom. 24 And he cried and said, Father Abraham, have mercy on me, and send Lazarus, that he may dip the tip of his finger in water, and cool my tongue; for I am* *tormented in this flame. 25 But Abraham said, Son, remember that thou in thy lifetime receivedst thy good things, and likewise Lazarus evil things; but now he is comforted, and thou art tormented.*

In death, the rich man is in Hades and Lazarus is being held in Abraham's bosom obviously within eyesight of each other. Unrelated, I had never thought about the fact that Hades and any place Abraham might be could be within eyesight of each other. This close proximity is not my point, however — it is just another observation I had never caught before. Anyway, the rich man still wants favors from his previous stature. Abraham tells the rich man he already received his favors in *life*, and now he deserves his new position of torment.

The rich man then asks Abraham to send Lazarus back to tell his brothers of the torments of Hades. The rich man believed that if someone from the dead came back and told his brothers of the torments of Hades then surely the brothers would believe and do whatever it took to not go there. It would be important, for the sake of credibility, that the rich man's brothers knew the messenger.

It seems reasonable that the rich man would ask Abraham to send Lazarus back to talk to all his brothers because Lazarus would have been readily recognized by the brothers as the beggar who laid at the rich man's father's house gate.

Luke 16:26-28 *26 And beside all this, between us and you there is a great gulf fixed, so that they who would pass from here to you cannot; neither can they pass to us, that would come from there. 27 Then he said, I pray thee, therefore, father, that thou wouldest send him to my father's house 28 (For I have five brethren), that he may testify unto them, lest they also come into this place of torment.*

Abraham responds to the rich man's request by telling the rich man that his brothers already have Moses and the Prophets, and they needed to listen to them.

Luke 16:29 *Abraham saith unto him, They have Moses and the prophets; let them hear them.*

The rich man argues with Abraham that if Lazarus returned from the dead and talked to his brothers, they would surely believe. Abraham says that if anyone rose from the dead, that his brothers would not believe what the message was. The key to this story is verse 31.

Luke 16:30-31 *30 And he said, Nay, father Abraham; but if one went unto them from the dead, they will repent. 31 And he said unto him, If they hear not Moses and the prophets, neither will they be persuaded, though one rose from the dead.*

I do remember being told a long time ago that I was not allowed to argue with God. However, I am going to disagree again and argue. Right now!

When Abraham tells the rich man that even though a person whom people knew had died, risen from the dead, and then went and had a conversation with someone, told that person about the afterlife and how terrible it could possibly be, and that the raised dead person *would not* be able to persuade that person of the existence of Hades, I have to argue.

I am not talking about a declaration of a *light at the end of a tunnel* experience. I am talking about being formally declared dead, with an obituary posted, being buried in a casket, covered with dirt, the life insurance check being cashed and *then* having been in the ground for so long that your body has surely started to decompose, and *then you rose from the grave.*

Abraham makes it very clear that if you then went visiting someone, after all that, *"neither will they be persuaded,"*

In the early 2000's there was a television personality who claimed he could communicate with the dead. John Edward had a TV program called *Crossing Over*. On this television program he was portrayed as a *psychic medium*. During the program, John Edward would attempt to communicate through *"readings"* with dead loved ones in his audiences. John Edward's television *readings* were mostly given in a group scenario, but he did occasional individual *readings* as well. The show was very entertaining, and it was also interesting to me because at that time I *wanted and needed* it to be true.

My mother died when I was 31. I missed my mother very much, but because I was not sure if she had accepted Jesus as her Savior, I was also not sure that I would ever see her again. The thought of not ever seeing my mother again made me very sad. I still believed that because she did not go to church, and she never had accepted Jesus as her personal Savior, she was surely in hell. I missed my mother then and I miss my mother still.

To have someone you love die and then be able to receive a message from that person or their spirit would be phenomenal! At that point in my life I was absolutely open to any possibility and it seemed possible that I could get in contact with my mother again with the assistance of John Edward and *Crossing Over*. I started to imagine that maybe there *was* a life after death that didn't include hell. An afterlife message without Jesus' message of heaven and hell seemed possible. The believability of an afterlife message from John Edward probably depended on who got the reading and how it affected them personally.

Keep in mind that I am specifically talking about people who claim they can communicate with the dead and then interpret the dead person's message to you.

I will keep my beliefs to myself, and let you choose your own beliefs about John Edward and other *psychic mediums*. I am just saying "If it were possible to communicate with the dead, that would be phenomenal."

The Bible tells about people being raised from the dead in both the Old Testament and the New Testament. The Bible tells us about people who *have been* raised from the dead and also about people who *are going to be raised* from the dead in the future. I will provide you with an astonishing example later in this chapter about a New Testament resurrection that was *not* Jesus.

The Bible tells us that we only get one life to accept Jesus as our Savior. If we do not accept Jesus as our Savior before we die, we will then be judged to hell. The Bible does *not* say that we get to die and then we get to live a second time, to get second chance to accept Jesus.

Hebrews 9:27 *And as it is appointed unto man once to die, but after this the judgment.*

Well, not exactly!

The Bible records that some people were given a *second* chance to die. These second chances to die are made possible through *resurrections.* Jesus was the most important resurrection story told in the Bible, and I can certainly understand God giving Jesus that opportunity.

Besides Jesus there have been many people who have been resurrected in Bible stories. It strikes me as contradictory and not in God's best interest for consistency to give people a second chance to die when the Bible states again in **Hebrews 9:27** *And as it is appointed unto man once to die, but after this the judgment.*

The Bible offers a very popular example of a resurrection in the New Testament that goes against the Bible's own mandate that we all live one life, then die and then we are judged. So the Bible does have exceptions to its own rule(s). It *is* okay with me, for the Bible to have exceptions to its own rule(s), *as long as* the exceptions are generously and equally applied to all of God's creatures, yesterday, today and tomorrow.

My example is that the Bible clearly and very thoroughly declares that a different man named Lazarus died and was raised from the dead to die a second time.

This may have been for the glory of God then and now, but my question is this: "Why can't *I* be that exception?" Why can't *you* be that exception? Why can't any *converted non-Christian* be that exception? If the Bible talks about resurrections as the pinnacle act of Jesus' power, why do we not have any resurrections today?

We are not talking about the rich man and Lazarus anymore. We are talking about another man named Lazarus, in the New Testament, John 11:11, who died and was raised from the dead, and who was the brother of Mary and Martha, who were very close friends of Jesus.

There are several verses in the New Testament that tell of Jesus' return to earth — also known as the Second Coming of Christ — and the subsequent resurrection of all dead Christians. I use the word *dead* in my sentence about telling of a resurrection because I believe you actually have to be *dead* before you can be resurrected.

Confusing? Sorry, but in the Bible verse I have chosen to explain the resurrection of Lazarus, brother of Mary and Martha, the Bible uses the word *asleep.*

Because I have tried to stay true to the promise of not using my own interpretations of words or verses to *prove my position to then serve my own purpose,* let me instead use a couple more verses to put the words *asleep, sleep, sleepeth,* and *sleeping* into the same context of meaning *dead* or *death.*

In John 11 we find the story of Lazarus, brother of Martha and Mary, who was resurrected by Jesus.

John 11:11 *These things said he; and after that he saith unto them; Our friend Lazarus sleepeth; but I go, that I may awake him out of sleep.*

The disciples thought that Jesus was actually saying that Lazarus was only sleeping (as we know sleeping,) but Jesus had to clarify that Lazarus was in fact dead and that in this case *asleep* meant the same as *dead*.

John 11:14 *Then said Jesus unto them plainly, Lazarus is dead.* In these verses Jesus said *sleepeth* and *sleep* meant *dead*.

Elsewhere, 1 Thessalonians 4:13-16 are the verses used to declare the Second Coming of Jesus when *everyone* who is asleep or dead in Christ will be resurrected in the last days.

1 Thessalonians 4:13-16 *13 But I would not have you to be ignorant, brethren, concerning them who are asleep, that ye sorrow not, even as others who have no hope. 14 For if we believe that Jesus died and rose again, even so them also who sleep in Jesus will God bring with him. 15 For this we say unto you by the word of the Lord, that we who are alive and remain unto the coming of the Lord shall not precede them who are asleep. 16 For the Lord himself shall descend from heaven with a shout, with the voice of the archangel, and with the trump of God; and the dead in Christ shall rise first.*

In these verses Jesus said *sleep* and *asleep,* meaning *dead*.

I am not just trying to twist a couple of verses to explain that sleep, sleeping, sleepeth, asleep, and slept are used interchangeably with dead and death. There are many other verses in the Bible that use the words asleep and slept interchangeably with dead and death. Acts 4:18 and Acts 4:20 are just a couple more.

The New Testament Book of Revelation prophesizes that two of God's witnesses will preach to the world for a thousand two hundred and threescore days.

Revelation 11:3 *And I will give power unto my two witnesses, and they shall prophesy a thousand two hundred and threescore days, clothed in sackcloth.*

I am amazed that God did not give these two witnesses a jet plane, an unlimited credit card and maybe some radio or television studio time so they could fulfill their obligation to preach the gospel! Seems all they got from God was sackcloth and death. The scripture also states that these two witnesses will be killed by the beast and that the world will leave their bodies laying in the street for three and a half days in full view of everyone.

Revelation 11:7-9 *7 And when they shall have finished their testimony, the beast that ascendeth out of the bottomless pit shall make war against them, and shall overcome them, and kill them. 8 And their dead bodies shall lie in the street of the great city, which spiritually is called Sodom and Egypt, where also our Lord was crucified.*

After three and a half days the two witnesses will come back to life and be resurrected for the entire world to see. It would be astonishing to see two dead people on Fox News or CNN rise from the dead. We would have a public viewing and even more amazing, a public record of a real resurrection that would give anyone hope of the possibility of their own personal resurrection.

2 Corinthians 4:1 *Knowing that he who raised up the Lord Jesus shall raise up us also by Jesus, and shall present us with you.*

1 Corinthians 15:52 *In a moment, in the twinkling of an eye, at the last trump; for the trumpet shall sound, and the dead shall be raised incorruptible, and we shall be changed.*

A widow's son is raised from the dead in **Luke 7:11-17** *11 And it came to pass, the next day, that he went into a city called Nain; and many of his disciples went with him, and many people. 12 Now when he came near to the gate of the city, behold, there was a dead man carried out, the only son of his mother, and she was a widow, and many people of the city were with her. 13 And when the Lord saw her, he had compassion on her, and said unto her, Weep not. 14 And he came and touched the bier; and they that bore him stood* *still. And he said, Young man, I say unto thee, Arise. 15 And he that was dead sat up, and began to speak. And he delivered him to his mother. 16 And there came a fear on all. And they glorified God, saying, A great prophet is raised up among us; and, God hath visited his people. 17 And this rumor of him went forth throughout all Judea, and throughout all the region round about.*

A certain ruler's daughter who was raised from the dead or sleep by Jesus is also recorded in Mark 5:21-43, Luke 8:40-56, as well as in **Matthew 9:18** and **23-26** *18 While he spoke these things unto them, behold, there came a certain ruler, and worshiped him, saying, My daughter is even now dead; but come and lay thy hand upon her, and she shall live. 23 And when Jesus came into the ruler's house, and saw the musicians and the people make a noise, 24 He said unto them, Give place; for the maid is not dead, but sleepeth. And they laughed him to scorn. 25 But when the people were put forth, he went in, and took her by the hand, and the maid arose. 26 And the fame of this went abroad into all the land.*

The Bible records that a couple of men were given the opportunity to really contradict **Hebrews 9:27** *And as it is appointed unto man once to die, but after this the judgment.*

These stories and verses are of two men who never had to die the first time. According to the Bible, Elijah and Enoch were two men who never died.

2 Kings 2:11 *And it came to pass, as they still went on, and talked, that, behold, there appeared a chariot of fire, and separated them, and Elijah went up by a whirlwind into heaven.*

Genesis 5:24 *And Enoch walked with God, and he was not; for God took him.* Enoch is also mentioned in the New Testament in **Hebrews 11:5** *By faith Enoch was translated that he should not see death, and was not found, because God had translated him; for before his translation he had this testimony, that he pleased God.*

More challenges concerning the man named Enoch will be covered in the chapter: *You can believe...*

Here are a couple of different verses that do not get much attention, but they should. We read about the events that follow Jesus' resurrection and the main point highlighted is that a centurion guard notices the events as they unfold and declares, "Whoa, this really was the Son of God."

I had personally read and preached these scripture verses before. We read the chapter and verses at face value, but again we miss a hidden verse. At least I never saw it before. In my 19-plus years of Christianity, I had never heard a sermon from a fellow preacher or ever had a Bible study conversation about this incredible verse!

Let's find and examine this verse together.

Matthew 27:50-52 *50 Jesus, when he had cried again with a loud voice, yielded up the spirit. 51 And, behold, the veil of the temple was torn in two from the top to the bottom; and the earth did quake, and the rocks were split; 52 And the graves were opened; and many bodies of the saints that slept were raised.*

Again, here we have the word "slept" where the word really intended is dead. I am not making this a personal interpretation of what slept really means, simply a declaration that the Bible uses sleep, sleeping, sleepeth, asleep, and slept interchangeably with dead and death in some verses.

But consider this: If these people were just sleeping, why were they put in graves that had to be opened by an earthquake?

Matthew 27:53-54 *53 And came out of the graves after his resurrection, and went into the holy city, and appeared to many. 54 Now, when the centurion, and they that were with him watching Jesus, saw the earthquake, and those things that were done, they feared greatly, saying Truly this was the Son of God.*

Previously, we were describing a psychic medium who would attempt to convey a message from a dead person's spirit. But, here in these verses we have something completely different from a psychic medium simply interpreting what my mother might be trying to say to me after 35-plus years.

Matthew 27:52-53 *52 And the graves were opened; and many bodies of the saints that slept were raised, 53 And came out of the graves after his resurrection, and went into the holy city, and appeared to many.*

Here we have not one, not two, not just a few, but *many* dead people that not only rose from the dead, but also went into the holy city of Jerusalem and visited other people! Where is this story in the records of history? Unbelievable!

Here comes the argument from me with God over Abraham's statement in **Luke 16:30-31** *30 And he said, Nay, father Abraham; but if one went unto them from the dead, they will repent. 31 And he said unto him, If they hear not Moses and the prophets, neither will they be persuaded, though one rose from the dead.*

The argument I am making is this: "I would be persuaded!"

If my mother bodily came back from the dead, fully resurrected, and she and I continued the fun talk we had at our last Thanksgiving, (a conversation that I would pay nearly anything in the world to continue) and then before she left said, "Son, I want you to believe in Jesus because he let me come back for a while and talk to you," I would not be writing *Disorganized Christianity*. I would be persuaded!

Now back to **Matthew 27: 50-54** *50 Jesus, when he had cried again with a loud voice, yielded up the spirit. 51 And, behold, the veil of the temple was torn in two from the top to the bottom; and the earth did quake, and the rocks were split; 52 And the graves were opened; and many bodies of the saints that slept were raised, 53 And came out of the graves after his resurrection, and went into the holy city, and appeared to many. 54 Now, when the centurion,* *and they that were with watching Jesus, saw the earthquake, and those things that were done, they feared greatly, saying Truly this was the Son of God.*

At Jesus' resurrection we have many people raised from the dead, and as if that wasn't enough, here's the truly phenomenal part: they came out of the graves after his resurrection, and went into the holy city, and appeared to many.

Today, we have the ability to be very mobile in the course of our lives and very rarely are we born and raised and die in the same town or same area. I would venture to say that in biblical times, however, most people were buried close to where they grew up or close to where they had the most friends and spent most of their lives.

Imagine if these many saints — after they died and were buried close to where they lived — suddenly were resurrected and went visiting in public in our day and age? There would be such a blockbuster, Pulitzer Prize, National Enquirer type story with Fox News and CNN running 24-hour coverage about it and it would be recorded in the archives for all time!

So I ask: Where is the historical story? The Bible makes a big deal about not only Jesus' resurrection, but also a guy named Lazarus and a couple of guys in the future? The Bible recorded the resurrection of the widow's son in Luke 7:11-17 with 7 verses. The Bible account of Jairus' daughter in Matthew 9:18-26, Mark 5:21-43, and Luke 8:40-56 warranted mention in three gospels amounting to a total of 26 verses.

In this recorded and translated verse in the King James Bible, why is there no historical mention of verses **52** *And the graves were opened; and many bodies of the saints that slept were raised,* **53** *And came out of the graves after his resurrection, and went into the holy city, and appeared to many.*

Why has this most phenomenal Bible story only received two hidden verses? Not one single Christian I have mentioned these verses to has ever read or even heard about Matthew 27:52-53.

Honestly, had you ever read or heard of Matthew 27:52-53 before today? You can get on the Internet and find a million stories about the smallest and most trivial of events from the beginning of time until today.

Didn't anyone who was visited that day keep a diary? Where is this story? I am not buying excuses like: God "has reasons" for not revealing this spectacular human event and we should just "not question God's perfect plan" or any other of *organized religion's* non-valid responses or made-up excuses of evasion of this valid question.

If this event were true and recorded in multiple documents by different people, I believe the story of many people raised from the dead and then went visiting would have changed the course of religion yesterday, today, and tomorrow.

The Internet is so full of information it almost seems impossible to not find some small detail to corroborate any story you could imagine. It seems that you can find the most trivial facts, along with the most monumental facts simply by using an Internet search engine.

Why in God's name do we not have an account of what I believe could be the most important and absolutely amazing religious story ever told in the history of mankind? We read about Moses parting the Red Sea and even have a theme park "ride" commemorating the act. We read about Noah building a boat and saving his family. We read about a whale swallowing a man. We read about a lady eating an apple, but we do not read about many people being raised from the dead and then went visiting in a large city? I challenge you to name a story that would have a bigger impact on an entire faith than a story of the resurrection of many who went visiting. Once again:

In **Matthew 27:52-53** *52 And the graves were opened; and many bodies of the saints that slept were raised, 53 And came out of the graves after his resurrection, and went into the holy city, and appeared to many.*

Man landing on the moon would pale in comparison to the event of many dead people being raised from the grave and then found to be visiting other people in a very large city.

If God wanted to prove the merits of Christianity and reintroduce those ten fundamental rules and then declare that He had the power to reward us with eternal life if we followed those ten rules or accepted his son Jesus as our Saviour; then I cannot understand why God did not make sure that this story of all stories did not have headline status in the Bible but instead was hidden in some obscure passage. Also amazing is the small detail that mankind has absolutely no record of the event!

No one has ever been resurrected in public in our modern times. Again, I am not talking about a near-death light at the end of the tunnel experience. I am not talking about some obscure person in a distant country who decided to become a loner and didn't want to talk about their miraculous resurrection.

I am talking about someone people knew, who has been buried in a pine box, covered with dirt, and then raised from the dead. An authentic resurrection would give a lot of glory to God and validation of God's power.

Satan has been called the great deceiver and beguiler.

2 Corinthians 11:3 *But I fear, lest by any means, as the serpent beguiled Eve through his craftiness, so your minds should be corrupted from the simplicity that is in Christ.*

What better deception to transfer all the attention away from Jesus and God and give that attention to some prophet who raised someone from the dead in full view of the world? Satan could surely deflect any sinner away from Jesus and God if Satan aided someone in raising a person from the dead. Satan could possibly manipulate events to even fake a death and a resurrection.

I believe Christianity could use some real, positive acts of God in our times. True acts of God to glorify God and not be twisted and manipulated as a catch phrase used to deny paying insurance claims. If the miracles were needed and performed and they were all for the glory of God in biblical days, why aren't healing miracles and resurrections being used today? From what I have been able to see, God could use some glorification and good Internet press!

If Jesus was to be crucified, then buried and then resurrected, and we are looking forward with confidence to the day when that eventually happens for us and we are believing in that sequence of events on faith, how tremendous would it be for the Bible to highlight the fact that such a thing already happened once. Instead, all we get is a couple of verses most Christians have never even read about in their own Bible!

BC and AD time lines are very important to this next series of thoughts. In biblical times there were many prolific writers of history. Not journalists, but historians; recorders of local events. Flavius Josephus and Tacitus to name a couple, and these historians were neither Republican or Democrat, Conservative or Liberal, and they didn't work for Fox News or CNN. There was a time when people simply wrote down what happened. These proclaimed biblical period historians have left *no* written record of *any* eyewitness biblical stories. Flavius Josephus (37- 100AD) and Tacitus (56AD –117AD) wrote about things they read about. They were interpolators.

Webster's New Collegiate Dictionary defines Interpolate as: "1 a: to alter or corrupt (as a text) by inserting new or foreign matter b: to insert (words) into a text or into a conversation."

None of these historians wrote about any actual eyewitness events because they weren't even *born* until after the crucifixion and claimed resurrection.

In the Christian circle of history we are told that there is "an abundance" of documents concerning Jesus, the global flood, the famines, the raising of the dead, the crucifixion and the nativity, etc.

Well, the truth is that there isn't. Sometimes the *lack* of history becomes so profound that it may just develop a voice of its own and whisper, "There probably isn't a real documented history, after all."

The reality could possibly be that Christian books are simply expressing what *organized religion* dictates that they are *supposed* to say. If I am wrong, then do bring out the original books — correctly dated — that fully and completely document an eye witness account of the crucifixion *exactly* as the Bible describes it, because the Bible should be the template upon which we base all truth. If there *were* true Christian historical clarity, there would not be so much Christian historical confusion.

If you are a Christian who absolutely despises what I am saying here, ask yourself one question; if you are a Christian who *kind of* agrees with what I am saying, ask yourself one question; if you are a Christian who emphatically states "Yes, *Disorganized Christianity* is saying what I have felt for a long time and wanted to say for a long time," please ask yourself this question:

Keeping in mind the story in Luke 16 regarding the rich man and Lazarus, and the absolute statement by Abraham that *you* would not believe — even if a person came back from the dead and talked to you — *wouldn't you actually believe a recognizable dead person* if they came visiting *you?*

If you physically and emotionally recognized your mother, father, spouse or child if they came back from the dead, sat in in your living room and talked with you for a while, *I think you would believe whatever they told you about the other side!* Be honest with yourself. No one is looking or judging! I think you would take this ressurection as proof of faith. I know I certainly would.

The Bible *clearly states that* there is no afterlife without Jesus. The Bible says there is only *one way* to heaven and that is through Jesus.

John 14:6 *Jesus saith unto him, I am the way, the truth, and the life; no man cometh unto the Father, but by me.*

I can see how a preacher, televangelist or faith healer raising a dead person would be beneficial to someone's ministry. I'm willing to bet that if someone were to raise anyone from the dead today, it would boost their ratings and cash flow. If raising the dead in Jesus' day was a means to prove Jesus and God, why not raise someone today?

CHAPTER 8

Angels and giants and creeping thing, oh my!

We call them giants. The Bible calls them Rephaim, Anakim, Zumzamin and Nephilim. Sometimes the Bible also calls them giants.

Giants play a very interesting role in Bible history. But who were the giants and how did these giants originate? Where did the giants go? Why did the giants go? Goliath is probably the most famous giant in the Bible.

1 Samuel 17:4 *And there went out a champion out of the camp of the Philistines, named Goliath, of Gath, whose height was six cubits and a span.*

Cubit, as defined by *Webster's New Collegiate Dictionary*, is "any of various ancient units of length based on the length of the forearm from the elbow to the tip of the middle finger and usually equal to about 18 inches, but sometimes 21 or more;" and span is "the distance from the end of the thumb to the end of the little finger of a spread hand; Also: an English unit of length equal to 9 inches." Using these calculations, Goliath would have been about 9 feet 9 inches tall.

Another Old Testament giant in Gath had special features.

2 Samuel 21:20 *And there was yet a battle in Gath, where was a man of great stature, who had on every hand six fingers, and on every foot six toes, four and twenty in number; and he also was born to the giant.*

The Old Testament also records some giants who kept the Israelites out of the Promised Land.

Numbers 13:33 *And there we saw the giants, the sons of Anak, who come of the giants; and we were in our own sight as grasshoppers, and so we were in their sight.*

God sent a group of Israelites to spy out the land that was promised them when they left Egypt. During the spies' 40 days of checking out the promised land of milk and honey, they discovered giants in the land, the children of Anak.

Numbers 13:28 *Nevertheless, the people are strong that dwell in the land, and the cities are walled, and very great: and moreover, we saw the children of Anak there.*

The Israelite spies came back to Moses and reported to the people of Israel that God had led them into even more danger than they ever had in Egypt. When the spies suggested they go back to Egypt, God got angry because the Israelites again questioned God's intentions for them. As a punishment for the Israelites' lack of faith, God told them that only the Israelites under the age of 20 and those who had not murmured against God could then enter into the Promised Land and the rest would wander and die in the desert for forty more years.

Numbers 14:29 *Your carcasses shall fall in this wilderness; and all who were numbered of you, according to your whole number, from twenty years old and upward, who have murmured against me.*

Numbers 14:33 *And your children shall wander in the wilderness forty years, and bear your harlotries, until your carcasses be wasted in the wilderness.*

Some interpretations try to argue that the giants the spies saw were actually just big men and not giants at all. In Numbers 13:28 the Bible refers to …the children of Anak. The children of Anak were giants.

The Israelites had escaped from Egypt and had only one goal on their mind.

Numbers 13:27 *And they told him, and said, We came unto the land to which thou sentest us, and surely it floweth with milk and honey; and this is the fruit of it.*

The Israelites' one goal was to get to the Promised Land; the land of milk and honey. God had been proven many times since the Israelites left Egypt, and it seems very odd these particular giants — or even simply big men — scared them so much as to cause them to not enter their Promised Land. God kept the Israelites wandering in the desert for forty more years simply because of giants. It seems, according to the *infallible* Bible, that giants were very real in the Old Testament.

God created and made giants, **Genesis 2:1-3** *1 Thus the heavens and the earth were finished, and all the host of them. 2 And on the seventh day God ended his work which he had made; and he rested on the seventh day from all his work which he had made. 3 And God blessed the seventh day, and sanctified it, because that in it he had rested from all his work which God created and made.*

After God made the heavens and the earth and the host of them, God rested and things seemed to go pretty well.

I am going to cite the Genesis story from creation to the fall of man right up to the global flood in a short form. Giants were the key ingredient that led to the global flood which destroyed mankind.

God made the Garden of Eden for man: **Genesis 2:8** *And the Lord God planted a garden eastward in Eden; and there he put man whom he had formed.*

Then God put a nice couple, Adam and Eve, in The Garden of Eden: **Genesis 2:8** *...and there he put man whom he had formed,* and **Genesis 2:21-22** *21 And the Lord God caused a deep sleep to fall upon Adam, and he slept; and he took one of his ribs, and closed up the flesh instead thereof; 22 And the rib, which the Lord God had taken from man, made he a woman, and brought her unto the man.*

God gave them trees that provided them food: **Genesis 2:9** *And out of the ground made the Lord God to grow every tree that is pleasant to the sight, and good for food;* God then allowed the temptation and fall of Adam and Eve with some sort of fruit tree. I have purposely made a very strong and bold statement when I say that God allowed temptation to enter into the Garden of Eden by way of the snake, Satan. *Organized religion*, with the introduction of man's first sin, tries to rationalize God allowing Satan to tempt Eve because in some sick way it is a way for man to prove — if they could withstand the temptation — their love for God.

The *organized religion* theory holds that as our parent, the more God tempts us, the more God shows how much he loves us, and it is our responsibility to repeatedly prove our love back to God by passing these tests or temptations.

If you think about it for a moment, I absolutely guarantee that you would not want your parents to validate your love to them like that, and I am pretty confident that is not how you have raised your own children, either. And if you have raised your children that way, how is it going? Incidentally, the Bible does not say it was an apple tree. Our Sunday School teachers told us that it was an apple tree.

Genesis 2:15-17 *15 And the Lord God took the man, and put him into the garden of Eden to till it and to keep it. 16 And the Lord God commanded the man, saying, Of every tree of the garden thou mayest freely eat; 17 But of the tree of the knowledge of good and evil, thou shalt not eat of it; for in the day thou eatest thereof thou shalt surely die.*

Well, not exactly!

Remember the heavenly creation, host of them, mentioned in Genesis 2:1? The host of them are the angels everyone glamorizes. I really do not know where the white wings and feathers came from, but the first angel that was introduced to Adam and Eve was in the form of a serpent, or the snake, in The Garden of Eden.

It didn't take long for the host of them, God's heavenly creations, to introduce themselves into God's earthly creation. God then allowed one of the host of them to come down and mess with Eve. Here is the introduction of the first fallen host of them, the serpent, Satan or the Devil:

Genesis 3:1-6 *1 Now the serpent was more subtle than any beast of the field which the Lord God had made. And he said unto the woman, Yea, hath God said, Ye shall not eat of every tree of the garden? 2 And the woman said unto the serpent, We may eat of the fruit of the trees of the garden; 3 But of the fruit of the tree which is in the midst of the garden, God hath said, Ye shall not eat of it, neither shall ye touch it, lest ye die, 4 And the serpent said unto the woman, Ye shall not surely die; 5 For God doth know that in the day ye eat thereof, then your eyes shall be opened, and ye shall be as God, knowing good and evil. 6 And when the woman saw that the tree was good for food, and that it was pleasant to the eyes, and a tree to be desired to make one wise, she took of the fruit thereof, and did eat, and gave also unto her husband with her; and he did eat.*

This Bible scripture verse says that Eve ate of the fruit of the tree that she felt would make her wise, not to sin, or to know what good and evil was.

I have emphasized the word allowed to describe God's continual actions of letting Satan tempt man and woman. If God is actually as powerful as the Bible says He is, why is God always allowing Satan to mess with His human creation? According to your description of an all-powerful God, Satan should not be allowed to do anything God did not want to happen. If we as humans are merely toys for Satan and God to argue over, debate over and tempt, then please keep your God and let us find a Father worth sending a Father's Day card to!

I want to share a couple of examples of God's judgment towards man for his failings.

God's reactions and punishments seem rather odd and inconsistent towards the host of them and mankind, both during and after the fall. God allowed a talking snake to beguile the woman. The snake beguiled the woman, and God just cursed the snake. God did not kill the snake. The woman then tempted man with some fruit, and God was so angry that He banished them both from His presence. God did not kill them. God just cast Adam and Eve out of the Garden.

Well, God did say Adam and Eve would die if they ate fruit from the tree, but not really die, just "sort of die." In another act of disobedience one of Adam and Eve's sons, Cain, killed his brother, Abel. Cain got off with only a curse from God. Again, God did not kill Cain. From Genesis 1 to Genesis 5 God just kind of put up with His creation.

God delivered a little cursing and did a lot of talking about how to be God's creation. But then, in Genesis 6, came the culminating and decisive expression of God's anger toward mankind, the universal global flood.

Okay, so what exactly happened to finally make God angry enough to destroy everything on the planet? What was that final act that made God decide to destroy all flesh? The final act wasn't that God's creation, Adam and Eve, disobeyed Him and destroyed the perfect condition He had created for them. This single act in the Garden of Eden of supposedly a willful act of disobedience seems to be *organized religion's* sole validation for their existence, to control and condemn us. Blame Adam and Eve. Condemn Adam and Eve and then transfer that condemnation onto us, but don't kill us.

The final act wasn't jealousy. The final action wasn't that another entity, the Snake; the serpent, had more power over Adam and Eve than God did, which could be construed as a jealous act. There are two verses in the Bible that express that jealousy is a trait of God, and it can have severe consequences.

One of those Ten Commandments, **Exodus 20:5** *Thou shalt not bow down thyself to them, nor serve them, for I, the Lord thy God, am a jealous God, visiting the iniquity of the fathers upon the children unto the third and fourth generation of them that hate me.*

The next verse tells us that God is capable of destroying the earth over jealousy.

Deuteronomy 6:14-15 *14 Ye shall not go after other gods, of the gods of the people who are round about you 15 (For the Lord thy God is a jealous God among you), lest the anger of the Lord thy God be kindled against thee, and destroy thee from off the face of the earth.*

Even though it is said that God would destroy man from the face of the earth because of jealousy, God didn't actually destroy anything for a while.

The final action that made God angry enough to destroy every living thing on the face of the earth was, in fact, the result of the introduction of giants. Giants on Earth ultimately led to the global flood.

Genesis 6:1-7 *1 And it came to pass, when men began to multiply on the face of the earth, and daughters were born unto them, 2 That the sons of*

God saw the daughters of men that they were fair; and they took them wives of all whom they chose. 3 And the Lord said, My Spirit shall not always strive with man, for that he is also flesh; yet his days shall be an hundred and twenty years. 4 There were giants in the earth in those days; and also after that, when the sons of God came in unto the daughters of men, and they bore children to them, the same, became mighty men who were of old, men of renown. 5 And God saw that the wickedness of man was great in the earth, and that every imagination of the thoughts of his heart was only evil continually. 6 And it repented the Lord that he had made man on the earth, and it grieved him at his heart. 7 And the Lord said, I will destroy man whom I have created from the face of the earth; both man, and beast, and the creeping thing, and the fowls of the air; for it repenteth me that I have made them.

Just who were these sons of God? My own understanding is that the sons of God are the angels in heaven, but let's see if the Bible tells us more about them. The chronological order of creation goes like this:

Genesis 1:1 *In the beginning God created the heaven and the earth.*

Genesis 2:1 *Thus the heavens and the earth were finished, and all the host of them.*

Genesis 2:7 *And the Lord God formed man of the dust of the ground, and breathed into his nostrils the breath of life; and man became a living soul.*

The Bible defines the order of creation as: God always was, creation of the heavens and the earth, creation of the host of them, and finally man. In Job we have the famous story of how Satan wanted to tempt Job and then see if Job would still love God even if it appeared God had forsaken Job. God said that Job would love God even if Satan took everything but Job's own life.

As the story unfolded, Satan did tempt Job. Job steadfastly declared his love for God, and Satan lost this attempt to ruin another of God's earthly creations. However, in this story we do find out who the sons of God were.

Job 1:6 *Now there was a day when the sons of God came to present themselves before the Lord, and Satan came also among them.*

These host of them *and* sons of God *are the same group of beings. The Bible states that no man has actually* seen *God.*

1 John 4:12 *No man hath seen God at any time. If we love one another, God dwelleth in us, and his love is perfected in us.*

God must have been seen by the sons of God and Satan when they presented themselves to Him in the heavens, so they could not be men. Again, I believe they were the angels.

In Job 38:7 *When the morning stars sang together, and all the sons of God shouted for joy?*

These beings God is talking about are the angels in the heavens. If they are not the angels in heaven, then who else is up in the heavens with God shouting for joy?

Genesis 6:4 *There were giants in the earth in those days; and also after that, when the sons of God came into the daughters of men, and they bore children to them, the same became mighty men who were of old, men of renown.*

Now these men of old and men of renown, were they good or bad? The giants had to have been on the earth for a long time because the Bible says that they were mighty men who were of old, men of renown. Adam ate an apple and was thrown out of the Garden immediately. Giants were on the earth for a long time, were called mighty men who were of old, men of renown and then because of them, eventually God destroyed the earth.

Evidently, some created beings get God's patience, while some created beings don't. Consistency would be a good trait for an *infallible* God to have. If God was consistent with blessings and curses, we might not have as many "Well, not exactly" verses.

Blasphemy? I don't think so. Read more about this inconsistency in the chapter *I believe in the separation of church and hate!*

Genesis 6:6-7 *6 And it repented the Lord that he had made man on the earth, and it grieved him at his heart. 7 And the Lord said, I will destroy man whom I have created from the face of the earth; both man, and beast, and the creeping thing, and the fowls of the air; for it repenteth me that I have made them.*

I get the reasoning that because it repented the Lord that he had made man on the earth, God then destroyed man. But what did the beasts and the fowls of the air and the creeping thing do to make God angry?

Genesis 1:26 *And God said, Let us make man in our image, after our likeness; and let them have dominion over the fish of the sea, and over the fowl of the air, and over the cattle, and over all the earth, and over every creeping thing that creepeth on the earth.*

What did the beast and the creeping thing and the fowls of the air do, that the fish didn't do? God created them all and repented they were all made. God said that everything was going to be destroyed, all flesh.

Genesis 6:17 *And, behold, I, do bring a flood of waters upon the earth, to destroy all flesh, wherein is the breath of life, from under heaven; and everything that is in the earth shall die.*

So why didn't God destroy the fish as well; weren't they flesh?

1 Corinthians 15:39 *All flesh is not the same flesh, but there is one kind of flesh of men, another flesh of beasts, another of fish, and another of birds.*

Maybe it was just inconvenient to destroy the fish when you use water to destroy the earth? But if fish are flesh and God says all flesh will be destroyed, where exactly does that leave us? Do we have yet another "Well, not exactly" verse, one more time?

But let's get back to the giants. There are two very strong Christian ideas about who the giants were:

(1) First thought: The sons of God were the men from the lineage of Seth, the good son of Adam and Eve. Abel was the first good son but Cain killed him, so now Seth was the good son. The daughters of men were the daughters of Cain, the bad son, and thus the union of Seth's good sons and Cain's bad daughters produced the giants. Remember, they didn't have a whole lot of marriage choices. Again, I say this is what some people think happened. This is what some people speculate might have happened. These people could just read their Bible and find out who the sons of God were.

Again we see the "patriarchal man rules, and matriarchal women loses" theme which is common in the Bible.

The sons of God refers to all the godly sons of Seth and daughters of men to all the ungodly daughters of Cain, and this union is used to try to excuse a very bizarre situation in God's plan which seems to have gone haywire. This explanation is in the *Scofield King James Version* footnotes on page 11 and contributed to the fundamental mindset instilled in us in 1967. The human element of this story is the most reasonable earthly answer, but still leaves a lot of holes in the explanation.

(2) Second thought. The sons of God were fallen angels of Satan that bred with the daughters of men and created giants.

This conclusion somewhat has its roots in the very thing I am rebelling against. It is the fact we have an interpretation of a story inside a Bible version of the Holy Bible.

I have been talking about only using the Bible verses themselves and no outside commentaries of any versions, but I choose to include this interpretation because it is actually included in the translated Bible version I used for 19-plus years. It had such a major impact on my teaching and preaching that the explanation needs to be addressed.

The fallen angels' breeding with earth women was the de-facto accepted explanation of giants in 1967. However, Giants were never really discussed in public. Giants took on approximately the same biblical importance as the dinosaurs. There was proof of their existence, but since *organized religion* couldn't explain it, and couldn't either condemn you for it or make money on it, they chose to just ignore it. You could take the explanations or leave them.

The *New Scofield King James Bible Version*, on page 11 in the footnotes, suggests that the sons of God were fallen angels who kept not their first estate.

Page 11: Accordingly, this intrusion into the human sphere produced a race of wicked giants. Others hold that since angels are spoken of in a sexless way, and that the words "took them wives" signifies a lasting marriage, the reference has to do with the godless line of Cain. A refinement of the latter view holds that the expression "sons of God" refers to all the godly, and "daughters of men" to all the ungodly, irrespective of their natural paternity. Whichever view is held, It is obvious that Satan attempted so to corrupt the race that the Messiah could not come to redeem man. But, God salvaged a remnant, Noah, Genesis 6:8.

Even this explanation falls all over itself, offering one conclusion that is baseless and then moves to a different conclusion that seems even more idiotic. The explanation — whether right or wrong, debated from any perspective — just doesn't make sense.

STOP! *Organized religion* has an unbelievable verse about angels breeding with earth women and the best you can do to explain this is "Whichever view is held?" Where is the next blockbuster movie produced by Steven Spielberg, Oliver Stone, or Ron Howard?

There is so much misinformation and ambiguity here! First of all, how could the translators let this sons of God story even get through? It shows that if the fallen angels theory is right, then God allowed heavenly creations to again ruin earthly creations. This "game playing" by God is getting really tiresome. I have wondered for a long time **about certain words used in** the Lord's Prayer:

Luke 11:2-4 *2 And he said unto them, When ye pray, say, Our Father, who art in heaven, Hallowed be thy name. Thy kingdom come. Thy will be done, as in heaven, so in earth. 3 Give us day by day our daily bread. 4 And forgive us our sins; for we also forgive everyone that is indebted to us. And lead us not into temptation; but deliver us from evil.*

Why are we praying to God to lead us not into temptation? Why would a good Father lead his children deliberately into temptation? The Bible describes its own parable of Fatherhood in Luke 11:11.

Luke 11:11 *If a son shall ask bread of any of you that is a father, will he give him a stone? Or if he ask a fish, will he for a fish give him a serpent? 12 Or if he shall ask an egg, will he offer him a scorpion? 13 If ye then, being evil, know how to give good gifts unto your children, how much more shall your heavenly Father give the Holy Spirit to them that ask him?*

I don't know whether at the time Adam and Eve were in the Garden of Eden they asked for a fish, but it seems they did get a serpent! Now which Father/Dad was that?

It seems to me that when God allowed angels to come down and defile mankind "as in the days of Noah" that there must have been a whole lot more defiling than Adam and Eve did in the Garden. The sons of God must have defiled God in a very provocative way because when Adam and Eve defiled the Garden, all the consequences they suffered was a separation from God that would require a Savior to fix. The angels and giants defiled mankind and God so severely that the Bible — God's *infallible* word — stated that all living creatures on the planet would be destroyed.

Well, not exactly!

I believe this to be a very important missing part of the Bible story. Where are the fallen angels, the sons of God and all the host of them that God proclaimed condemnation on and where is their Savior? When anyone did something bad against God, which the Bible calls a sin, there is always a condemnation followed by a punishment. Where in God's word, after the angels and giants committed sins against God, is the condemnation? There isn't one!

Let's say that again.

Adam and Eve ate an apple and were banished from the garden and separated from God. Adam's sin resulted in God providing a Savior for mankind. Adam and Eve were condemned forever for an apple.

The angels came down and bred with the daughters of men and the Lord eventually destroyed the entire planet including all men, beasts and fowls, but we have no immediate condemnation or actions taken against the angels. Nowhere is there a mention of the angels needing or getting a Savior for themselves, for their misdeeds or sins. Doesn't there need to be a Savior for all of God's creatures, not just man? There is no Savior provided for the fallen angels, but there is a punishment in about a zillion years, but subsequently only for a little while.

Revelation 20:1-2 *1 And I saw an angel come down from heaven, having the key of the bottomless pit and a great chain in his hand. 2 And he laid hold on the dragon, that old serpent, who is the Devil and Satan, and bound him a thousand years.*

2 Peter 3:8 *But, beloved, be not ignorant of this one thing, that one day is with the Lord as a thousand years, and a thousand years as one day.*

The Bible claims that one day is like a thousand years and a thousand years is like one day to God. Are you seriously telling us *converted non-Christians* that after man is condemned forever for eating an apple, the angels that bred with Eve's daughters and created the giants that led to God destroying all living flesh on the face of the Earth, may have to go to jail for one day for thousands of years of continued disobedience?

This is your verse, and you have used it to prove your point of God and God's timing. I will use the same verse to prove my point! Even if Satan and the angels had to put in their full 1,000 year sentence — which would seem like only one day — I still do not like the fact that the angels and Satan ultimately get out of jail anyway. See the chapter *You can believe...*

There is also a story in which angels come down from heaven and visit Lot in Sodom.

Genesis 19:1-3 *1 And there came two angels to Sodom at evening, and Lot sat in the gate of Sodom; and Lot seeing them rose up to meet them; and he bowed himself with his face toward the ground; 2 And he said, Behold now, my lords, turn in, I pray you, into your servant's house, and tarry all night, and wash your feet, and ye shall rise up early, and go on your ways. And they said, Nay; but we will abide in the street all night. 3 And he pressed upon them greatly; and they turned in unto him, and entered into his house; and he made them a feast, and did bake unleavened bread, and they did eat.*

Angels, or sons of God, or the host of them had feet — they were washed in verse 2 — and they had digestive tracts, tongues, mouths, bowels and in verse 3 they did eat.

Genesis 2:1-3 *1 Thus the heavens and the earth were finished, and all the host of them.*

We have heavens and the earth and the host of them created before Adam and Eve. Who are "the host of them?" The host of them were the created angels. Satan was the fallen angel that beguiled the woman, Eve. Satan was the first of God's creation that sinned in the Garden of Eden.

Organized religion says that man is solely responsible for the sin that separated us from God and that Adam and Eve made a conscious choice to disobey God. *Organized religion* says that the angels and Satan were not responsible for man's sin. I will give my complete explanation of why Adam and Eve did not make a conscious, willful decision to eat the apple in the chapter *You can believe...*

Even after all the previous explanations attempting to offer you an understanding of the importance of giants in the Bible and where the giants may have come from, aside from the host of them creation theory, no one really knows. And what they came here to do we can only guess. Did the angels come to earth just to have sex with our daughters?

If, I am wrong about where giants came from, or who the giants really were, that is OK! My earthly existence and my future spiritual existence do not appear to be connected with giants.

What I really am interested in and what I do care about is their continuing role with mankind. From a biblical perspective, we know that giants existed on this planet. First, the Bible tells us that giants existed. Second, there is proof of giants by the discovery of skeletons and then through earthly historically documented accounts. But what happened to giants, and where are they now?

I care about what happened to them because it sounds like man was doing all right until the giants arrived, took over, and then God got angry with man. In his anger, God then destroyed man and the original creation.

In **Genesis 6:7** *And the Lord said, I will destroy man whom I have created from the face of the earth; both man, and beast, and the creeping thing, and the fowls of the air; for it repenteth me that I have made them.*

It is not stated anywhere that God will specifically destroy the giants. It does not say anywhere that God repenteth him that he allowed the sons of God to breed with earth women and create giants. If giants were not the result of breeding of angels — sons of God — and the daughters of men as the Bible states, then who were they, and why does it seem like God is afraid of the giants? Whoever they really were, did God really not have power over the giants? And what earthly good have giants been to mankind?

In the Garden of Eden: **Genesis 2:16-17** *16 And the Lord God commanded the man, saying, Of every tree of the garden thou mayest freely eat; 17 But of the tree of the knowledge of good and evil, thou shalt not eat of it; for in the day that thou eatest thereof thou shalt surely die.*

We read that if Adam and Eve eat from the tree of the knowledge of good and evil, they will die. We, today, understand the word "die" to mean that we cease living and breathing.

But in biblical contexts? Not exactly!

Genesis 6:7 *And the Lord said, I will destroy man whom I have created from the face of the earth.*

The verse is quite explicit and direct in that God will destroy man from the face of the earth. This verse says man will be destroyed, not "some" of man or "most" of man, but man. Period.

Genesis 6:8 *But Noah found grace in the eyes of the Lord...* Put your thinking caps on, folks! Here comes the question for the ages! If God destroyed man, and beast, and the creeping thing and the fowls of the air and the total obliteration of all living creatures including the giants, except for Noah and his family and the fish, then why was Goliath in 1 Samuel 17:4? And why was the six fingered and six toed giant in 2 Samuel 21:20, and the sons of Anak that kept the Israelites out of the Promised Land in Numbers 13:33? Did the global flood destroy everything or in this case, again, does "everything" really not mean everything?

The Bible declares with its *infallible* words that the global flood actually did destroy everything from the face of the earth: man, beast, the creeping thing, the fowls of the air, and all living things including the giants God had created. If that is true, why are giants mentioned in the Old Testament after the global flood? If all the giants were killed as a result of the global flood, did God have a hand in creating them again? Why? Did God allow some DNA from a Seth/son to transfer to a Cain/daughter and accidentally bring into being another giant? Did God let the angels, the host of them, come down after the global flood and have sex with earth women again? Did God not learn a lesson? Why would God want to send down another bunch of heavenly creations to tempt and mess up His earthly creation, one more time? Does God really have control over Satan and the "host of them"?

A reasonable answer for the giants of the post-global flood Old Testament can be found in The *Book of Enoch*. It states that 200 angels came down from Mount Hebron and bred with the daughters of Eve again. The only problem with this answer to my question: "if all living things, including giants were killed in the global flood, where did the giants of the post-global flood Old Testament come from?" is that you cannot use The Book of Enoch because it is not canonized or recognized as an authority by *organized religion*. Besides, if you insist on using The *Book of Enoch* to satisfy the question about giants, then you become obligated to validate all the other claims made by The *Book of Enoch* and believe me when I say that *organized religion* is not ready to tackle those claims!

It is frustrating to read in the Bible that God allows Satan to freely come down to Earth and tempt us simply so that we have to continually prove that we love God.

More on the Garden of Eden, Job, giants and who really is stronger — God or Satan — to come in the chapter *You can believe...*

CHAPTER 9

Noah and the Ark.

Genesis 6:9 *These are the generations of Noah: Noah was a just man and perfect in his generations, and Noah walked with God.*

Genesis 7:1 *And the Lord said unto Noah, Come thou and all thy house into the ark; for thee have I seen righteousness before me in this generation.*

Genesis 6:1-7 *1 And it came to pass, when men began to multiply on the face of the earth, and daughters were born unto them, 2 That the sons of God saw the daughters of men that they were fair; and they took them wives of all whom they chose. 3 And the Lord said, My Spirit shall not always strive with man, for that he also is flesh; yet his days shall be an hundred and twenty years. 4 There were giants in the earth in those days; and also after that, when the sons of God came in unto the daughters of men, and they bore children to them, the same became mighty men who were of old, men of renown. 5 And God saw that the wickedness of man was great in the earth, and that every imagination of the thoughts of his heart was only evil continually. 6 And it repented the Lord that he had made man on the earth, and it grieved him at his heart. 7 And the Lord said, I will destroy man whom I have created from*

the face of the earth; both man, and beast, and the creeping thing, and the
fowls of the air; for it repenteth me that I have made them.

I will now attempt to tell the Noah and the Ark story in a very simple
Sunday School way.

God created man, and after a while man started to be bad and sin a
lot. God does not like sin, so God decided to cleanse the earth from all of
this sin by killing everything and start over with the only good guy left on
the planet, Noah. God told Noah to build a boat that could carry Noah's
family and a male and female of every living creature on the planet. Noah
built the boat, and after he put his family and all the animals on the boat,
God closed the door of the boat and then let the rain come down and flood
the entire Earth. God, of course, knew that once Noah and his family got
off the boat, then everything would be right with the world.

Hey, that's the way I remember the story being told!

Let us now tell the story using a new set of eyes while searching for
the truth with a different heart.

In Verse 1 — in a roundabout way — God blames women for the
impending doom of mankind. It is stated that *daughters* were born unto
men. Jumping a little bit ahead of the analysis: if women hadn't tempted
the angels by simply being pretty or fair, then the problem of giants and
wicked thoughts by man may never have presented itself. Just like Eve was
the scapegoat in the Garden of Eden, here we have the *daughters of men*
being the instrument by which the angels — God's heavenly creation —
again starting beguiling and bringing down God's earthly creation.

Verse 2 states that the *sons of God*, whom we have already proven
were angels, lusted after our daughters and were *allowed* to come down to
earth and have sex with them. I say that the angels, like Satan, were *allowed*
to come to our earth and mess it up.

DISORGANIZED CHRISTIANITY

The angels were not only *allowed* to come down and have sex with our daughters, but they were not given any boundaries as to which daughters they could breed with; *and they took of them wives of all whom they chose.* The angels had free will, free desire, and free reign. So *who* is really in charge of this planet, the bad angels or God? Either God is in charge with no power, or the bad angels — including Satan — are just not afraid of God's actions.

Verse 3 is typically the verse used to justify why the Bible does not have to actually *prove* that man did live to be from 500 to 969 years old.

Genesis 5:27 *And all the days of Methuselah were nine hundred sixty and nine years: and he died.* No one *after* the global flood is claimed to have lived to be 969 years old.

Verse 4 arguably one of the hardest verses of the Bible to explain. If you want to maintain the illusion of a superior God who is in complete control, the angels really messed up God's illusion. We already addressed this in the chapter *Angels and giants and creeping thing, oh my!* but to refresh your memory: *sons of God* — angels — came in to the daughters of men, got them pregnant, and created giants. Once again, it seems like man and God were doing just fine until angels entered the picture, and even though the giants are touted as being "mighty men who were of old, men of renown," God is going to destroy the entire planet because *man* was bad.

I have not found a verse in which women went up to heaven, flirted with the *sons of God* and brought the angels into them, and then God got angry with the angels!

Verse 5 has the angels and the giants stirring up problems that man had never, or at least not up to that point, even *thought* of. Here again, we have God angry with *man.*

Verse 6 is the verse that really makes *me* angry with God. God allowed the angels to come down to earth, wreak their havoc, go unpunished, and

God *repents* that he even made *man*. Show me where God cursed those angels? Show me where God even *admonished* those angels? Show me, in these verses of God's anger towards *man*, where God even *condemns* those angels? Show me where God repents that he made those angels, or did God even really *create* angels, in the first place?

Verse 7 declares that God *will destroy man whom I have created from the face of the earth; both man, and beast, and the creeping thing, and the fowls of the air.* A couple of thoughts on this: What did the animals do to deserve total destruction, and in the end, what fate was given to the animals? With angels, daughters of men, giants, and man each playing some part in the days that led up to the flood, what did the cattle and birds and all the other creatures (except fish!) on Earth do to merit destruction? Why would God repent the creation of the little kitty cats and the cute little puppies and the parakeets and the crocodiles? God could have commanded the destruction of all *humans* because they were bad and since the animals were not bad, but just in the way, include them in the destruction but without the condemning curse.

God said that *all* creation was bad, and he repented having created them ALL. We don't know what was bad about the animals, but they must have been bad, because God said it, right?

Genesis 9:15-17 *15 And I will remember my covenant, which is between me and you and every living creature of all flesh; and the waters shall no more become a flood to destroy all flesh. 16 And the bow shall be in the cloud; and I will look upon it, that I may remember the everlasting covenant between God and every living creature of all flesh that is upon the earth. 17 And God said unto Noah, This is the token of the covenant, which I have established between me and all flesh that is upon the earth.*

In verses 15, 16 and 17 the Bible repeats "ALL living flesh upon the earth" four times. If a message was ever suppose to have been delivered, you would think "ALL living flesh upon the earth" would be that absolute message. But it is not! Because you forgot about the fish. Are the fish important to biblical accuracy concerning the flood? The Bible cannot say "ALL" when it doesn't really mean ALL anymore. We are not ALL sinners. We are not ALL condemned to hell. We are not ALL guilty. There is no more biblical ALL!

Two of each kind of *all* flesh representing male and female — except fish — were to be saved. Even though fish are flesh, and all flesh was to be destroyed, why were they not included in the all flesh-destroyed verses? Could God have destroyed the fish too, if he really wanted to fulfill his own curse of "all living creatures?"

1 Corinthians 15:39 *All flesh is not the same flesh, but there is one kind of flesh of men, another flesh of beasts, another of fish, and another of birds.*

If fish are flesh and God says *all flesh* will be destroyed are we back to yet another "*Well, not exactly*" situation?

Genesis 9:2-3 *2 And the fear of you and the dread of you shall be upon every beast of the earth, and upon every fowl of the air, upon all that moveth upon the earth, and upon all the fish of the sea; into your hand are they delivered. 3 Every moving thing that liveth shall be food for you; even as the green herb have I given you all things.*

It seems we don't know what the beasts and the fowls did in order for *all* to be destroyed, but we do know now that after they replenished the earth they were all invited to man's breakfast, lunch, and dinner tables, not as guests but as the meal.

We are not sure whether there were two birds, four birds, nine birds, or 18,000 birds on the Ark. The Bible says two of every bird, one male and one female, and then the Bible says seven of every clean bird, and then the Bible says in **Genesis 7:14** *They, and every beast after its kind, and all the cattle after their kind, and every creeping thing that creepeth upon the earth after its kind, and every fowl after its kind, every bird of every sort.*

Webster's New Collegiate Dictionary, defines fowl as 1: "a bird of any kind." My confusion is that the Bible says to bring into the Ark "fowls and birds." Not being a fowl or bird expert, but then reading definitions in the dictionary, it sounds like they are the same thing. Even if you can explain the difference between a fowl and a bird to me, why should you have to? The Bible should be clear!

Genesis 6:19 *And of every living thing of all flesh, two of every sort shalt thou bring into the Ark, to keep them alive with thee, they shall be male and female.*

A bird is a fowl is a bird. Well, not exactly!

According to our Noah story, we at least had two cats, two elephants, two spiders, two cows, but we could have had four birds. There were two doves and two ravens. It appears that birds were the only multiple species of animals on the ark. *Which* two birds replenished the earth, then?

Genesis 8:11-12 *11 And the dove came in to him in the evening; and, lo, in her mouth was an olive leaf plucked off: so Noah knew that the waters were abated from off the earth. 12 And he stayed yet another seven days; and sent forth the dove, which returned not again unto him any more.*

One dove never came back to the Ark. Did the male of the dove pair go out and find the missing female dove to complete the pair? He must have found her because we have doves today!

You can believe that two birds, one male and one female, on the Ark replenished the bird population on the entire planet and actually recreated all of the 9,000 to 10,000-plus species of birds found today.

Animals.about.com/od/zoologybasics/a/howmanyspecies.htm

That web site tells us that evolution takes *millions* of years. Did these two birds have to mate at least 9,000 to 10,000 times and then do the impossible, procreate a species *different from their own*, not just *once* but 9,000 to 10,000 times in a span of 3,000 to 4,000 years since the flood? That is a whole lot of procreating going on!

Okay, more realistically, where did the thousands of different species of birds come from? If the "two bird" theory is absolutely the "truth," how could *any* two birds procreate a hummingbird and a bald eagle? And let's not forget the multiple species of dogs and spiders and cats and elephants and horses. Just how did the penguins get to Antarctica from the Mesopotamian Valley?

Genesis 7:13-15 *13 In the very same day entered Noah, and Shem, and Ham, and Japheth, the sons of Noah and Noah's wife, and the three wives of his sons with them, into the ark; 14 They, and every beast after its kind, and all the cattle after their kind, and every creeping thing that creepeth upon the earth after its kind, and every fowl after its kind, every bird of every sort. 15 And they went in unto Noah into the ark, two and two of all flesh, wherein is the breath of life.*

The concern I have here is pretty simple: have you ever tried to move from a three-bedroom house, with teenagers and their stuff, in one day? Noah had to load eight people, enough clothes, food and water for a 150 day and night journey, as well as oversee the embarkation of 3 to 30 million animals and their provisions, *in the very same day.*

See ***Animals.about.com/od/zoologybasics/a/howmanyspecies.htm***

Along with the traditional animals we can imagine were on the ark like cats and dogs and elephants and tigers and bears, there must have been some very unique animals. As with the giants we mentioned earlier, if certain animals were present *after* the flood and the flood indeed was global, they must also have been present *before* the flood and thus included on the ark. This is simple logic.

When *organized religion* cannot answer a question, they *make up* an answer or try to defer an answer until God tells them it is all right to answer. In Genesis 1:21 the Bible says "sea monster" and *organized religion* translators think of the most logical animal and choose a whale.

In Job 41:1 the Bible mentions a "leviathan" and *organized religion* chooses a crocodile. Leviathans are mentioned in Job 41:1, Psalm 74:14 and Psalm 104:26.

In Job 40:15 the Bible mentions a "behemoth" and *organized religion* chooses that to mean a hippopotamus.

In this instance, my *organized religion*'s choice of "whale," "crocodile," and hippopotamus" are based on the footnotes in the *King James Bible* I have been quoting since page one of *Disorganized Christianity*. Now, the translators may think that those are very wise choices, but if they keep reading the scriptures, they will find that their hasty jump to a conclusion, as usual, cannot possibly be correct.

In the case of the leviathan, a crocodile does not *breathe fire*:

Job 41:1 and **18-21** *1 Canst thou draw out leviathan with an hook, or his tongue with a cord which thou lettest down? 18 By his sneezing a light doth shine, and his eyes are like the eyelids of the morning. 19 Out of his mouth go burning lamps, and sparks of fire leap out. 20 Out of his nostrils goeth smoke, as out of a boiling pot or cauldron. 21 His breath kindleth coals, and a flame goeth out of his mouth.*

In the case of the behemoth, a hippopotamus does not have the *tail of a cedar*:

Job 40:15-17 *15 Behold now behemoth, which I made with thee; he eateth grass as an ox. 16 Lo, now, his strength is in his loins, and his force is in the muscles of his belly. 17 He moveth his tail like a cedar; the sinews of his thighs are knit together.*

The Bible mentions certain animals or creatures we do not see today, but they must have been real. In *my* version of the Bible, the *New Scofield Reference Bible, Authorized King James Version*, sometimes the translators use a familiar word to describe a different or unusual animal. Hegoat was used to describe a satyr, ostrich was used for an owl, jackal was used for a dragon, wild oxen were used for a unicorn and adder was used for a cockatrice.

Now whether or not an adder is *really* a cockatrice or a cockatrice is *really* an adder, the fact that the Bible mentions this animal and offers the following description is amazing.

An adder or cockatrice is described in **Isaiah 14:29** *Rejoice not thou, O Philistia, because the rod of him who smote thee is broken; for out of the serpent's root shall come forth an adder, and his fruit shall be a fiery, flying serpent.*

I haven't actually seen one of those lately, but I will keep looking! With all the already established very hard to believe "facts" about Noah and the Ark set aside, I want to show why I believe that Noah was the absolute worst man God could have used as His agent to replenish a sinful earth.

Genesis 6:8-9 *8 But Noah found grace in the eyes of the Lord. 9 These are the generations of Noah: Noah was a just man and perfect in his generations, and Noah walked with God.*

While God was so angry with man on the Earth that he decided to destroy all flesh on the planet as punishment for ungodliness, He somehow decided that man needed another chance. My first question is *"Why?"*

If man was truly so bad, **Genesis 6:5** *And God saw that the wickedness of man was great in the earth, and that every imagination of the thoughts of his heart was only evil continually,* then destroy *all* mankind like you said you would, no exceptions! No more "well, not exactly!" Why have an exception, especially if your exception is in no way better than your proclaimed bad creation?

My concerns are based on what the Bible reveals about Noah after the global flooding and the destruction of the earth were complete. At this point, Noah is the person in charge of replenishing mankind, physically and spiritually.

The Bible states that one of the first things Noah did after leaving the ark was to plant a vineyard.

Genesis 9:20 *And Noah began to be a farmer; and he planted a vineyard.*

Now, was the allegedly all-knowing God aware in advance that Noah would plant a vineyard, make wine and get drunk and then proceed to do all the things drunks do? If Noah simply wanted fruit, why not plant an apple orchard? Well, maybe an apple wasn't such a good choice either! But why a grape vineyard, unless you wanted the wine?

Show me a verse or passage from the Bible where making or drinking wine turned out well. I suppose you could choose the miracle of Jesus turning water into wine at the wedding feast. When the wine provided for the feast ran out, Jesus "made" more wine, but we never heard what happened after the consumption of more wine.

In Noah's example the end result was not left up to the imagination; Noah got drunk. In fact, Noah got drunk in the very next verse:

Genesis 9:21 *And he drank of the wine, and became drunk; and he was uncovered in his tent.*

In the very short space of two verses, we have Noah getting off the ark, planting a vineyard and then getting drunk. Where was this perfect and righteous man who was praised by God? Noah was a *just man and perfect in his generations*, and Noah walked with God. Walked *where?* Walked through God's vineyards?

To demonstrate that Noah was grateful and understood why God had saved him and his family, shouldn't Noah have felt inspired to set the example for the new creation by obeying God's statutes and ordinances? Instead, Noah decided to get drunk. Let's consider that Noah engaged in an activity that was *specifically* mentioned by God as one of the major reasons the entire Earth was flooded: drinking. At least that is what *your* Bible thought was important enough to record.

If you go back to *your* Bible verses, **Matthew 24:37-38** *37 But as the days of Noah were, so shall also the coming of the Son of man be. 38 For as in the days that were before the flood they were eating and drinking, marrying and giving in marriage, until the day that Noah entered into the ark.*

Drinking was the second leading activity that led God to destroy the planet. Are you going to try to tell me that God did not know about Noah's drinking when He called him righteous? It is not like Noah merely had a case of the jitters from just getting off the boat. Noah had to plant a vineyard, wait for the harvest, squeeze the grapes, and then wait for the fermentation process. Then Noah drank. Then Noah got drunk.

Meanwhile, *nowhere* in that process is it recorded in the Bible that Noah taught his sons about God's statutes and ordinances. If Noah *did* instruct his sons on how to live on the Earth and how to please God, why not record the new way to live for his sons and for all of us?

Up to this time in the Old Testament, we have not been given a very clear and accurate understanding of what God actually wanted from us. The New Testament verses are not much better at explaining in detail precisely what is expected of us, either. Given all the contradictions, misinterpretations, and mistranslations throughout the Bible, seems to me that the rest of us are pretty much left up a creek without a paddle or perhaps in a flood without an ark!

The Bible does not spend any time celebrating this new beginning. Noah goes directly from redeemer to drunk and mankind goes from redeemed to cursed once more, all in the space of just two verses. Not a very good second chance!

Now that Noah is drunk, we have a very interesting Bible twist on words. We have already shown that the Bible's translators tend to not pay attention to God's inspired revelations, so they interpret their own words to soothe the times. The translators certainly did not pause to explain to us what *"and he was uncovered in his tent"* really meant. Yet this short phrase led to the worst curse of all time.

Adam and Eve were not cursed, they were *punished*; the snake was cursed, and the ground was cursed. But why would God or the translators shy away from telling us what *"uncovered in his tent"* meant unless they were just leaving that curse available for anyone to interpret and use against us whenever they felt it was necessary?

My point here is that the average Bible reader does not know what *"and he was uncovered in his tent"* really means. Oh yes, there are plenty of explanations and theories, but I had never been told the actual definition of the sin that led to the Noah/Canaan curse. We do have several clues though.

Genesis 9:20-27 *20 And Noah began to be a farmer; and he planted a vineyard. 21 And he drank of the wine, and became drunk; and he was uncovered within his tent. 22 And Ham, the father of Canaan, saw the nakedness of his father, and told his two brethren outside. 23 And Shem and Japheth took a garment, and laid it upon both their shoulders, and went backward, and covered the nakedness of their father; and their faces were backward, and they saw not their father's nakedness. 24 And Noah awoke from his wine, and knew what his younger son had done to him. 25 And he said, Cursed be*

Canaan; a servant of servants shall he be unto his brethren. 26 And he said. Blessed be the Lord God of Shem; and Canaan shall be his servant. 27 God shall enlarge Japheth, and he shall dwell in the tents of Shem; and Canaan shall be his servant.

Words used in biblical days can have quite different meanings from the same word used today. One such example would be the word "knew."

Genesis 4:1 *And Adam knew Eve his wife; and she conceived, and bore Cain, and said, I have gotten a man from the Lord.*

Today we would define the word "knew" as some form of intelligence, e.g. "I knew the answer to the question." In biblical days the word "knew" also meant that someone had sexual relations to create life.

With this kind of dual meaning as part of the process comes the increased possibility of someone choosing to interpret any given word to mean what they *want* the word to mean and support the message they want the word to convey.

The curse from Noah to Canaan came from a sentence that has many interpretations. Some of the translations come from very bold and brazen people who are not afraid to "tell it like it is," while other interpretations come from a crowd that did not want to unduly instill any sexually provocative statements into their Bible translations. If the translators of the Bible had just said what Ham *actually* did in Noah's tent, then we would not have had this confusion for thousands of years.

The words *"uncovered the nakedness"* of their father are the focal point of the curse. What does *"uncovered the nakedness"* of their father mean? In this verse we do not have a clear understanding of precisely what the sin was, significant enough to justify a multi-generational everlasting curse. But we could go to other verses in the Bible that express *"uncover their nakedness"* and see in what context the words are being used there.

Leviticus 18:5-6 *5 Ye shall therefore keep my statutes, and mine ordinances, which if a man do, he shall live in them: I am the Lord. 6 None of you shall approach to any that is near of kin to him, to uncover their nakedness: I am the Lord.*

Not being a professor of languages and cultures, I would still venture to say that this verse tells everyone to not have sexual relations with anyone who is related to you. Because these verses and this curse are so important, I am going to give you another very long set of verses to further explain my conclusion as to the meaning of *"uncover their nakedness."* This is one of those times when God got very explicit in his commandment of who not to *"uncover the nakedness"* of.

Leviticus 18:7-23 *7 The nakedness of thy father, or the nakedness of thy mother, shalt thou not uncover: she is thy mother; thou shalt not uncover her nakedness. 8 The nakedness of thy father's wife shalt thou not uncover: it is thy father's nakedness.* (could be the clue) *9 The nakedness of thy sister, the daughter of thy father, or daughter of thy mother, whether she be born at home, or born abroad, even their nakedness thou shalt not uncover. 10 The nakedness of thy son's daughter, or of thy daughter's daughter, even their nakedness thou shalt not uncover: for theirs is thine own nakedness. 11 The nakedness of thy father's wife's daughter, begotten of thy father, she is thy sister; thou shalt not uncover her nakedness. 12 Thou shalt not uncover the nakedness of thy father's sister: she is thy father's near kinswoman. 13 Thou shalt not uncover the nakedness of thy mother's sister: for she is thy mother's near kinswoman. 14 Thou shalt not uncover the nakedness of thy father's brother; thou shalt not approach to his wife: she is thine aunt. 15 Thou shalt not uncover the nakedness of thy daughter-in-law: she is thy son's wife; thou shalt not uncover her nakedness. 16 Thou shalt not uncover the nakedness of thy brother's wife: it is thy brother's nakedness. 17 Thou shalt not uncover the nakedness of a woman and her daughter, neither shalt thou take her son's daughter, or her daughter's daughter, to uncover her nakedness; for they are her near kinswomen: it is wickedness. 18 Neither shalt thou take a wife to her sister, to vex her, to uncover her nakedness, beside the other in her lifetime.*

19 Also thou shalt not approach unto a woman to uncover her nakedness, as long as she is put apart for her uncleanness. 20 Moreover thou shalt not lie carnally with thy neighbor's wife, to defile thyself with her. 21 And thou shalt not let any of thy seed pass through the fire to Molech, neither shalt thou profane the name of thy God: I am the Lord. 22 Thou shalt not lie with mankind, as with womankind: it is abomination. 23 Neither shalt thou lie with any beast to defile thyself therewith; neither shall any woman stand before a beast to lie down thereto: it is confusion.

There are several more verses in the Bible that command anyone to not *"uncover their nakedness."* I believe this extensive block of verses clearly identifies *"uncover their nakedness,"* with sexual misconduct.

Regardless of the details surrounding the actions of Ham, precisely *who* gave Noah the authority to curse anyone? Noah did not have the authority to place a curse on Canaan that would force a multi-generational lifetime of servitude to his uncles. Noah was just an embarrassed drunk who lashed out at the first person he felt deserved punishment, for any reason. Have you ever been around an angry drunk? Remember that God just finished forgiving and sparing Noah for his pre-flood sins and earthly actions, and now Noah does not even show any mercy or forgiveness towards Ham for his seeing or being a party to whatever *"uncovered the nakedness of his father"* meant?

Luke 6:36-37 *36 Be ye, therefore, merciful, as your Father also is merciful. 37 Judge not, and ye shall not be judged; condemn not, and ye shall not be condemned; forgive, and ye shall be forgiven.*

Ezekiel 18:19-20 *19 Yet say ye, Why? Doth not the son bear the iniquity of the father? When the son hath done that which is lawful and right, and hath kept all my statutes, and hath done them, he shall surely live. 20 The soul that sinneth, it shall die. The son shall not bear the iniquity of the father, neither shall the father bear the iniquity of the son; the righteousness of the righteous shall be upon him, and the wickedness of the wicked shall be upon him.*

The son shall *not* bear the iniquity of the father. Well, not exactly!

Numbers 14:18 *The Lord is long-suffering, and of great mercy, forgiving iniquity and transgression, and by no means clearing the guilty, visiting the iniquity of the fathers upon the children unto the third and fourth generation.*

Deuteronomy 5:9 *Thou shalt not bow down thyself unto them, nor serve them; for I the Lord thy God am a jealous God, visiting the iniquity of the fathers upon the children unto the third and fourth generation of them who hate me.*

Exodus 20:5 *Thou shalt not bow down thyself to them, nor serve them; for I, the Lord thy God, am a jealous God, visiting the iniquity of the fathers upon the children unto the third and fourth generation of them that hate me.*

Ham will serve his brothers for how long? This one curse by Noah begat on mankind hatred, intolerance, anger, and slavery among others. Christianity's dirty little secret is that this curse from a *man*, not God, has been the basis for slavery in America and the world. Yes, our churches used this curse to justify their intolerance of Black people. More on this thought will follow in the chapter *I believe in the separation of church and hate!*

In Ezekial 18 we are told that the son *shall not* bear the iniquity of the father but in Numbers 14, Deuteronomy 5, and Exodus 20 God says that the children *will* bear the iniquities of the father for three and four generations. Right now, I am not too concerned about this contradiction. What I *am* concerned about is the fact that God, *the creator of the universe*, only passes the iniquities of the father to children for three and four generations, yet *Noah's* curse of Canaan, the son, because of Ham, the father's sin, was *forever*. Who did Noah really think he was and why would God choose such an arrogant, angry, and self-serving person to replenish the earth?

Genesis 6:9 *These are the generations of Noah: Noah was a just man and perfect in his generations, and Noah walked with God.*

Was Noah, really the best God could find to replenish the earth?

I have an idea: "God, if you are going to really destroy the entire planet and all the living creatures that breathe, why not start over with a new Garden of Eden. Hey, try another sinless Adam and Eve. Only this time don't *allow* Satan, one of your heavenly creations, to beguile Eve or *allow* any other angels to come down to earth and breed with earth women! Seems like all the really bad stuff we humans get blamed and condemned for started with God's heavenly angels being *allowed* by God to have their unheavenly way with us."

Noah and his sons sound like a pretty bad remnant to task with replenishing the earth. How much better were Noah and his sons than Adam and Eve? Adam and Eve ate an apple and were banned forever from the Garden of Eden. Noah got drunk, had some sort of sexual encounter with Ham, and Ham's lineage got punished forever. Sounds like another case of transference of guilt to me. Is this the best God could do or did God really just say, "I don't want to start over, so I will settle for Noah?"

CHAPTER 10

I believe in the separation
of church and hate!

I strongly believe that the Bible has instructed and influenced those who want to hate in how to claim a *righteous validation* to hate.

My three major examples will be hatred of women, hatred towards Black people, and hatred towards homosexuals, all in the name of God's Christian *love* and *order*. My conviction is that if I am to believe in a God who demonstrates such a hateful spirit and then *organized religion* tries to pass off this hateful spirit as being necessary for God's *will to be done*, then I do not want to have any part of *that* God. If I am expected to stand back and watch the hatred, bigotry, belittlement, and condemnation of any group of people by intolerant Christians in the name of Jesus and the Bible's God, then I choose to find a different God!

I am in no way claiming that the Bible's God should do things my way or explain unclear verses in the same manner I would. I am just saying that because there is biblical confusion and misinterpretation of many translations, we have unclear verses. We *converted non-Christians* choose not to believe these verses anymore, and until *organized religion* can answer to our satisfaction any questions we have, just leave *us* alone!

Organized religion has the right to teach their dogma, no matter the source. I do believe though, that because of the hate and punishments *organized religion* perpetuates in their faith that — one day very soon — their members' or leaders' karma will run over their dogma.

John 3:16 *For God so loved the world, that he gave his only begotten Son, that whosoever believeth in him should not perish, but have everlasting life.*

The message in John 3:16 is declared as being the single verse that proves God's love for mankind. We are to believe that God loves us *so* much that after He *allowed* Satan to beguile Eve and then condemned all mankind, God's love was proven by His sending down Jesus to die for our sins if we believe in him.

I believe this verse is unclear and full of ambiguities because many Christian denominations can't even agree on exactly what it means to *believe in Jesus*. Each denomination is defined by the differences in what they want to *believe* about Jesus.

Mark 12:30-31 *30 And thou shalt love the Lord thy God with all thy heart, and with all thy soul, and with all thy mind, and with all thy strength: this is the first commandment. 31 And the second is this: Thou shalt love thy neighbor as thyself. There is no other commandment greater than these.*

Verse 31 is also referred to as the *"greatest commandment."*

I have found far too many biblical verses that define why I believe God is not *really* a God of love, but actually a God of self-serving anger and vindictiveness toward anything or anyone who gets in His way. If God wants to prove the point that He is in control and all things are proven in God's time and way, then why does He usually use death and destruction to prove His power, if God is truly a God of love?

The God of the Old Testament was a very mean, jealous, and angry God. Entire civilizations, right down to the animals, were killed simply because people would not worship God.

Talking to Israel about how to annihilate Babylon; God says in **Jeremiah 51:20-26** *20 Thou art my battle-axe and weapons of war; for with thee will I break in pieces the nations, and with thee will I destroy kingdoms; 21 And with thee will I break in pieces the horse and its rider; and with thee will I break in pieces the chariot and his rider; 22 With thee also will I break in pieces man and woman; and with thee will I break in pieces old and young; and with thee will I break in pieces the young man and the maid. 23 I will also break in pieces with thee the shepherd and his flock; and with thee will I break in pieces the farmer and his yoke of oxen; and with thee I will break in pieces captains and rulers. 24 And I will render unto Babylon and to all the inhabitants of Chaldea all their evil that they have done in Zion in your sight, saith the Lord. 25 Behold, I am against thee, O thou destroying mountain, saith the Lord, that destroyeth all the earth; and I will stretch out mine hand upon thee, and roll thee down from the rocks, and will make thee a burnt mountain. 26 And they shall not take of thee a stone for a corner, nor a stone for foundations, but thou shalt be desolate forever, saith the Lord.*

You could argue that God didn't really kill the people and cattle, and that the Israelites *actually* did the killing. The problem with that excuse is that the Israelites did God's bidding because their leaders said they should, through commandments from God. Today, God's anger or displeasure with man is delivered by whichever Christian dogma has the loudest voice or strongest following. Today's judgments may not be from God to Moses to the Israelites, but it seems to have a familiar pattern, from God's Bible to preachers and televangelists to congregations including television and radio audiences.

The God of the New Testament didn't attack or kill entire civilizations. But with selective verses as justification, our modern-day *organized religion's* members —obeying God's Bible — attack and yes, attempt to spiritually kill specific groups of people in the name of God.

Back in Noah's time God destroyed the entire planet for man's bad behavior for a lot less than what it looks like we have going on today. You can argue that I have no idea how bad Noah's times *were* compared to today and I would concede: "You are right." But is the lack of discernable information *that leaves me lacking clarity* my fault or the Bible's?

What I can read in **Genesis 6:5** *And God saw that the wickedness of man was great in the earth, and that every imagination of the thoughts of his heart was only evil continually* is certainly left open to interpretation by anyone with a position to prove and a purpose to fulfill.

We get a *little* more information regarding how bad man had to be in the eyes of God, in order for Him to destroy all of mankind in **Matthew 24:37-38** *37 But as the days of Noah were, so shall also the coming of the Son of man be. 38 For as in the days that were before the flood they were eating and drinking, marrying and giving in marriage, until the day that Noah entered into the ark.*

Another descriptive clue as to just how bad the days leading to the global flood really were can be found in **Luke 17:26-27** *26 And as it was in the days of Noah, so shall it be also in the days of the Son of man. 27 They did eat, they drank, they married wives, they were given in marriage, until the day that Noah entered into the ark, and the flood came and destroyed them all.*

"As in the days of Noah eating, drinking and marrying wives," does not exactly hold a candle to the 5:00 news today. If you think news channels might be biased and current events are not really as bad as biblical days, go ahead and pick the news channel you want to believe, CNN or Fox.

As of 2018 the United States is on record as having had an estimated 54,559,615 abortions since Roe vs. Wade in 1973. "Thou shalt not kill" (www.lifenews.com).

Listen to any Congressman or Congresswoman try to get their special bill passed that will put us further under their thumbs. "Thou shalt not lie."

Money managers stealing millions from pensions of the citizens of our country and the government. "Thou shalt not steal."

Meanwhile, *organized religion* has expanded to 34,000 different *understandings*. God said, "Thou shalt have no other Gods before me."

Preachers and televangelists peddle their charms, saying, "Send me your money so we can evangelize the world!" and then spend those fortunes on *things*. "Thou shalt not covet."

Oh yes, these sound like some of those Old Testament Ten Commandments again!

It does *not* sound like **Mark 12:30-31** *30 And thou shalt love the Lord thy God with all thy heart, and with all thy soul, and with all thy mind, and with all thy strength: this is the first commandment. 31 And the second is this: Thou shalt love thy neighbor as thyself. There is no other commandment greater than these.*

I am not trying to give a radical preacher the ability to give a doomsday message for the planet by these comparisons. I *am* saying that your Bible says the Son of man will come when times become as they were in the days of Noah. By the verses given in Matthew 24 and Luke 17 it seems we are way past "eating, drinking and marrying." My point is that the God of the Old Testament would have already destroyed the entire planet by now or maybe we have arrived at another point of "Well, not exactly!"

We have a cute little story being told every Christmas and presented in every church's nativity scene. But is the birth of Christ in a stable in Bethlehem accurate? Why would a loving God at such a joyous time — the birth of God's only begotten Son —allow one of the worst mass murders ever to take place?

At Jesus' birth, King Herod decreed that every male child, up to two years of age, be killed so the King would not feel threatened by a potential overthrow of his throne. Did this mass murder of every male child below age two have to take place in order to fulfill God's eternal plan for mankind? If the baby was just born why was the decree for "up to two years of age?"

I am not saying that God was right or wrong by letting such an event happen. I am just questioning whether these murders were necessary. I believe my conviction about not believing in a true, loving God of the Bible will be understood just a little better after you read this story.

Prophesy was given in the Old Testament that the threat to King Herod, was to be born in the town of Bethlehem.

Micah 5:2 *But thou, Bethlehem Ephrathah, though thou be little among the thousands of Judah, yet out of thee shall he come forth unto me that is to be ruler in Israel, whose goings forth have been from old, from everlasting.*

Well, that much is written. But let's see how much of this story is biblical and how much of this story is traditional.

The story goes like this: Jesus, the only begotten Son of God, was to be born of a virgin in the town of Bethlehem. There was no room in the inn, so the baby Jesus had to be born in a stable. There was an unusual cast of characters supposedly present at the birth of Jesus. We had Joseph, the not real father, Mary, the virgin mother, Jesus, the Son of God, three wise men with treasures, camels, goats, and sheep. There was also a particularly bright star up in the sky and a bunch of shepherds in the field. For now, I am willing to go along with the goats and sheep being in the stable. I will allow the goats and sheep because they probably lived in the stable.

The Bible does not mention the wise men's camels. Yet, almost every nativity scene has camels. We do not know exactly *who* was in the stable, but we do know who *wasn't* in the stable. My first concern is with respect to the three wise men.

Matthew 2:8 *And he sent them to Bethlehem, and said, Go and search diligently for the young child; and when ye have found him, bring me word again, that I may come and worship him also.*

These wise men were ordered by Herod, the King, to find this new born baby that would some day rise up and threaten his kingdom. Of course Herod told the wise men that he wanted to worship the newborn baby. After reading the entire story, we find that Herod lied and actually wanted the baby Jesus killed. The wise men came from the east and were told to follow a star.

The Bible does not tell us *how many* wise men came to see the baby Jesus. The claim that gifts of gold, frankincense and myrrh were given at their visit probably puts the number of wise men at three. The Bible does not give any names for the wise men. Historical writings other than the Bible offer the names of these three wise men as Gaspar, Melchior and Balthasar. Another Christian tradition, but not biblical. The wise men are portrayed as giving the *baby* Jesus gifts *in* the stable. Another Christian tradition, but not biblical.

Matthew 2:11 *And when they were come into the house, they saw the young child with Mary, his mother, and fell down and worshipped him; and when they had opened their treasures, they presented unto him gifts: gold, and frankincense, and myrrh.*

This verse states that when the wise men finally found Jesus they met him and Mary in a house, not a manger. Moreover, the verse says that the wise men saw a young child, not a newborn infant. Were our Sunday School teachers and our annual nativity scenes accurate? Well, not exactly!

Now the actual *number* of wise men and whether or not they had names or camels and the actual *time* when they gave Jesus his treasures are not my only concern. My other concern centers on what happens *after* the wise men presented the *"young child"* Jesus with his gifts.

These wise men were warned by God — in a dream — about the dangers of returning to King Herod with the news of their finding Jesus. So the three wise men took a different route to their own country and bypassed King Herod completely.

Matthew 2:12 *And being warned of God in a dream that they should not return to Herod, they departed into their own country a different way.*

My ongoing concern is that an angel of the Lord had also appeared to Joseph in a dream and warned him of the immediate danger presented by King Herod and his intention of killing Jesus. The angel told Joseph to flee to Egypt.

Matthew 2:13 *And when they were departed, behold, an angel of the Lord appeareth to Joseph in a dream, saying, Arise, and take the young child and his mother, and flee into Egypt, and be thou there until I bring thee word; for Herod will seek the young child to destroy him.*

Twice in this verse Jesus is referred to as a *young child*, not a newborn infant wrapped in swaddling clothes.

My deepest and most sorrowful concern can be found in **Matthew 2:16** *Then Herod, when he saw that he was mocked of the wise men, was exceedingly angry, and sent forth, and slew all the children that were in Bethlehem, and in all its borders, from two years old and under, according to the time which he had diligently inquired of the wise men.*

Why was King Herod *exceedingly angry*? The wise men were supposed to tell King Herod exactly where the *baby* Jesus was so he could kill him. King Herod knew that it was foretold that a baby would grow up to someday become the ruler and Governor of King Herod's kingdom.

These prophesies were recorded in **Micah 5:2** *But thou, Bethlehem Ephrathah, though thou be little among the thousands of Judah, out of thee shall he come forth unto me that is to be ruler in Israel, whose goings* *forth have been from old, from everlasting* and again in **Matthew 2:6** *And thou Bethlehem, in the land of Judah, art not the least among the princes of Judah; for out of thee shall come a Governor that shall rule my people, Israel.*

Although the *infallible* Word of God stated that Jesus would be the ruler of Israel and the Governor of Israel, look at what Jesus *himself* said:

John 18:36 *Jesus answered, My kingdom is not of this world; if my kingdom were of this world, then would my servants fight, that I should not be delivered to the Jews; but now my kingdom is not from here.*

An earthly kingdom was never meant to be. Jesus preached that he did not come to set up a kingdom on Earth. Jesus preached that he came to set up a kingdom in heaven. At least that is what the *infallible* Word of God says:

John 14:2-3 *2 In my Father's house are many mansions; if it were not so, I would have told you. I go to prepare a place for you. 3 And if I go and prepare a place for you, I will come again, and receive you unto myself, that where I am, there ye may be also.*

Which *infallible* Bible verse is right? In this case, since Jesus never became the ruler and Governor of Israel, I guess the latter verse must be the more *infallible* Word of God.

To summarize: The wise men who were participants in Jesus' birth story were warned of danger. They escaped. Joseph was warned of danger. He escaped with Mary and the *young child*, Jesus. All the male children under the age of two that died to complete this story were not warned. They all just died. No, they were all killed! I am not telling God what should or shouldn't have happened. But the simple fact that the male children under two years old in Bethlehem and within all its borders were summarily killed because King Herod got *exceedingly angry* is not acceptable with me, given that you are trying to convince me that God is a *loving* God!

I challenge any preacher to try to explain to me how killing all these children could in any way be considered directly beneficial to the Jesus' birth story or mankind's salvation. Would Jesus' birth story and mankind's salvation message somehow be hindered if all these Christmas children under the age of two were *not* killed and instead allowed to live? It does not say anywhere in the Bible that all these children were bad. It does not say anywhere in the Bible that all these children had rejected the birth of Christ and therefore must be punished.

The *only* explanation for killing all these children —and I believe they actually had *nothing* to do with Jesus' birth — was that some guy in power got *exceedingly angry* because he did not get his own way or his future was potentially threatened.

Another question of mine is this: "After the killing all of these children under the age of two, was there some great revelation explaining the cause and effect or purpose for the murders?"

No! This mass murder allowed by a perceived loving God warranted no more than one verse of attention!

I lost a son in infancy. I do not know why Sean Michael died. But I can relate to **Matthew 2:18** *In Ramah was there a voice heard, lamentation, and weeping, and great mourning, Rachael weeping for her children, and would not be comforted, because they are not.*

When Sean Michael died, I did not curse God, but I did not feel much love from God either.

THE TREATMENT OF WOMEN
Old Testament

The Old Testament surely must be the single largest documentation base of instruction for the ill treatment of women ever assembled!

There are more verses in the Old Testament given to God's commanded abuses towards women than I care to cover. I believe almost anyone could write *volumes* outlining the numerous examples of how women are not equal to men — and never would be — if the Old Testament were allowed to stand as the protocol for keeping women in their place. I will address only a *few* of the scariest and saddest examples of how a so-called "loving God" instructed men to treat women.

Virgin girls and virgin women were definitely held in a higher esteem than non-virgins, but that higher esteem did not necessarily lead to a better life. After God directed battles with scorched earth instructions given to Moses, all virgin captives were spared their lives, but they were subsequently used by God's victors.

God told Moses to take 1,000 men from each tribe of Israel to go and destroy the Midianites.

Numbers 31:9-11 *9 And the children of Israel took all the women of Midian captives, and their little ones, and took the spoil of all their cattle, and all their flocks, and all their goods. 10 And they burned all their cities wherein they dwelt, and all their encampments with fire. 11 And they took all the spoil, and all the prey of men and of beasts.*

After conquering the Midianites, Moses told the warriors of Israel that any virgins could be theirs for the taking.

Numbers 31:17-18 *17 Now therefore kill every male among the little ones, and kill every woman that hath known man by lying with him. 18 But* *all the female children, that have not known a man by lying with him, keep alive for yourselves.*

Let us be perfectly clear: God *told* Moses to take these actions:

Numbers 31:1 *And the Lord spoke unto Moses, saying.*

Deuteronomy 20 is a chapter about the law of warfare. Here is a chapter that clearly explains: "If you ever go to war for the Lord, do not be afraid because God will deliver you and give you victory along with some fringe benefits." A few of these fringe benefits include women, little ones and cattle.

Deuteronomy 20:14 *But the women, and the little ones, and the cattle, and all that is in the city, even all the spoil thereof; shalt thou take unto thyself; and thou shalt eat the spoil of thine enemies, which the Lord thy God hath given thee.*

God also offered an "optional steal-to-own" program with respect to captured beautiful women who were provided to the Israelite men. If a warrior saw a woman of the conquered tribe whom he liked, he could take her home for a month and then have his way with her. If she didn't please him, he could simply let her go to fend for herself! Since he *stole* her, he didn't even need to produce a "receipt of return."

Deuteronomy 21:11 and **13-14** *11 And seest among the captives a beautiful woman, and hast a desire for her, that thou wouldest have her as thy wife. 13 And she shall put the raiment of her captivity from off her, and shall remain in thine house and bewail her father and mother a full month; and after that thou shalt go in unto her, and be her husband, and she shall be thy wife. 14 And it shall be, if thou have no delight in her, then thou shalt let her go where she will. But thou shalt not sell her at all for money; thou shalt not make merchandise of her, because thou hast humbled her.*

He humbled her! You can be absolutely sure that a woman did not translate that particular *infallible* Bible verse!

In Judges we find another massive virgin capture.

Judges 21:10-12 *10 And the congregation sent there twelve thousand men of the most valiant, and commanded them, saying, Go and smite the inhabitants of Jabesh-gilead with the edge of the sword, with the women and the children. 11 And this is the thing that ye shall do, Ye shall utterly destroy every male, and every woman who hath lain by a man. 12 And they found among the inhabitants of Jabesh-gilead four hundred young virgins, who had known no man by lying with any male; and they brought them unto the camp to Shiloh, which is in the land of Canaan.*

You would think that a loving God — not just of the Israelites, but of the entire planet's population regardless of ethnicity — would not punish that part of a nation that was the purest. These girls were told not to lose their virginity to just any guy, but do the right thing and wait for marriage. And now, because they obeyed the law of celibacy, they got rewarded by being taken and ravaged by God's invading army?

Now, I suppose you could argue that everything was all right because the invading army at least took them as wives. But we do not know whether they were taken as wives as stated earlier, nor whether if God's invading army did not find further pleasure with their now "used" virgins, could they simply *discard* them. If *organized religion* wants to stand by and condone this as "loving" behavior, then I invite you to put up *your own* daughters!

The rest of the story tells that the four hundred virgins were not enough to go around, so the Israelites sent another bunch of guys off to capture more virgins from an annual celebration in Shiloh. Leave *our daughters and us* alone!

God actually gives rules and conditions for a Father to sell his daughter to another man.

Exodus 21:7 *And if a man sell his daughter to be a maidservant...*

Leviticus 27:1 *And the Lord spoke unto Moses, saying.*

I repeat these words, because the Bible repeats these words. It is very clear that it is *God* speaking and commanding these awful deeds and not *Moses* misspeaking on behalf of God.

Leviticus 27:3-4 *3 And thy valuation shall be of the male from twenty years old, even unto sixty years old, even thy valuation shall be fifty shekels of silver, after the shekel of the sanctuary. 4 And if the female, then thy valuation shall be thirty shekels.*

I guess "equal pay for equal work" is not acceptable to God either.

I find this next thought to be absolutely disgusting! Again, note that these words are coming directly from the Lord to Moses.

Leviticus 12:1-2 and **5** *1 And the Lord spoke unto Moses, saying, 2 Speak unto the children of Israel, saying, If a woman have conceived seed, and born a male child, then she shall be unclean seven days; according to the days of the separation for her infirmity shall she be unclean. 5 But if she bear a female child, then she shall be unclean two weeks, as in her separation.*

Of course I don't understand this. I don't *want* to understand this, especially if the explanation comes from dogma with a patriarchal agenda attached. I am father to a boy and a girl and at their birth there was nothing you could have done to convince me that one was any "cleaner or dirtier" than the other.

And the ultimate putdown for woman can be found in Genesis. We have already showed that Eve was *not* the first of God's creation to sin in the Garden of Eden, and yet she still gets the punishment.

Genesis 3:16 *Unto the woman he said, I will greatly multiply thy sorrow and thy conception; in sorrow thou shalt bring forth children; and thy desire shall be to thy husband, and he shall rule over thee.*

I have shown that while the Bible is even confused as to whose transgression resulted in the condemnation of mankind, Eve was ultimately blamed and put in subjection to her husband, every day in sorrow.

New Testament

Remember the story of my mother and the *Blue Sequin Dress*, and the way women in the 1960's were told what to wear and what not to wear; women were also told not to speak in church.

What follows are some verses that tell women to be quiet and submit. There was a time when women could not — and did not — talk in church. Women certainly did not preach or have authority over Christian men in church. However, today there are a lot of women who talk in church and preach in church and have authority over men in church.

I Timothy 2:11-12 *11 Let the woman learn in silence with all subjection. 12 But I permit not a woman to teach, nor to usurp authority over the man, but to be in silence.*

Did the Bible rules change over time because someone found a new verse or did *organized religion's* men finally realize that they could not mandate their *organized religion's* women to be silent doctrinally?

God wrote these verses about women. Did God mean for these verses to apply for all time? What biblically changed over time? Has modern man finally seen the light and realized that in the context of today's world they actually now *know more than God* about women?

I Corinthians 14:34-35 *34 Let your women keep silence in the churches; for it is not permitted unto them to speak, but they are commanded to be under obedience, as also saith the law. 35 And if they will learn anything, let them ask their husbands at home; for it is a shame for women to speak in church.*

From the beginning of time it sounds like women have been put in their place over and over again. The Bible is very clear about the hierarchy of New Testament women in church.

I Corinthians 11:3 *But I would have you know that the head of every man is Christ; and the head of the woman is the man; and the head of Christ is God.*

The Bible tells wives to submit to their husbands in *everything*. OK, Christian husbands, try to pull that one off today! With all of the power you claim God has given you, **Philippians 4:13** *I can do all things through Christ, who strengtheneth me* and the Bible telling women to submit to you in everything, how's that Bible verse working for you today?

Ephesians 5:22-24 *22 Wives, submit yourselves unto your own husbands, as unto the Lord. 23 For the husband is the head of the wife, even as Christ is the head of the church; and he is the savior of the body. 24 Therefore, as the church is subject unto Christ, so let the wives be to their own husbands in everything.*

I ask again, "How do you Christian men translate that commandment from God, and make it happen in today's society? How do you intolerant Christian men who try to usurp authority and condemn us *converted non-Christians* using your chosen but proven invalid Bible verses, then turn around and allow your wives to usurp authority over you which goes against a *real* Bible verse?

Colossians 3:18 *Wives, submit yourselves unto your own husbands, as it is fit in the Lord.*

I Timothy 2:11-14 *11 Let the woman learn in silence with all subjection. 12 But I permit not a woman to teach, nor to usurp authority over the man, but to be in silence. 13 For Adam was first formed, then Eve. 14 And Adam was not deceived, but the woman, being deceived, was in the transgression.*

The Bible states that it was Eve who transgressed against the law, not Adam. If the first sin *was* Eve's fault and if it was Eve's *transgression*, then why does the Bible say:

Romans 5:12-14, 19 *12 Wherefore, as by one man sin entered into the world, and death by sin, and so death passed upon all men, for all have sinned. 13 For until the law sin was in the world; but sin is not imputed when there is no law. 14 Nevertheless, death reigned from Adam to Moses, even over them that had not sinned after the similitude of Adam's transgression, who is the figure of him that was to come. 19 For as by one man's disobedience many were made sinners, so by the obedience of one shall many be made righteous.*

1 Timothy clearly states that Eve was in the transgression, not Adam. Romans 5:14 clearly states it was Adam's transgression, not Eve's. Just a gentle reminder.

Again, *organized religion* tells us we are supposed to obey certain verses chosen by them or we will be condemned by certain verses that are also chosen by them. We *converted non-Christians* are just confused as to which *infallible* verses we are supposed to follow.

What about the notion of Christian women fearing their husbands if they are not in subjection to his rule?

I Peter 3:1-2 *1 In the same manner, ye wives, be in subjection to your own husbands that, if any obey not the word, they also may without the word be won by the behavior of the wives. 2 While they behold your chaste conduct coupled with fear.*

1 Peter 3:5-6 *5 For after this manner in the old time the holy women also, who trusted in God, adorned themselves, being in subjection unto their own husbands, 6 Even as Sarah obeyed Abraham, calling him lord; whose daughters ye are, as long as ye do well, and are not afraid with any terror.*

So, as long as women obey and are in subjection to their husbands they have nothing to fear.

1 Peter 3:7 *In like manner, ye husbands, dwell with them according to knowledge, giving honor unto the wife, as unto the weaker vessel.*

This sounds like nothing more than a back-handed commandment based on disrespect and fear to me.

Jesus was questioned by a group of Sadducees. Sadducees were a group of Jews who did not believe in the resurrection.

Luke 20:27 *Then came to him certain of the Sadducees, who deny that there is any resurrection; and they asked him.*

The central figure in the questioning was about a woman who had been married seven times and then died. Their question was, "Whose wife would she be after she is resurrected?"

Luke 20:33 *Therefore, in the resurrection whose wife of them is she? For seven had her as wife.*

They were always trying to trick Jesus, but Jesus answered the question in his own way.

Luke 20:34-35 *34 And Jesus, answering, said unto them, The sons of this age marry, and are given in marriage; 35 But they who shall be accounted worthy to obtain that age, and the resurrection from the dead, neither marry, nor are given in marriage.*

Jesus made a statement that it would be better for a man to not marry in this age if he wanted to be resurrected from the dead and go to heaven. Was Jesus including a *woman* who wanted to be resurrected from the dead to also not marry in this age? No! Jesus was not using the word *man* in place of mankind.

Instead of it just being better for "sons" to not marry, why is it not better for a "daughter" to not marry? Again, it seems that women are just not as important.

John 3:16 *For God so loved the world, that he gave his only begotten Son, that whosoever believeth in him should not perish, but have everlasting life.*

Nowhere in this *infallible* Bible verse of love, does it say *anything* about having a better chance to get to *everlasting life* by being single or male.

The New Testament sure puts "aged" women in their place! Of course "aged" Christian men cannot keep them there.

Titus 2:3-5 *3 The aged women likewise, that they be in behavior as becometh holiness, not false accusers, not given to much wine, teachers of good things, 4 That they may teach the young women to be sober minded, to love their husbands, to love their children, 5 To be discreet, chaste, keepers at home, good, obedient to their own husbands, that the word of God be not blasphemed.*

Christian men of today, why don't you start by trying to tell your wife that she is aged, then try and put her back in the kitchen!

1 Timothy 2:9 *In like manner, also, that women adorn themselves in modest apparel, with godly fear and sobriety, not with braided hair, or gold or pearls, or costly array.*

Who is going to interpret the value of modest apparel? What man is going to stop his wife from going to *her* hairdresser and how many men are even going to try to control their wife's jewelry box? These are rules that were set up for the New Testament church, the same church that many men in *organized religion* are always touting they represent.

Christian men may believe they have the Bible — God's infallible word — on their side to give them the rules, validation and strength to treat women as their subordinates, but you men are wrong. In the depths of your soul, when you are alone, you know it. Eve did not sin in the Garden of Eden and women are better and deserve better than the image with which *organized religion* portrays them.

The Bible contains verses that tell women what to eat, drink, wear and how to act.

Organized religion interprets these mandates and then enforces them using scriptures. This control used to work, but it will not work anymore. I have read even more control verses that I have not included in this book, but with all of this researching, I could not find the verse concerning *Blue Sequin Dresses!*

SLAVES

In Genesis 6, God talks about destroying the entire earth with a global flood because man was bad. In Genesis 8, God talks about not *ever* destroying the earth again, even though man's heart is *evil from his youth.*

Genesis 8:21 *And the Lord smelled a sweet savor; and the Lord said in his heart, I will not again curse the ground any more for man's sake; for the imagination of man's heart is evil from his youth; neither will I again smite any more every thing living, as I have done...* except, of course, for the fishes, Noah, Ham, Shem, Japheth and their wives.

Organized religion tells *us:* "We are all sinners from birth, and we are *born* sinners." However, the *Bible* does not back up that declaration. Your statements based on misinterpreted verses that allow you to *claim* that we are *born* sinners is actually incorrect. The Bible does say that man is evil from his youth, not birth. I could only find two verses that come even *close* to declaring that we are "sinners from birth" and each of those verses is reflecting either man talking to man, man talking to God, but *not* God talking to man.

Organized religion has tried to use these verses to prove their position in the past, but since then we have started reading with a new set of eyes and a different heart, and we now know what these verses really mean.

Psalm 51:3 *Behold, I was shaped in iniquity, and in sin did my mother conceive me.*

Let's put this "sinner from birth" declaration in perspective or context. I will offer a detailed version of the explanation of David and his sins later in this chapter, but for now King David had many wives and concubines. King David was basically a peeping Tom and saw Bathsheba naked taking a bath and ordered her to be brought to him where he impregnated her. King David then ordered Bathsheba's husband Uriah to be put in a dangerous situation where he would certainly be killed on the battlefield, in order to cover up his sin, and then he wanted to lament his sins to God and be forgiven.

This sounds a lot like a self-proclaimed bad boy's way of finding mercy with God and then being allowed to have a great and prosperous life all the while condemning everyone else because "the devil made him do it" from conception. *Nowhere* does this verse say, "and God commanded" or "the Lord declared that David was a sinner from birth."

Psalm 58:3 *The wicked are estranged from the womb; they go astray as soon as they are born, speaking lies.*

This verse does not declare or even imply that the message of being a "sinner from birth" is given by *God*. It is also quite ignorant in its assertions about babies. Babies do not go astray and lie as soon as they are born. Babies cry; they don't lie.

It seems to me that in order to even *imagine* being evil, that thought has to have its basis in some external origin and thus come from "somewhere" first. For example, I had never *imagined* landing on the moon until I read *From the Earth to the Moon* by Jules Verne; *after* that I imagined being a space traveler. I did not imagine until I had a basis for that imagination.

I had never even imagined a cell phone when I was a teenager and was dialing with a *rotary phone.* Anyone under the age of thirty can look up a rotary phone on the Internet. I was using a phone that could communicate with friends and family across town and across the country and it was amazing. I never imagined talking on the phone while being in a car or walking down the street. Someone saw the rotary phone and then imagined a cell phone.

We have to have a basis of origin before the imagination becomes possible.

Now, you could argue that Jules Verne imagined space travel from talking to someone about flight and that someone imagined flight from talking to someone interested in birds or maybe the first person's basis in origin of space travel was just in their brain after they saw the moon. We may never know where it really started, but it did have an *origin!*

I guess you could say that my basis in origin was from my mother, and her basis in origin came from her mother, and a long time ago Adam's basis of origin came from God, and God's basis in origin came from… oh!

Which came first, the chicken or the egg? Which came first, *your* God or the universe?

It is not really the initial basis in origin of the universe that I am concerned with in this line of thought. My concern is about the nature of the basis in origin and the follow through that contributes to **Genesis 8:21** *And the Lord smelled a sweet savor; and the Lord said in his heart, I will not again curse the ground any more for man's sake; for the **imagination** of man's heart is evil from his youth; neither will I again smite any more every thing living, as I have done,* (except for the fishes, Noah, Ham, Shem, Japheth and their wives).

I am not willing to accept that the evil mankind does arises purely from our imagination or is just thought up with no basis of origin, devoid of basis in reality or example first. Eve lived in the Garden of Eden peacefully, had a daily communion with God and had no thoughts of disobeying God until Satan was *allowed* to beguile her. Is the evil imagination of Eve's heart to eat an apple in question here or is it Satan's *previous* imagination that we should be addressing?

When did the imagination basis of origin for slavery start? And does it even have anything to do with the Bible? If you examine history and consider how it has turned out Black religious race instigators, it sounds like slavery was "invented" around the time the United States became a country, at least in the eyes of *organized religion*. Was it invented before the cotton gin was invented because we needed a large free labor force in the South? This is generally the time frame most people think of when considering when slavery started. But I have an alternative thought regarding slavery's origin.

Where did the *actual* basis in origin for slavery come from? The popular sentiment is against slavery in the *world* today. Of course, we still see the remnants of the United States of America's long and shameful slave history.

I worked with a gentleman named George, who was Black, African-American, Negro or whatever politically correct name you want me to use. I just called him *friend*. I said, "George, I believe what my great, great Grandfather did to your great, great, Grandfather was absolutely awful.

But, I did not do it, and I am not doing it today, so don't be mad at me. Be mad at my great, great, Grandfather."

Old Testament

I have already shared my thoughts on Noah and his curse of Canaan the son, through Ham the father:

Genesis 9:24-27 *24 And Noah awoke from his wine, and knew what his younger son had done unto him. 25 And he said, Cursed be Canaan; a servant of servants shall he be unto his brethren. 26 And he said, Blessed be the Lord God of Shem; and Canaan shall be his servant. 27 God shall enlarge Japheth, and he shall dwell in the tents of Shem; and Canaan shall be his servant.*

The use of this word *servant* throughout the Bible is crucial to understanding the story of Noah and the subsequent actions taken by *organized religion* in the name of God and the Bible with regards to slavery, both in America and the world.

If the word *servant* was chosen by God's translators and interpreted by your preachers to simply mean maids, cooks, butlers, and chauffeurs, then US history would be very different today.

I will not accept the fact that slavery took place, according to the Bible, but has been pervasively diminished in importance through use of the word "servant," as used in the Bible, yet not immediately accepted as *"slavery."*

Luke 12:47-48 *47 And that servant, who knew his lord's will, and prepared not himself, neither did according to his will, shall be beaten with many stripes. 48 But he that knew not, and did commit things worthy of stripes, shall be beaten with few stripes. For unto whomsoever much is given, of him shall be much required; and to whom men have committed much, of him they will ask the more.*

I do not believe it is biblically saying that we should "beat with many stripes" maids, cooks, butlers and chauffeurs.

Permit me to show how the curse made by Noah and the resulting hatred, bigotry, belittlement, and condemnation of Black people was condoned and encouraged by *organized religion* to the great detriment of this country.

Where exactly did Noah get his "basis of origin" to imagine the concept of slavery that enabled him to so quickly and recklessly throw out the curse of servitude or slavery on Canaan, the son of Ham, to his uncles Shem and Japheth?

Abraham was regarded as the father of many nations.

Genesis 17:4-5 *4 As for me, behold, my covenant is with thee, and thou shalt be a father of many nations. 5 Neither shall thy name any more be called Abram, but thy name shall be Abraham, for a father of many nations have I made thee.*

In this case, I am willing to concede that "father of many nations" means that God will — figuratively speaking — bless Abraham's people with lots of family and not that Abraham will father most of them. But Abraham did have a wife Sarah and a handmaid named Hagar. Each of these women gave Abraham sons with non-nuclear family consequences.

The Middle East wars that have spread around the world are actually the extension of a single war raging since the beginning of time between these two brothers. Abraham had two sons: Isaac, born of Abraham's real wife Sarah and Ishmael, born of Hagar, an Egyptian handmaiden. Clearly, these two women came from very different ethnic groups.

One group became the chosen group of God. The Bible states that God actually communicated verbally with these chosen people. The other group was blessed, but not chosen to be God's favorite. Each group has been fighting to prove their superiority ever since.

Genesis17:15-22 *15 And God said unto Abraham, As for Sarai, thy wife, thou shalt not call her name Sarai, but Sarah shall her name be. 16 And I will bless her, and give thee a son also of her: yea, I will bless her, and she shall be a mother of nations; kings of people shall be of her. 17 Then Abraham fell upon his face, and laughed, and said in his heart, Shall a child be born unto him that is an hundred years old? And shall Sarah, that is ninety years old, bear?*

I usually quote the entire scripture passage before commenting, but this statement is so outrageous that I have to mention it immediately and keep the spirit of the verses present. God verbally communicated with Abraham. I don't care *what* God tells Abraham in this instance; what matters is that *God* was talking and Abraham had the lack of respect to not only question Him, but then laugh at God!

You can argue that Abraham was laughing about the fact that a hundred year old man and a barren wife could produce an heir and that was funny. However, I didn't read anywhere that on this particular day God was doubling as a stand up comic! My impression is that God was talking to one of the leaders of the world to come and that it would have been appropriate for Abraham to have listened with reverence and respected God and the communication.

I believe this is a blatant example of the way members of God's chosen people did not really have respect for God and perhaps reason why God had to — in Exodus 20 — deliver a commandment *(one of those Ten Commandments)* that He had better not be second place in their hearts and lives.

Continuing with **Genesis Chapter 17**... *18 And Abraham said unto God, Oh, that Ishmael might live before thee! 19 And God said, Sarah, thy* *wife, shall bear thee a son indeed; and thou shalt call his name Isaac: and I will establish my covenant with him for an everlasting covenant, and with his seed after him. 20 And as for Ishmael, I have heard thee: behold, I have blessed him, and will make him fruitful, and will multiply him exceedingly; twelve princes shall he beget, and I will make him a great nation. 21 But my covenant will I establish with Isaac, whom Sarah shall bear unto thee at this set time in the next year. 22 And he ceased talking with him, and God went up from Abraham.*

If you take a moment to *really* think about the world and where the major conflicts have — and are — coming from, we can trace them back to God's chosen people. If the Bible is correct and Isaac represents Israel and Ishmael represents Muslim nations then they are the same family. God established one family as the future ruler and then just *"blessed"* the other family to be great — but not the *rulers* — which certainly creates the basis for much of the tension we see in the world today.

If this sounds far-fetched, let me remind you that all this unrest and all these wars have taken place in the name of religion and conflicting interpretations of the will and intention of God!

Come on Dad, make these kids behave! The unrest between Israel and Muslims — as sad as it may be — does not address my point about the non-nuclear family of Abraham. It appears that while Sarah and Abraham took matters into their own hands with Hagar in order to create the heir that God would send in His own time; and that even though Abraham broke God's commandment of one woman and one man for marriage, God *still* turned around and blessed them with Isaac, thus creating the non-nuclear family conflict we have in the world today.

Abraham and Sarah not only broke the marriage union commandment of one man and one woman, but they also created the foundation for the longest and most ruinous war ever visited upon the planet.

Malachi 2:10 *Have we not all one father? Hath not one God created us? Why do we deal treacherously, every man against his brother, by profaning the covenant of our fathers?*

To add to the mess, Abraham also had concubines.

In **Genesis 25:6** *But unto the sons of the concubines, Whom Abraham had, Abraham gave gifts, and sent them away from Isaac, his son, while he yet lived, eastward, unto the east country.*

Remember that from the beginning of mankind, God ordained that the Word of God be passed down verbally to Israel, and the Israelites were told to pass the Words of God on to their sons and their son's sons.

If the Words of God had been passed down as they were commanded to be, and the Words of God were true and exact, wouldn't the basis of origin for slavery have been passed down to Noah and his sons before the flood? Noah and his sons were the only remnant left to carry on the Words of God. If God wrote the Bible before the foundations of the Earth were even formed, and the Words of God were not changed up until Noah's time, then it follows that Noah could only have gotten his basis of origin for slavery from God.

If the original imagination of slavery was inspired as a bad and unacceptable thing in Noah's brain before God flooded the earth, why would the all-knowing God describe Noah as a righteous and perfect man if one of the first things Noah did was to perpetuate slavery on Canaan?

I contend Noah believed that slavery was an acceptable form of punishment, approved by God. And if God approved of ancient biblical slavery, then it would be very reasonable to believe that *organized religion* would follow in Noah's footsteps today.

God's message to man, which was actually written before the ages and before the foundations of the Earth were laid, should surely have been the same before the flood as well as after the flood. God's message has been characterized as being the same yesterday, today, and tomorrow.

1 Corinthians 2 *7 But we speak the wisdom of God in a mystery, even the hidden wisdom, which God ordained before the ages unto our glory.*

After the flood and Noah's curse on Canaan, it is recorded that God encouraged and instructed on the matter of how slaves should be bought, sold and taken in the Old and New Testaments. Regardless of whether these slaves were called servants, maidservants, manservants, bondsman, maids, cooks, butlers, and chauffeurs or any other title that would allow an apologetic mistranslation, the act of practicing slavery is still wrong.

I am not trying to be the one who draws the distinction between good slavery and bad slavery. I do understand that some people in ancient times did sell themselves into slavery as an option to keep themselves and/ or their families from starving. The key to understanding this particular idea of enslavement is that they sold *themselves.*

I also have read in the Bible how God demands that men, women, and children captured from any civilization that God did not like — for any reason — were to be made slaves. I believe this is most likely where the slavery imagination basis of origin started. However, I will not attempt — in this short book — to fully clarify or justify my personal reasoning for or against any form of slavery, especially in America. I simply believe that God's translators were guilty of confusing the use of the words slaves, servants, maidservants, manservants, and bondsman among others.

These mistranslations represent the fundamental reasoning behind the confusion that has led *organized religion* to *prove its own position to then use that position to serve its own purpose,* when it comes to slavery.

Using exact Bible words, how interesting is it that we have this practice of slavery actually included in the Ten Commandments?

Exodus 20:17 *Thou shalt not covet thy neighbor's house; thou shalt not covet thy neighbor's wife, nor his manservant, nor his maidservant, nor his ox, nor his ass, nor anything that is thy neighbor's.*

I understand the words "manservant" and "maidservant" to also mean slaves and not just the hired help. These next few verses will shed some light on why I believe this to be true.

Exodus 21:2 *If thou buy an Hebrew servant, six years he shall serve; and in the seventh he shall go out free for nothing.*

Exodus 21:7 *And if a man sell his daughter to be a maidservant, she shall not go out as the menservants do.*

Menservants could be freed after six years of service, but maidservants were indentured forever.

Exodus 21:26-27 *26 And if a man smite the eye of his servant, or the eye of his maid, that it perish; he shall let him go free for his eye's sake. 27 And if he smite out his manservant's tooth, or his maidservant's tooth; he shall let him go for his tooth's sake.*

If the manservant or the maidservant are not really slaves, why would the Bible state that they should be set "free?"

Leviticus 25:44-46 *44 Both thy male and female slaves, whom thou shalt have, shall be of the nations that are round about you; of them shall ye buy male and female slaves. 45 Moreover, of the children of the strangers who do sojourn among you, of them shall ye buy, and of their families that are with you, which they begot in your land; and they shall be your possession. 46 And ye shall take them as an inheritance for your children after you, to inherit them for a possession; they shall be your slaves forever; but over your brethren, the children of Israel, ye shall not rule one over another with vigor.*

This pretty clearly states that an Israelite cannot make another Israelite a slave, but any Gentile living round about them is fair game to be taken as a slave.

Deuteronomy 23:15 *Thou shalt not deliver unto his master the servant who is escaped from his master unto thee;*

Joel 3:8 *And I will sell your sons and daughters into the hand of the children of Judah, and they shall sell them to the men of Sheba, to a people far off; for the Lord hath spoken it.*

Countries that enslaved Israel, Judah, will now have their sons and daughters delivered to Judah to be sold to other far away countries as slaves and God hath spoken it.

New Testament

In the Bible, servants and slaves seem to be the same, in most cases. This presents the occasion for *Disorganized Christianity* to find and explore that one misinterpretation that discredits what is written throughout.

I expect an attempt by *organized religion* to actually prove that one or more of these biblical servants, maidservants, man servants, or bondsmen were really just a live-in part of the family. However, the Bible's description of a servant's or slave's place in the family — and his or her obligations — does not sound like he or she is being part of the family or even just a minimum wage-paid worker.

Ephesians 6:5 *Servants, be obedient to them that are your masters according to the flesh, with fear and trembling, in singleness of your heart, as unto Christ.*

Servants/slaves obey with the fear and trembling and at minimum wage!

Colossians 3:22 *Servants, obey in all things your masters according to the flesh; not with eyeservice, as men-pleasers, but in singleness of heart, fearing God.*

Servants/slaves obey in all things with fear of God, and at minimum wage!

Colossians 4:1 *Masters, give unto your servants that which is just and equal, knowing that ye also have a Master in heaven.*

Masters be fair to your servants/slaves because God just may give *you*, masters, in accordance to what you give your servants/slaves.

I Timothy 6:1 *Let as many servants as are under the yoke count their own masters worthy of all honor, that the name of God and his doctrine be not blasphemed.*

A paid servant/slave, maid, cook, butler or chauffer is not under a yoke!

Titus 2:9 *Exhort servants to be obedient unto their own masters, and to please them well in all things, not answering again; not purloining, but showing all good fidelity, that they may adorn the doctrine of God, our Savior, in all things.*

The Apostle Paul, the supposed writer of Titus, tells all servants to act in certain ways in order to please their *masters* and to adorn the doctrine of God.

Luke 12:47-48 *47 And that servant, who knew his lord's will, and prepared not himself, neither did according to his will, shall be beaten with many stripes. 48 But he that knew not, and did commit things worthy of stripes, shall be beaten with few stripes. For unto whomsoever much is given, of him shall be much required; and to whom men have committed much, of him they will ask the more.*

I do not believe that by following the Bible's instructions, *organized religion* can condone giving non-slave servants "stripes." *Organized religion* may argue that the Bible allows you to give *slaves* stripes, but we know that does not include *paid servants*. Go ahead and pick the word you need to *prove your needed position to then serve your own purpose*. Today, slavery cannot be *organized religion's* purpose, regardless of whether they try to use chains or scriptures.

1 Peter 2:18 *Servants, be subject to your masters with all fear; not only to the good and gentle but also to the perverse.*

I very much doubt this verse is talking about a servant choosing voluntary slavery.

My next thought is based on a personal experience I had in the early 1970's and then with my continual study of *organized religion's* stance on slavery in America.

As I stated in the first sentence of this chapter, I believe the Bible has instructed and influenced anyone who wants to hate to claim a righteous validation *to hate*. I contend that *organized religion* used Bible verses to condone the treatment of Black people from the very beginnings of America, even before the United States became a country. The atrocities that man could do to man in the name of biblical imaginations is shameful and really should stop. Racial bigotry has *not* stopped in America's churches. I am not claiming that it is widespread by any means, but there are still pockets of bigotry that should be cleansed from the doctrines of some *organized religions*.

As I mentioned earlier, my personal experience occurred in my own church in the early 70's. I wrote in my Bible the notes from a sermon that was given from Genesis Chapter 9 where Noah cursed Canaan. My notes read that this is the scripture that mandated that Ham, who moved to

Africa with his descendants and became the black race, would be slaves to the world forever.

The curse was actually on Canaan, the *son*, but in the 1960's I wrote Ham, the *father*. I am ashamed to admit that in the early 70's I repeated this claim in a small Bible study group with a bunch of college students who were just trying to have a decent Bible study discussion. To all of them, I apologize and have repented of my thoughts. *It is my duty* to change what I have said if I know it to have been false and can back up the real truth with scripture. I can and I have.

In my ongoing study of the subject of slavery in *organized religion*, the scripture passage that seems to be the most conflicting about a slavery/ non-slavery theme is in the Book of Philemon. Philemon is a one chapter book, but I will not cite the entire book.

While the Apostle Paul was in prison, he met another prisoner — a slave named Onesimus — and they became brothers in Christ. The Apostle Paul then wrote a letter to Philemon, the slave's owner, and urged him using a number of pleas to free Onesimus from bondage when he was released from prison. The Apostle Paul first clearly acknowledged that Onesimus was Philemon's slave, but then suggested the slave's freedom.

Philemon 16 *Not now as a servant but above a servant, a brother beloved, specially to me but how much more unto thee, both in the flesh, and in the Lord?*

In verse 16, the Apostle Paul then tried to convince Philemon that Onesimus would benefit Philemon more as a free man, serving Christ, than he would as a slave.

Philemon 19 *I, Paul, have written it with mine own hand, I will repay it; albeit I do not say to thee how thou owest unto me even thine own self besides.*

The Apostle Paul then, in verse 19, tries to guilt Philemon into freeing Onesimus by reminding Philemon that he himself was beholden to the Apostle Paul.

Philemon 21 *Having confidence in thy obedience I wrote unto thee, knowing that thou wilt also do more than I say.*

After applying all the salesmanship techniques, Paul gives Philemon an advance "thank you" for doing more than he even asked, in verse 21. We do not know whether Onesimus was actually freed.

My concern or dismay arises from the fact that we have Jesus spreading a message of *love and forgiveness* and the Apostle Paul — spreading the Jesus message to the Gentiles (who previously were shut out of the salvation message) — yet why did the Apostle Paul simply try to *convince and cajole* Philemon to free Onesimus? Why didn't the Apostle Paul *condemn slavery and command* that Philemon free his imprisoned slave?

The Bible message of slavery being wrong, at least in the New Testament, would have left no room for *organized religion* to validate slavery or bigotry of any kind anywhere; not yesterday, not today, not tomorrow. This exchange between Philemon and the Apostle Paul could have been the perfect correction needed at that time and could then have served as future instruction for a righteous non-slavery practice in the Bible.

2 Timothy 3:16-17 *16 All scripture is given by inspiration of God, and is profitable for doctrine, for reproof, for correction, for instruction in righteousness, 17 That the man of God may be perfect, thoroughly furnished unto all good works.*

While we debate whether or not the Bible completely endorses slavery because God commanded it in the Old Testament, or whether the Bible allows slavery with the condition that masters be kind to their slaves as we read in the New Testament, the Bible definitely has an underlying slavery theme. I will leave it up to the Bible scholars and language experts to implement any further condemnations or apologies.

With all these commandments and instructions for slavery from God, how can Man — and in our earlier example, Noah — *not* have "evil imaginations from his youth," even about slavery? Parents teach their children core values; those children then teach their own children values. We could teach to love one another instead.

Mark 12:30-31 *30 And thou shalt love the Lord thy God with all thy heart, and with all thy soul, and with all thy mind, and with all thy strength: this is the first commandment. 31 And the second is this: Thou shalt love thy neighbor as thyself. There is no other commandment greater than these.*

HOMOSEXUALITY

Imagine that you are walking down a major street in San Francisco, and you find yourself approaching a very large building with a courtyard open to the street. This courtyard is full of men and several of them are kissing each other. Would any member of *organized religion* not be offended by these actions?

Is this gathering place the entrance to one of those *San Francisco bathhouses* we have all heard about? Is this a male escort service gathering place? No, it is neither. This could just be an ordinary, regular God-fearing *organized religion's* church.

Here I go again! Blaspheming again and now immorality has even found its way into *Disorganized Christianity!* But wait: instead of immediately exercising your holier-than-thou attitude and condemning me for my example, how about reserving your condemnation of my San Francisco gathering place until *after* you read several Bible verses that tell Bible loving and God-fearing men to *greet one another with an holy kiss.*

Romans 16:16 *Greet one another with an holy kiss. The churches of Christ greet you.*

1 Peter 5:14 *Greet ye one another with a kiss of love. Peace be with you all that are in Christ Jesus.* Amen.

1 Corinthians 16:20 *All the brethren greet you. Greet ye one another with an holy kiss.*

2 Corinthians 13:12 *Greet one another with an holy kiss.*

1 Thessalonians 5:26 *Greet all brethren with an holy kiss.*

I did not include these verses so that some particular group of people could *prove its own position to then serve its own purpose.* These verses were actually given by the Apostles and disciples of Jesus to the newly formed churches that were springing up in the wake of Jesus' crucifixion. This unusual instruction of greeting one another with an holy kiss of love was being given as an example of how Jesus acted and wanted the church to act. The wording of these verses is very plain and clear, and any excuses about "today being a different time" and kisses meaning different things today than back in biblical times are not valid for use as condemnation.

It would be a hard argument to make that "male-kissing-male" in a biblical scenario is the same as a "male-kissing-male" in a lover's scenario, and that either circumstance could validate or condemn the other, but I am not trying to prove that. I am proving by the *reactions* to this thought process that *organized religion* has already determined that they will not even *consider* the possibility that "male-kissing-male" is even remotely biblical. *Organized religion* will jump to the immediate conclusion that this "male-kissing-male" scenario *has to be* an abomination. I draw this conclusion because it has already been pointed out to me.

I really do not think you can argue much about the reality of *holy kissing.* I am not telling you to *greet one another with an holy kiss.* I am just enlightening you, that *your infallible* Bible tells you to *greet one another with an holy kiss.*

ET TU, JUDAS?

Matthew 26:48-49 *48 Now he that betrayed him gave them a sign, saying, Whomsoever I shall kiss, that same is he; hold him fast. 49 And forthwith he came to Jesus, and said, Hail, master; and kissed him.*

Men kissing men must have been a normal Christian activity, particularly if we consider that Judas' subtle way of identifying Jesus for the ultimate betrayal, was just a kiss.

Acts 20:37 *And they all wept much, and fell on Paul's neck, and kissed him.*

The Apostle Paul was leaving Miletus and the congregation and elders there were sad to see him leave. They prayed with the Apostle Paul and kissed him on the neck. Men kissing men sounds like a normal, sinless biblical activity to me.

Luke 7:38 *And stood at his feet behind him, weeping; and began to wash his feet with tears, and did wipe them with the hair of her head, and kissed his feet, and anointed them with the ointment.*

Luke 7:44-45 *44 And he turned to the woman, and said unto Simon, Seest thou this woman? I entered into thine house; thou gavest me no water for my feet. But she hath washed my feet with tears, and wiped them with the hair of her head. 45 Thou gavest me no kiss. But this woman, since the time I came in, hath not ceased to kiss my feet.*

Jesus rebukes Simon because Simon had not kissed him since he had entered his home, but the woman in the home had not stopped kissing Jesus' feet since he had arrived. Furthermore, it seems as though Jesus even *questioned* Simon as to why Simon had not greeted Jesus with a kiss even though they were not from the same church. It appears that Jesus would not have been at all shocked if Simon had kissed him. Jesus almost certainly *expected* Simon to kiss him, or why would he bring up the chastisement of Simon for not kissing him, yet praise the woman for continually kissing his feet? Men kissing men just appears to have been a normal, sinless biblical activity as far as I can read in God's *infallible* Bible.

I am not taking any of these verses out of context. I am not trying to make naughty things nice or bad things into acceptable things. I am merely stating that the Bible has examples for it to be all right to have men kissing men. These are *your* Bible verses.

Organized religion could counter with: "Yeah, God might have said those things back then, but today is different, and gays messed up the true meaning of *greet one another with an holy kiss.*"

Okay, prove it!

I didn't say "Suggest it." I didn't say "Relate an embarrassing story that would totally validate why men shouldn't *greet one another with an holy kiss.*" I said, "Prove that it is not God's commandment and was not Jesus' practice!" Use *your* Bible to prove that the New Testament message of *holy kissing* is not valid for today!

Now, as usual, you *mean spirited and intolerant* Christians will likely jump to the erroneous conclusion that because the Bible says to *greet one another with an holy kiss,* I must be trying to *prove my position so that I can use it to serve my own purpose* for selfish reasons.

Organized religion is wrong, again! I personally witnessed one Christian man question *"Greet one another with an holy kiss"* during a Bible study session, and saw him get completely chastised and ridiculed for even *thinking* that a Christian man would do such a disgusting thing! I felt sad for this man who was not gay, and was just questioning a scripture verse.

This good Christian man ended up leaving *organized religion,* and at the time I did nothing to support him. I apologize to him today and guarantee him I will not ever stand by and watch any person be chastised and condemned by any *organized religion* member again. You may rest assured that *Disorganized Christianity* will be my weapon of choice.

Organized religion can continue to believe that homosexuals are ruining the nuclear family and the basis of marriage as God ordained it in the Bible. But if the infallible Bible account of the way marriage should be holds true and firm, and one man can only marry one woman for all time — except for death — and Christians *want to* honor that scenario, then maybe *organized religion* could have a basis for homosexuals destroying the nuclear family. But *organized religion* will have to uphold its part of God's *infallible* word before anyone can whine that the marriage model is being destroyed by homosexuals.

Old Testament, Genesis 2:23-24 *23 And Adam said, This is now bone of my bones, and flesh of my flesh; she shall be called Woman, because she was taken out of Man. 24 Therefore shall a man leave his father and mother, and shall cleave unto his wife; and they shall become one flesh.*

New Testament, Matthew 19:3-9 *3 The Pharisees also came unto him, testing him, and saying unto him, Is it lawful for a man to put away his wife for every cause? 4 And he answered and said unto them, Have ye not read that he who made them at the beginning, made them male and female; 5 And said, For this cause shall a man leave father and mother, and shall cleave to his wife, and they two shall be one flesh? 6 Wherefore, they are no more two, but one flesh. What, therefore, God hath joined together, let not man put asunder. 7 They say unto him, Why did Moses then command to give a writing of divorcement, and to put her away? 8 He saith unto them, Moses, because of the hardness of your hearts, permitted you to put away your wives, but from the beginning it was not so. 9 And I say unto you, Whosoever shall put away his wife, except it be for fornication, and shall marry another,* *committeth adultery; and whosoever marrieth her who is put away doth commit adultery.*

The first thought I want to address is that while the Bible is declared as the *infallible* Word of God and thus what God says or writes should be the absolute rule, these preceding verses demonstrate that this is just not the case. As we move through *Disorganized Christianity*, we have already read several scriptures where God repented that He even did or thought of certain things.

In the case of divorce, God does not ever repent of the exact rules on marriage. God *explicitly* states that one man and one woman shall become one, for all time. Is this another misinterpretation where ALL really means *ALL* or something else, like divorce?

Jesus reaffirms God's declaration of one man and one woman becoming one by reminding the Pharisees: "From the beginning of time that was the rule." Now the problems begin when the Bible states that Moses and Jesus allowed the marriage rules to *change*. Even *Jesus* is changing the *infallible* Word of God!

Wait a moment, I read somewhere that Jesus was God.

1 John 5:7 *For there are three that bear record in Heaven, the Father, the Word, and the Holy Spirit; and these three are one.*

Now I am confused. Since Jesus represents God in the flesh in the New Testament, can Jesus now change the rules of the God in the Old Testament? Why would Jesus *want* to change the rules of God or his own beliefs just to accommodate man's desire for divorce?

The Pharisees were constantly testing Jesus and trying to get his understandings of Old Testament writings. In the case of Matthew 19, the Pharisees are asking Jesus about divorce. Please pay close attention to what I am trying to attempt to explain, as a clarification on Bible divorce. I will do my best to find some solid ground because the Bible stumbles all over itself, when it comes to discussing divorce.

Matthew 19:3-9 *3 The Pharisees also came unto him, testing him, and saying unto him, Is it lawful for a man to put away his wife for every cause? 4 And he answered and said unto them, Have ye not read that he who made them at the beginning, made them male and female; 5 And said, For this cause shall a man leave father and mother, and shall cleave to his wife, and they two shall be one flesh? 6 Wherefore, they are no more two, but one flesh. What, therefore, God hath joined together, let not man put asunder. 7 They say unto him, Why did Moses then command to give a writing of divorcement, and to put her away? 8 He saith unto them, Moses, because of the hardness of your hearts, permitted you to put away your wives, but from the beginning it was not so. 9 And I say unto you, Whosoever shall put away his wife, except it be for fornication, and shall marry another, committeth adultery; and whosoever marrieth her who is put away doth commit adultery.*

Why didn't Jesus simply say, "Moses let you divorce because of the hardness of your hearts, but I am saying that Moses was full of himself and God said no divorce." God said that under no circumstances, and God gave no reasons for man to put asunder this holy union. Yet, Moses said divorce was all right. Moses won, God lost!

Jesus added to God's Word with his own specific circumstances, namely fornication and adultery, to declare divorce allowable. Judging by the number of Christian divorces since then, Jesus won, God lost! I cannot find *anywhere* in God's *infallible* word that Moses or Jesus had the authority to entertain the possibility of divorce.

Proverbs 30:5-6 *5 Every word of God is pure; he is a shield unto those who put their trust in him. 6 Add thou not unto his words, lest ye reprove thee, and thou be found a liar.*

By inserting their own personal conditions for divorce, were Moses and Jesus actually guilty of *proving their own positions to serve their own purposes,* to appease the crowd? God never gave either of them permission to approve divorce.

John 12:49-50 *49 For I have not spoken of myself; but the Father, who sent me, he gave me a commandment, what I should say, and what I should speak. 50 And I know that his commandment is life everlasting; whatsoever I speak, therefore, even as the Father said unto me, so I speak.*

Again, in each of the personal declarations by Moses and Jesus concerning divorce, it is not recorded that "God told Moses" or "God told Jesus" that divorce was an option under certain circumstances.

Adam and Eve were accused of being the first who sinned against God. God made a big deal of condemning Adam and Eve. Cain was accused of being the first to murder in the Bible. God made a big deal of cursing Cain. Adam, Eve and Cain's trespasses against God were *vague* at best, yet God *absolutely* defined what marriage should be and how sacred it was supposed to be for all time. If marriage was to be the most holy of institutions that a man and a woman could enter into on this planet and God explicitly defined that union, then why didn't God curse Lamech?

Lamech, a descendant of Cain, was the first man recorded in the Bible to have two wives.

Genesis 4:19 *And Lamech took unto him two wives; the name of the one was Adah, and the name of the other, Zillah.*

Not a single curse or rebuke against Lamech is recorded for his breaking God's holy marriage union. *I* didn't say that the marriage union was holy. *Organized religion* and the *infallible* Bible say that the marriage union is holy.

Well, not exactly!

Let us not excuse or pass over the broken rules for a marriage union by Lamech merely because maybe God or the translators just overlooked Lamech as a minor player. Many men and women have been mentioned in the Bible only once and usually just in passing. Lamech caught the Bible's attention for a different reason in scripture, not for his non-nuclear family multiple marriages, but for killing one man and injuring another.

Genesis 4:23 *And Lamech said unto his wives, Adah and Zillah, Hear my voice; ye wives of Lamech, hearken unto my speech; for I have slain a man who wounded me, and a young man for hurting me.*

The Bible recorded *three times in two verses* the fact that Lamech had two wives, a reality in direct disobedience against God's holy marriage union. With Lamech proudly announcing his non-nuclear marriages and Moses — then Jesus — changing God's absolute commandment in **Matthew 19:4-6** *4 And he answered and said unto them, Have ye not read that he who made them at the beginning, made them male and female; 5 And said, For this cause shall a man leave father and mother, and shall cleave to his wife, and they two shall be one flesh? 6 Wherefore, they are no more two, but one flesh. What, therefore, God hath joined together, let not man put asunder.*

Where is the curse — or at least a rebuke — on having two wives?

It seems a little too convenient that homosexuals of today are given the blame for trying to change the basis of marriage and the sanctity between one woman and one man when over 4,000 to 6,000 years ago — just six generations removed from the Garden of Eden and God's ordained marriage union declaration — some of the most revered men of early Bible days started ruining the nuclear family by having several wives and mistresses and illegitimate children. These men not only got away with their multiple non-nuclear families, but also were blessed and honored by God.

The Book of *Genesis* tells a story of how a man named Jacob eventually wound up with two wives, Leah and Rachel. Precisely *how* Jacob got two wives is not terribly important, but the fact that while having two wives God still blessed him is puzzling.

Genesis 32:28 *And he said, Thy name shall be called no more Jacob, but Israel; for as a prince hast thou power with God and with men, and hath prevailed.*

Even most non-Christians have heard the miraculous story of David and Goliath; where a little shepherd boy slew the Philistine giant Goliath with a slingshot. To me, the miracle of this story is not that a little boy used a rock to kill a giant. What I want to know is *where* the giant came from because God supposedly killed all the giants in the global flood of Noah. The miracle is that Goliath was not even supposed to be a *possibility*. As noticeable as they are, two giants are not mentioned as being on the ark or getting off the ark.

From slaying the giant, David went on to become the King of Israel and one of the Bible's greatest heroes. David has many stories chronicling his life, but one stands alone on account of his lust, treachery, and nuclear family destruction.

2 Samuel 11:2-4 *2 And it came to pass at eventide, that David arose from his bed, and walked upon the roof of the king's house. And from the roof he saw a woman washing herself, and the woman was very beautiful to look upon. 3 And David sent and inquired about the woman. And one said, Is not this Bathsheba, the daughter of Eliam, the wife of Uriah, the Hittite? 4 And David sent messengers, and took her. And she came in unto him, and he lay with her; for she was purified of her uncleanness. And she returned unto her house.*

Bathsheba's visit to David resulted in a pregnancy. King David sent for Uriah, her husband, to come home from the battlefield to sleep with his wife and get her pregnant to cover up the infidelity. Uriah would not sleep with Bathsheba, so David then had him killed on the battlefield to cover up his sin of adultery.

I just don't understand why God punishes the sinner by killing an innocent unborn child: David and Bathsheba's first born child is killed as punishment for David's sin. God then turns around and gives David and Bathsheba a second son, Solomon, who becomes another great Bible hero.

David taking multiple wives and concubines seemed to be a regular activity even before Bathsheba, as we read in **2 Samuel 5:13** *And David took him more concubines and wives out of Jerusalem, after he was come from Hebron; and there were sons and daughters born to David.*

The Bathsheba story goes on to reveal that Nathan, a very close friend to King David, was sent by God to spiritually convict David for his sin. In 2 Samuel Chapter 12, Nathan told David about a rich man and a poor man in a city. The rich man took one of the poor man's lambs and used it for his own purposes. David was exceedingly angry with the rich man and declared that the rich man should be killed for his treacherous actions. When Nathan then revealed that David was the rich man and Uriah was the poor man and Bathsheba was the lamb, David forgave himself. This, even after David *admits* that whoever did this terrible thing should be killed, he of course excuses himself from the death sentence he would so readily have given anyone else.

Mean spirited and intolerant Christians will condemn us, *converted non-Christians*, and give us their death sentence, but when they find out that biblically they are not much better than that which they condemn, they then allow themselves a convenient spiritual "get out of jail free card."

Solomon had a very large non-nuclear family and was blessed by God for a long time. The Bible does say that God finally grew displeased enough with Solomon that he took his kingdom away, but that was for worshipping other Gods, not for having 700 wives and princesses and 300 concubines.

1 Kings 11:1-3 *1 But King Solomon loved many foreign women; in addition to the daughter of Pharaoh, women of the Moabites, Ammonites, Edomites, Sidonians and Hittites, 2 Of the nations concerning which the Lord said unto the children of Israel, Ye shall not go into them, neither shall they come in unto you; for surely they will turn your heart after their Gods. Solomon clung unto these in love. 3 And he had seven hundred wives, princesses, and three hundred concubines; and his wives turned away his heart.*

1 Kings 11:9 *And the Lord was angry with Solomon, because his heart was turned from the Lord God of Israel, who had appeared unto him twice.*

Solomon was so blessed in his life that God appeared to him *twice* and yet Solomon's punishment was not for the multitude of wives and concubines he kept, but for the idolatry of other Gods. This is not a very strong argument for the nuclear family crowd.

You *mean spirited and intolerant* Christians should spend time making *organized religion* and the translations and interpretations of *your* Bible better. Getting rid of gays and lesbians by putting them in their "right place" using the same Bible and the same Bible prejudices *organized religion* used to put women and Blacks in their right place for centuries will not work this time!

Disorganized Christianity may be a small glowing ember engulfed by the Christian forest of hatred, but I truly believe it will help fan the flames, "*of love thy neighbor.*"

Mark 12: 31 *And the second is this: Thou shalt love thy neighbor as thyself. There is no other commandment greater than these.*

When loving your brother and your sister as thyself truly catches fire, the dead roots, branches and leaves of that Christian forest of hatred will burn and be consumed by that fire. Not exactly fire and brimstone, but we *converted non-Christians* will take it.

Mean spirited and intolerant Christians may argue that it is their personal spiritual responsibility to cleanse the world — or at least their little corner of the world — from gays and lesbians. It may look like their home is better after they straighten out that gay or lesbian child, especially before anyone finds out. It may look like their neighborhood is better. It may look like their office at work is better. It may look like their city is better. It may look like their state is better. It may look like their country is better. Yes, it may even look like *organized religion* is better. But defined by the hatred you spew, is it really?

I believe *mean spirited and intolerant* Christians should stop spending their time and energy trying to condemn gays and lesbians, which they actually have no right to do anyway.

Luke 6:36-37 36 *Be ye, therefore, merciful, as your Father also is merciful. 37 Judge not, and ye shall not be judged; condemn not, and ye shall not be condemned; forgive, and ye shall be forgiven.*

I have tried to simply give Bible verses and then let everyone interpret the verses and the significance of those verses in the context of their own life. If you have read a verse and acted on that verse, then the verse was clear, and it had a value.

I am not going to follow that approach with Luke 6:36-37.

I am going to offer my explanation of these verses in a very basic down to earth way because I believe they are actually two of the most important verses in the entire Bible. If you cannot see how Luke 6:36-37 might be two of the most important verses in the Bible, then I believe that *mean spirited and intolerant* Christians may just be destined to *not separate church and hate.*

Verse 36, *Be merciful,* sets the stage for being able to fulfill verse 37. You may insist that you are already merciful. My question for you is this: In the corner of your own little world where no one can enter or see, if you look back on your life, can you remember the three or four things you have done that you hope your spouse or your children or your parents or your best friend will *never* find out about? Can you vividly recreate those stupid, wrong, sinfully disgusting acts and remember how you felt when you had finished carrying them out? Did you want to die but then realized that you did need to go on with life? Did you then ask, plead and pray that God would forgive you for those acts? Do you remember when you promised God that you would *never* do anything like that again, and that if only God *would* forgive you — and hopefully not allow the natural order of events to take place and make you publicly suffer for those acts — that you would do *anything* for forgiveness? If your act was so bad and you *begged* God to forgive you, what you were effectively asking for was *mercy from God.*

Verse 36 says that as much mercy as you ask from God you *have to* give that much mercy to everyone else. In my example, gays and lesbians on this planet are *the everyone else.*

Let me say that again.

If you won't *give* mercy, the Bible says you will *not* get mercy.

James 2:13 *For he shall have judgment without mercy, that hath shown no mercy; and mercy rejoiceth against judgment.*

Verse 37: *Judge not and ye shall not be judged.*

I will concede that in the overall story of Adam and Eve and the apple, and the Old Testament animal sacrifices for the atonement of sins, and then with the New Testament birth, life, and death on the cross of Jesus for the atonement of everyone's sins, certain judgments need to be accounted for. But those judgments can only come from *God*, not from *mean spirited and intolerant* Christians, with their agenda.

Would *mean spirited and intolerant* Christians really judge others as harshly as they do if they actually believed this verse? Would *mean spirited and intolerant* Christians *really* judge others if every time they judged someone else, God would judge them? If each of you really believed *"to judge not"* with the fear of God in your heart, I believe *mean spirited and intolerant* Christians would choose to *judge not* and then *they could* separate church and hate.

Verse 37: *Condemn not and ye shall not be condemned.*

I was always amazed by the *mean spirited and intolerant* Christian who condemned the most. These judgmental Christians typically had the most to *hide* from condemnation by others.

Romans 2:1-3 *1 Therefore, thou art inexcusable, O man, whosoever thou art that judgest; for wherein thou judgest another, thou condemnest thyself; for thou that judgest doest the same things. 2 But we are sure that the judgment of God is according to truth against them who commit such things. 3 And thinkest thou this, O man, that judgest them who do such things, and doest the same, that thou shalt escape the judgment of God?*

There was that *mean spirited and intolerant* Christian lady who had an abortion years ago, but was always ready to give an ear full to the divorced or single young lady in church who maybe "dated more than she should." How about the deacon who always chastised other men for not setting as good of an example as a father and husband and bread-winner as he was, and all the while he thought the sins he was committing were well hidden. Would certain *mean spirited and intolerant* Christians really condemn others if every time they condemned someone else, God would condemn *them?* If they really believed it with the fear of God in their heart, I believe some *mean spirited and intolerant* Christians would choose to *condemn not* and then they *could* separate church and hate.

Verse 37: *Forgive and ye shall be forgiven.* Oh yes, I want to be forgiven. To be clear, I want to be forgiven by the people I have hurt. I see no reason to ask the Bible's God for any forgiveness.

Remember those personal sins of ours that we talked about earlier? Yes, the ones that only *we* know about? Well, except for God! God not only saw those sins, but he recorded them until a later date and for a specific purpose.

Revelation 20:12 *And I saw the dead, small and great, stand before God, and the books were opened,; and another book was opened, which is the book of life. And the dead were judged out of those things which were written in the books, according to their works.*

If some *mean spirited and intolerant* Christians really do need those sins forgiven, then they need to forgive the sins of others who honestly offend them. It really is that simple. Your Bible says to forgive everyone's sins. If any Christian can get through life on this Earth and keep those awful, disgusting sins hidden and then — as believers in the Bible — that he or she will only have to let them be revealed by God for one viewing at the end of time, maybe that is a good strategy.

If any Christian truly feels that his or her life would be better having shared those awful, disgusting sins with someone, then share them only with God. No one has to go into a closet and share them with anyone less than God.

Would some *mean spirited and intolerant* Christians start truly forgiving others if every time they truly forgave someone else, God would truly forgive *them?* If you really believed it with the love of God in your heart, I believe some *mean spirited and intolerant* Christians would choose to *forgive* and then *some of them would* be able to separate church and hate.

For those *mean spirited and intolerant* Christians who believe they are already perfect in both God's and their own eyes — and the previous three paragraphs mean absolutely nothing to them — it seems they feel the need to make it their mission to clean up society and get rid of all the putrid sins of mankind. God calls these putrid sins of mankind, *abominations.*

Luke 6:41-42 *41 And why beholdest thou the mote that is in thy brother's eye, but perceivest not the beam that is in thine own eye? 42 Either how canst thou say to thy brother, Brother, let me pull out the mote that is in thine eye, when thou thyself beholdest not the beam that is in thine own eye? Thou hypocrite, cast out first the beam out of thine own eye, and then shalt thou see clearly to pull out the mote that is in thy brother's eye.*

First, I think we should identify all of our own motes and beams and *then* we can work on a strategy to clean up the world. While no one is looking and you are not showboating that self-righteous attitude of yours for all to see, ask yourselves what *really* offends some of *YOU, mean spirited and intolerant* Christians?

Let's find out what constitutes an *abomination* in the eyes of God and then which ones *really* offend you.

"Abomination," as defined by *Webster's New Collegiate Dictionary* is "1: something abominable; 2: extreme disgust and hatred."

Well, homosexuality would certainly fit that definition, according to some *mean spirited and intolerant* Christians, but let's see what else we can come up with that is just as great or greater *abomination* with God than homosexuality, as defined by your *infallible* Bible.

In the course of studying the Bible, I have discovered over 50 *abominations* to God. There are a lot more abominations in the Old Testament than in the New Testament. I am sure there are more *abominations to the Lord,* but I believe the ten I list next are more than enough to get my point across.

One: **Proverbs 12:22** *Lying lips are an abomination to the Lord, but they that deal truly are his delight.*

OK, I guess we could stop right there! When some *mean spirited and intolerant* Christians lie about our committed sins, our punishments and our eternal condemnation to *prove your own position and then use those lies to serve your own purpose,* your Bible declares that to be an *abomination.* I am not even suggesting that some Christians may just *lie* in their everyday existence because that would also be an *abomination* to *your* Lord. Does this *abomination* of God *really* offend you?

Two: **Proverbs 20:10** *Diverse weights and diverse measures, both of them are like an abomination to the Lord.*

In biblical days people bought and sold in open courtyard markets and the transactions were metered by the values each commodity had according to balance scales with weights and measures. Of course, they did not have a *Universal Product Code* label to make all business deals fair. I don't think we would be too far off the mark if we interpreted this verse as talking about cheating someone out of his or her fair share in a business deal, even if you do have a fish symbol on your business card. Could this *abomination* include money managers defrauding clients of their pensions and investments in order to build their own fortunes? How about large family owned companies where the major stockholders build their portfolios into the "billions of dollars" instead of giving workers enough working hours to qualify for basic health insurance for their families! Do these *abominations* of God *really* offend you?

Three: **Deuteronomy 22:5** *The woman shall not wear that which pertaineth unto a man, neither shall a man put on a women's garment; for all that do so are abominations unto the Lord thy God.*

This seems to me like a pretty silly and frivolous *abomination,* but then I didn't establish it, God did. Is a Scottish kilt a women's garment? Are cowboy boots only for boys? Are blue jeans really only for men? Must women wear dresses to church in the sub-zero weather of Alaska? Are these *abominations* outdated and just not valid for today's fashion world? Could this verse really have anything to do with *blue sequin dresses*? Does this *abomination* of God *really* offend you?

Four: **Leviticus 11:9-10** *9 These shall ye eat of all that are in the waters: whatsoever hath fins and scales in the waters, in the seas, and in the rivers, them shall ye eat. 10 And all that have not fins and scales in the seas, and in the rivers, of all that move in the waters, and of any living thing which is in the waters, they shall be an abomination unto you.*

Well, there goes the all-you-can-eat seafood buffet of crab legs, lobster tails, shrimp, and clam chowder, especially on Friday. Does this *abomination* of God *really* offend you?

Five: **Proverbs 11:20** *They that are of a perverse heart are an abomination to the Lord, but such as are upright in their way are his delight.*

Interesting, but who exactly gets to define perverse? This verse seems perfect for anyone with an inclination to *prove his or her own position to then serve his or her own purpose.* If you *mean spirited and intolerant* Christians knew what this *abomination* meant, would this *abomination* of God *really* offend you?

Six: **Deuteronomy 24:1-4** *1 When a man hath taken a wife, and married her, and it come to pass that she find no favor in his eyes, because he hath found some uncleanness in her; then let him write her a bill of divorcement, and give it in her hand, and send her out of his house. 2 And when she is departed out of his house, she may go and be another man's wife. 3 And if the later husband hate her, and write her a bill of divorcement, and giveth it in her hand, and sendeth her out of his house; or if the latter husband die, who took her to be his wife, 4 Her former husband, who sent her away, may not take her again to be his wife, after that she is defiled; for that is abomination before the Lord.*

I have known a few Christians that remarried their ex-spouses. Does this "bill of divorcement" *abomination* of God *really* offend you?

Seven: **Luke 16:15** *And he said unto them, Ye are they who justify yourselves before men, but God knoweth your hearts; for that which is highly esteemed among men is abomination in the sight of God.*

Who gets to define *highly esteemed*? Does highly esteemed mean the lust for riches at all cost? Does highly esteemed mean movie star status? Does highly esteemed include our spouse, children or family? This is another verse that seems perfect for anyone wanting to *prove his or her own position to then serve his or her own purpose.* If Christians knew what this *abomination* meant, would this *abomination* of God *really* offend you?

Eight: **Ezekial 18:10-13** *10 If he beget a son that is a robber, a shedder of blood, and that doeth the like to any one of these things, 11 And that doeth not any of those duties, but even hath eaten upon the mountains, and defiled his neighbor's wife, 12 Hath oppressed the poor and needy, hath spoiled by violence, hath not restored the pledge, and hath lifted up his eyes to the idols, hath committed abomination, 13 Hath given forth upon interest and hath taken increase, shall he then live? He shall not live; he hath done all these abominations; he shall surely die; his blood shall be upon him.*

This verse has a whole lot of *abominating* going on! But does this verse mean that Christians should not charge interest or have a business that accepts credit cards because their Christian customers will be charged interest?

Here are a couple more verses for Christians and their banks. Are you going to have two separate loan officers: one for Christians and one for non-Christians?

Exodus 22:25 *If thou lend money to any of my people who is poor among you, thou shalt not be to him as an usurer, neither shalt thou lay upon him usury.*

Deuteronomy 23:19-20 *19 Thou shalt not lend upon interest to thy brother; interest of money, interest of victuals, interest of anything that is* *lent upon interest. 20 Unto a foreigner thou mayest lend upon interest, but unto thy brother thou shalt not lend upon interest, that the Lord thy God may bless thee in all that thou settest thine hand to in the land to which thou goest, to possess it.*

How do you feel when your bank charges you interest? Does this *abomination* of God *really* offend you?

Nine: **Proverbs 6:16-19** *16 These six things doth the Lord hate; yea, seven are an abomination unto him: 17 A proud look, a lying tongue, and hands that shed innocent blood, 18 An heart that deviseth wicked imaginations, feet that are swift in running to mischief, 19 A false witness that speaketh lies, and he that soweth discord among brethren.*

Strange that while homosexuality is not mentioned in this list of *abominations* God hates, simple lying is mentioned *twice*. Do these *abomination*s of God *really* offend you?

Ten: **Leviticus 20:13** *If a man also lie with mankind, as he lieth with a woman, both of them have committed an abomination: they shall surely be put to death; their blood shall be upon them.*

And *there* is your *organized religion's* verse to condemn all gays and lesbians! Odd that it does not mention women that lieth down with women. There is only one verse in the Bible that I could find that vaguely expressed such womanly behavior.

Romans 1:26-27 *26 For this cause God gave them up unto vile affections; for even their women did exchange the natural use for that which is against nature; 27 And likewise also the men, leaving the natural use of the woman, burned in their lust one toward another, men with men working that which is unseemly, and receiving in themselves that recompense of their error which was fitting.*

Is this the only *abomination* that *really* offends you?

If *organized religion* still does not like gays and lesbians because they sincerely believe they are sinners and one just cannot condone sinners in any form, which other sin of your heterosexual brothers and sisters are you going to *not* condone today? While homosexuality is not mentioned as a sin in the Ten Commandments, which Ten Commandment sins are you glad God will not judge you for today?

If the Christians who *really* feel that gays and lesbians deserve all the hardships they endure — and further, that the Bible supports such hate — be glad that the Bible doesn't *really* make you pay for lying. Practically *everyone* commits the *abomination* of lying and because in my experience practically everyone lies, does that mean God will treat anyone who lies with an equal degree of guilt as gays and lesbians for homosexuality? I bet you hope not!

In review; *your* Bible verses state that two *abominations* to God are homosexuality and lying. Pick a sin, just not both. The question remains: who gave *organized religion* the authority to define which *abominations* are worse than others? It seems that for some *abominations* they want to condemn everyone, while some *abominations* they merely scoff at.

I wonder whether you *mean spirited and intolerant* Christians even *know* a gay or lesbian person? I am not asking if you know where one lives or works. I am asking if you actually *know* a gay or a lesbian person. Do you go bowling or hiking or camping or swimming or play on the same softball team with a gay or a lesbian? Do you actually sit in a boardroom or eat in the same lunchroom or work on the same loading dock with a gay or a lesbian? Have any of you *Christians* ever had a flat tire in the middle of the night on a lonely highway and had your children screaming from the back seat: "We want to go home!" In this scenario would you ask whether the man or woman who stopped to help you was gay or lesbian, before accepting their help? If they *were* gay or lesbian would you let them help you change your tire, so you could get *your* nuclear family home?

Do you think gays and lesbians are *not normal people* because you think their attraction to the same sex is weird or disgusting? OK, let's consider a few gays and lesbians I personally know and see how different their lifestyles are from yours. At what point in these scenarios are you *really* offended?

Imagine one man and one woman who each have that special feeling in the pits of their stomachs that says "I really love this person, they make me feel special and wanted, and I would like to feel that way for the rest of my life."

Now consider one man and one man or one woman and one woman each having that special feeling in the pits of their stomachs that says, "I really love this person, they make me feel special and wanted, and I would like to feel that way for the rest of my life." Does this *really* offend you?

One man and one woman *married* to each other, for what seems like forever, but one partner gets in a car accident and the paramedics take him or her to the hospital emergency room in critical condition. The doctor comes into the lobby and quietly tells you that your partner will not live through the night so you had better go in Room 19 so you can say goodbye and get some closure. YOU DO!

One man and one man or one woman and one woman, *committed* to each other for what seems like forever, and one partner gets in a car accident and the paramedics take him or her to the hospital emergency room in critical condition. The doctor comes into the lobby and quietly tells you that your partner will not live through the night so you had better go in Room 19 so you can say goodbye and get some closure. The law says "YOU CAN'T!"

Does this *really* offend you? Is your little Christian corner of the world "safer" because this law exists? Clarification is needed on the point of law I just mentioned. In some states it is now legal to be with a partner in the above mentioned hospital room. But that hasn't always been the case. Yes, laws are changing to provide equality, and that is good for all men and women, Christian or non-Christian, gay, lesbian or straight.

One man and one woman, *married* to each other, for what seems like forever, build a relationship along with a successful business that keeps them off the government entitlement rolls. One partner dies and the government steps in to take its share of this *married* couple's wealth. The government *cannot* take a penny of the *married* couple's estate because of the unlimited marital deduction, which is a provision in the United States Federal Estate and Gift Tax Law. The surviving spouse lives on, financially secure because of the deceased spouse's hard work and the government's rules. Are you glad *you* have this government-mandated protection because you were heterosexually married?

One man and one man or one woman and one woman, *committed* to each other, for what seems like forever, build a relationship along with a successful business that keeps them off the government entitlement rolls. One partner dies and the government steps in to take its share of this *committed* couple's wealth. The government *can and will* take as many dollars as they can because the unlimited marital deduction which is a provision in the United States Federal Estate and Gift Tax Law does not apply to a *committed* couple. The surviving partner has to come up with death taxes needed to satisfy the government and usually loses the business the partners built together.

Does this *really* seem fair and does it *really* offend you that two people who love each other and make a living for themselves and DO NOT live off the government should be treated so differently?

If you want to *really* understand the impact of discrimination on gays and lesbians for your pleasure or your remorse, look up the 1,138 individual freedoms that are denied gay and lesbian couples at *gaymarriage.procon. org/* and then type in "1138 freedoms."

If *organized religion* does not want to accept gays and lesbians because they are rude, crude, dirty, obnoxious, skanky, repulsive, gross, nasty, degenerate, and creepy, then just say so and with your so-called Christian love deny gays and lesbians everything you would expect and demand for yourselves and for other Christians.

I may not appreciate your stance, but I could then respect that stance as being something that truly bothered you or made you uncomfortable. Just don't use *your* Bible to back up *your* personal selective prejudices. What I cannot respect is *your* stance of hating gays and lesbians because *your* Bible falsely told you it was all right to hate gays and lesbians.

By the way, how many of those descriptive gay and lesbian characteristics that I listed above have you personally been called in your lifetime, even by those who love you the most? I bet at least one!

I was very aware that two very important things were taken from Christians in the 1960's. At the time there was an uproar, but today there is barely a whisper.

A question I have asked dozens of Christians over the last 25 years is this: what year did Madalyn Murray O'Hair get prayer taken out of schools? The most common answer I have gotten is "The early 1960's." The *actual* answer is that Madalyn Murray O'Hair did not get *prayer* taken out of schools; she got *Bible reading* taken out of schools. This is not intended to be a trick question, but rather a question designed by me to validate that a lot of Christians are not even aware of their basic heritage. Madalyn Murray O'Hair did contribute to the confusion by taking credit for getting prayer out of schools, but she was just a minor player in the case

Abington School District v. Schempp. Madalyn Murray O'Hair petitioned the Supreme Court, *Murray v. Curlett,* to prevent the school her son William was attending from forcing him to read Bible verses. *Abington School District v. Schempp* was the actual Supreme Court case that ended Bible reading in schools. The *Murray v. Curlett* case was included in the Supreme Court decision in 1963 (*see:* thoughtco.com/abington-school-district-v-schempp-and-murray-v-curlett-250694).

Prayer was taken out of schools in 1962 in the Supreme Court case *Engel v. Vitale. (see* uscourts.gov/educational resources/get-involved/consti-tution-*activities/first-amendment/freedom-religion/facts-case-summary. aspx).*

When I was growing up, there was such outrage over prayer and Bible reading being banned from public schools, along with fears that those actions were going to result in the destruction of the United States, and that God would punish Christians for allowing the government to keep our children from God. That is what I was taught, and that is what I believed. I did *not* read the Supreme Court decision at that time. I have since read the Supreme Court decision and have determined that Christians should have had better lawyers; then and now.

If *organized religion* really felt that these two issues were so important, it is odd to me that there has been no grassroots movement to get them back. If someone stole something from your house and you knew where your possessions were, would you just let the thief keep your possessions or would you fight to get them back? These two fundamental Christian practices were taken away. I don't care whether *organized religion* ever gets them back, but even *I* could at least put up an argument or two. I may not win, but at least everyone would know that school prayer and Bible reading was important to me. Where were you, Christians at the time… and where are you now?

Women are still not treated equally in the minds and actions of many men, and it took a Constitutional amendment to legally give women the right to vote. The 19th Amendment to the Constitution at least gave power to women to implement change.

Black people are still not treated equally in the minds and actions of many men and women, and it took a Constitutional amendment to abolish slavery and involuntary servitude. The 13th Amendment to the Constitution at least gave power to Blacks to implement change.

Although gays and lesbians are not treated equally in the minds and actions of many heterosexual men and women, it will probably take a Constitutional amendment to *legally* give them the right to be treated equally in the eyes of the law. The ??th amendment to the Constitution is undoubtedly on its way, so some of you *mean spirited and intolerant* Christians get ready! Your hearts and minds may not change with the law, but your actions will soon have to be tempered.

Are some of *you Christians really* offended by gays and lesbians or are you merely looking for the weakest battle opponents still remaining? After all, Madalyn Murray O'Hair, the Supreme Court, women and Blacks have already beaten you.

When *organized religion* gets its *"Jesus is love and preached a message of love"* moral compass back to pointing at true North, *then* we will see what we should do about those gays and lesbians.

John 8:7 *So when they continued asking him, he lifted himself up, and said unto them, He that is without sin among you, let him first cast a stone at her.*

Whenever *organized religion* cannot offer a factual and reasonable explanation for a question we may have concerning knowing or understanding why God does this or that, and you can only say "God knows all things, and they will be revealed in God's own time," I'm afraid that game is over. We *converted non-Christians* will no longer let you escape with such a lame excuse.

John 8:31-32 *31 Then said Jesus to those Jews who believed on him, If ye continue in my word, then are ye my disciples indeed; 32 And ye shall know the truth, and the truth shall make you free.*

If I stand before God and give Him an accounting of the things I have done, so be it.

Again we read **Revelation 20:12** *And I saw the dead, small and great, stand before God, and the books were opened; and another book was opened, which is the book of life. And the dead were judged out of those things which were written in those books, according to their works.*

Disorganized Christianity has not abused one person. *Disorganized Christianity* has not cursed one person for their actions or beliefs. *Disorganized Christianity* has not subjected one soul to damnation in the hereafter. Can *organized religion* say that?

Understand that, by your *infallible* Bible verses, one day *you* will stand before your God! Some Christian preachers need to worry more about standing before their God and the final judgment, instead of standing in front of their congregations spewing hate.

While some of you *mean-spirited and intolerant* Christians may be thinking of ways to condemn me and have God strike me down with a bolt of lightning, remember or read — perhaps for the first time — **Romans 14:10** and **12** *10 But why dost thou judge thy brother? Or why dost thou set at naught thy brother? For we shall all stand before the judgment seat of Christ. 12 So, then, everyone of us shall give an account of himself to God.*

If I had to stand in front of God one day, I would confess: "I did not feel that it was right for *organized religion* to condemn others for not living the exact way *organized religion* demanded they should live." But I won't have to stand before God and have to explain why I tried to *control and abuse others on this earth and preached their damnation in the hereafter.*

1 Corinthians 13:13 *And now abideth faith, hope, love, these three; but the greatest of these is love.*

If we *really* believe in the separation of church and hate, this is a verse worth claiming!

CHAPTER 11

You can believe...

Y*ou can believe* and express that I have no right to talk about the Bible the way I do! *You can believe* that I have no right to interpret the Bible the way I do! You can actually believe anything you want, because we *converted non-Christians* give you that freedom. I cannot stop you from believing what you want, anymore than you can stop *me* from believing whatever I want, from now on.

There is a freedom we *converted non-Christians* have now taken back from *organized religion*. It is a freedom we should never have let slip away, in the first place. It is our freedom to not be *controlled and condemned by you on this earth and then have to listen to you declare our damnation in the hereafter.* I no longer believe that the Bible and *organized religion* even have a "*hereafter.*"

I am going to share some new personal opinions that will be very controversial. I do not believe that any one contradiction, misinterpretation, or mistranslation will turn Christianity on its ear. Christianity will not die because of *Disorganized Christianity.* Christianity will simply have a whole lot more questions to answer. Again, the primary goal of *Disorganized Christianity* is just to have *organized religion* leave us alone!

I will attempt to give my personal opinions and feelings just like *organized religion* used to give me their personal opinions and feelings. The difference is that *organized religion* could not give me a true Bible verse to back up what they spouted. They were just their personal opinions based on their special understanding of the Bible. Well, in my case, I will give you my opinions and feelings based on an actual Bible verse or two. You may not agree with my interpretation of the verses I choose to back up my opinions and feelings, but at least I am giving you an actual true and relevant Bible verse.

You can believe that because of Adam's original sin all men and all women are condemned to hell. We have addressed this question before, but let's ask it again so we can illustrate a very important issue. My question: *Who* was the first of God's creation to sin in the Garden of Eden and thereby causing all men to be condemned to hell? Adam?

1 Corinthians 15:22 *For as in Adam all die.*

Well, not exactly! It wasn't Adam as the *infallible* Bible says. The Bible states that Eve took of the fruit and then gave it to Adam:

Genesis 3:6 ... *she took of the fruit thereof, and did eat, and gave also to her husband with her; and he did eat.*

1 Timothy 2:14 *And Adam was not deceived, but the woman, being deceived, was in the transgression.*

The Bible didn't even address Eve by name, referring to her just as "*the woman.*" So, Eve was the first of God's creation to sin. Well, not exactly! It wasn't Eve as the *infallible* Bible says. The answer is actually *Satan*, the devil or the fallen angel, one of the *host of them.*

Genesis 2:1 *Thus the heavens and the earth were finished, and all the host of them.*

Genesis 3:1 *Now the serpent was more subtle than any beast of the field which the Lord God had made. And he said unto the woman, Yea, hath God said, Ye shall not eat of every tree of the garden?*

The serpent was in fact Satan, one of God's heavenly creations. The Bible says that God created the Garden of Eden for Adam and Eve, but I say that God *allowed* Satan to come into *our* Garden of Eden and mess things up.

There is absolutely no account in the Bible of Adam and Eve disobeying or transgressing against God, during the time when it was just God and Adam and Eve. Adam and Eve, by the absence of an account of a different first sin, appear to have been content to live in the perfect Garden of Eden. An interesting point that is never talked about is that after God *created* Adam and Eve, how long did they peacefully live in the Garden of Eden before Satan was *allowed* to tempt them?

Is the length of time Adam and Eve lived without sin in the Garden of Eden even important? I think it is. If God created Adam and Eve as adults and then in a matter of days or weeks or months they decided to eat from the tree of the knowledge of good and evil, then perhaps your biblical claim that Adam and Eve had an inherent lust for evil and sin could be valid. But, if Adam and Eve actually had lived for a year or ten years or a hundred years or a thousand years within the perfect framework of God's plan and did not sin against God until Satan was *allowed* to have his way with them, then your inherent sinful nature claim could not hold up to be factual.

I would say that Adam and Eve were actually in the Garden of Eden for a very long time. My conclusion is based on the fact that Adam's first job was to name ALL the animals on the Earth.

Genesis 2:19-20 *19 And out of the ground the Lord God formed every beast of the field, and every fowl of the air; and brought them unto Adam to see what he would call them: and whatsoever Adam called every living creature, that was the name thereof. 20 And Adam gave names to all cattle, and to the fowl of the air, and to every beast of the field; but for Adam there was not found an help fit for him.*

A couple of thoughts concerning this *infallible* Bible declaration of how every animal on the planet was named. Several Internet sites claim that there are 8.7 million specific different species of animals in our world. If there are 8.7 million different species of animals on the planet *now* and Noah put one male and one female of every animal on the boat, it follows that there must have been 8.7 million animals for Adam to name before the flood.

Various totals of animal species range from 1.3 to 8.7 million; some website studies put their estimates as high as 100 million species (see n*ytimes. com./2011/08/30/science/30species.html).*

That is a *lot* of animals, so naming them would have taken a lot of time. Even if you chose the lower number of 1,300,000 animals, it would still be very time consuming.

Now, anyone could argue that we should not take the *infallible* Bible *literally* in this case and that we should understand that it would be impossible for Adam to name *ALL* the animals on the planet. Maybe Adam really only named *MANY* animals and not *ALL* animals like God commanded him to do. By a similar token, maybe Jesus died for *MANY* sinners and then maybe Jesus died for *ALL* sinners.

Choose your *infallible* words carefully because we will now be listening and holding *organized religion* just a little more accountable for its claims.

But let us return to the question at hand: How long would it take Adam to name just 1,300,000 different animals? And that's followed by my next question: Did Adam have to share the names of ALL the animals with Eve when she came around and then did Adam have to repeat the process for Cain and Abel and everyone else until everyone on the planet was familiar with Adam's chosen names? After 4,000 to 6,000 years of all the animals being on the planet, who knows all the names of the animals even today?

Genesis 1:26-27 *26 And God said, Let us make man in our image, after our likeness; and let them have dominion over the fish of the sea, and over the fowl of the air, and over the cattle, and over all the earth, and over every creeping thing that creepeth upon the earth. 27 So God created man in his own image, in the image of God created he him; male and female created he them.*

If God made man in His own image, *did God have a sinful nature,* as well? We have read that God killed lots of people for a variety of reasons. We have read God is both an angry God and a jealous God. We have read God repented of God's mean and evil intentions towards mankind several times. Could any of these traits be defined as sinful?

In my fallible Bible, God did *not* say, "Let's create man in Satan's image." God said, Let's create man in *our* image" but just exactly *who* are the "our" beings in this *infallible* verse?

Organized religion wants to say that the "our" includes Jesus Christ and the Holy Spirit. Yet the Bible does not actually state that conclusion anywhere. I would say that the verse could very well claim: *"And man said, Let us make God in our image, after our likeness;"* because there are so many religious definitions of who and what God is.

It appears that after Satan had tempted Adam and Eve in the Garden of Eden, God's anger was poured out on man. But the anger from God and the judgment that followed was absolutely misguided. Man was cast out of

Eden, a specific area given to man from God. Man's ability to go wherever he wanted was now limited. But God allowed Satan — the instigator of the original sin — to travel anywhere he wanted to go in Heaven and on the Earth.

Job 1:7 *And the Lord said unto Satan, From where comest thou? Then Satan answered the Lord, and said, From going to and fro in the earth, and from walking up and down in it.*

If God truly is as all knowing as the Bible claims, why did he even have to ask Satan where he had been? I am not expecting or demanding that God reveal Satan's thoughts, but certainly God had perfect knowledge of where Satan had been.

According to the Bible story of God and Job, Job was doing just fine with God.

Job 1:1 *There was a man in the land of Uz, whose name was Job; and that man was perfect and upright, and one that feared God, and shunned evil.*

Job 1:6-11 *6 Now there was a day when the sons of God came to present themselves before the Lord, and Satan came also among them. 7 And the Lord said unto Satan, From where comest thou? Then Satan answered the Lord, and said, From going to and fro in the earth, and from walking up and down in it. 8 And the Lord said unto Satan, Hast thou considered my servant, Job, that there is none like him in the earth, a perfect and upright man, one who feareth God, and shunneth evil? 9 Then Satan answered the Lord, and said, Doth Job fear God for nothing? 10 Hast not thou made an hedge about him, and about his house, and about all that he hath on every side? Thou hast blessed the work of his hands, and his substance is increased in the land. 11 But put forth thine hand now, and touch all that he hath, and he will curse thee to thy face.*

As with Eve, it appears that Satan enjoyed tempting God, and he tried it again by challenging Job's love toward God because God gave Job everything. Satan said "Of course Job loves you, look what you have given him."

Job 1:10 *Hast not thou made an hedge about him, and about his house, and about all that he hath on every side? Thou hast blessed the work of his hands, and his substance is increased in the land.*

God allowed Job to be physically harmed and his family to be killed because of a challenge by Satan! Satan didn't even start the challenge. God did. Satan was running freely around the heavens and the earth and God said to Satan: "Hey, look at Job, he sure loves me."

Job 1:8 *And the Lord said unto Satan, Hast thou considered my servant, Job, that there is none like him in the earth, a perfect and an upright man, one who feareth God, and shunneth evil?*

The Bible's God sounds like a little kid with an inferiority complex. Oh, there goes that blasphemy again! But we already know that Satan does not fear God. If God is truly the Creator of all, including everything in the universe, why should God care whether Satan believes that Job loves God or not? Who is God trying to convince, Satan or himself?

This next statement is very important. Job proved his love to God because Job knew to do right or wrong and he chose right.

Job 1: 20-22 *20 Then Job arose, and tore his mantle, and shaved his head, and fell down upon the ground, and worshipped, 21 And said, Naked came I out of my mother's womb, and naked shall I return there. The Lord gave, and the Lord hath taken away; blessed be the name of the Lord. 22 In all this Job sinned not, nor charged God with folly.*

Job knew who he was and who God was, to him. Job did it right! But then, here came his three best friends Eliphaz, Bildad, and Zophar. Here come the *mean spirited and intolerant Christians* who know our life and business and faith better than we do. Eliphaz told Job that the innocent do not suffer. Bildad took 22 verses in Job 8 to explain to Job that God only likes the good guys, and if his evil were to be told to God, then God would help him. In chapter 11, Zophar told Job that he should not declare innocence because Zophar knew better. Most of us *converted non-Christians* have known an Eliphaz, Bildad, and/or Zophar in our lives.

Who is this Satan anyway, that he can manipulate God? Just as Satan challenged God with Job, I believe Satan challenged God into letting him come down to earth where he was allowed to beguile Eve. If we are actually to believe that God created everything and God has dominion over everything, shouldn't He have absolute control over everything?

According to the Bible, Adam, Eve, and Job loved and were blessed by God and were provided everything they needed and wanted. Living what appeared to be a blessed life, they were visited by Satan, with God's permission, and then their troubles began. Wait a minute!

Aren't God's blessings of grace, abundance, and a happy life what we ask for in our prayers every day? Are we now to assume that if we pray for the things we need or even want, and God answers our prayers, that we can also expect a visit from Satan just as it happened to Job?

Organized religion, you can keep your abundant blessings and just let me live my life untested by Satan while I try to find a kinder God to believe in, whoever he is, or she is, or they are, or we are. There seems to be a biblical pattern of getting God's blessings and then ending up on the receiving end of Satan's beguiling —with God's approval!

God loved Job. God blessed Job and gave Job everything. Satan was allowed to challenge Job's love towards God. Job proved his love towards God by doing right. It does not matter to me whether Job succeeded in loving God or failed. What matters to me is that this sounds a lot like the way God loved Adam and Eve. God blessed Adam and Eve and gave Adam and Eve everything. Satan was allowed to challenge Adam and Eve's love towards God and then when they failed, mankind was condemned forever.

You may have taken offense at *Disorganized Christianity* whenever I have said that God allowed Satan to beguile Eve in the Garden of Eden. Well, go ahead, but your only alternative reasoning is that Satan snuck by the all-knowing, all-loving, and always-present God and then beguiled Eve. The choice is yours.

You may jump out of your seat and assert that God didn't just allow Satan to tempt Adam and Eve. Really, do you know that for a fact? Are you going to try to tell us that after defying God in heaven and then getting thrown out of heaven and then having proved by your Bible verses that Satan was allowed to freely run around between heaven and earth, that God did not have enough sense to keep Satan away from Adam and Eve?

In 2016 the world population was estimated at over seven billion people. In the early days of creation and the Garden of Eden, the world population was two. With only two people to keep an eye on, I just can't imagine that God's time management was an issue here.

Why was Satan even allowed in the Garden of Eden? The Garden of Eden was ours not Satan's. Was God absent that day? Was there no one else among the host of them who could have kept Satan away from Adam and Eve? What about the "in our own image" beings? Were they missing in action too?

Deuteronomy 34:5-6 *5 So Moses, the servant of the Lord, died there in the land of Moab, according to the word of the Lord. 6 And he buried him in a valley in the land of Moab, over against Bethpeor; but no man knoweth of his sepulcher unto this day.*

When Moses died, God buried his body because Satan wanted it, and God had the Archangel Michael watch over and protect it.

Jude 1:9 *Yet, Michael, the archangel, when contending with the devil he disputed about the body of Moses, dared not bring against him a railing accusation but said, The Lord rebuke thee.*

Where was the Archangel Michael for Eve? It appears that — because the Bible states that even the Archangel Michael would not bring a railing accusation against Satan — that the most powerful good Archangel Michael was even wary of Satan. With all the host of them available in heaven, why not send an army to watch over and protect Eve if God had to be absent?

Eve was alive. Eve was innocent. Where was God our Father who is supposed to lead us not into temptation and deliver us from evil?

Was God just sitting there watching as Satan beguiled Eve into eating the fruit of the tree of the knowledge of good and evil, just like God idly stood by and watched while Satan killed all of Job's family? Was God watching as Satan beguiled Eve, while thinking to Himself: "I could not control Satan. Let's see if Eve can resist him, but if she can't, I am going to kick her out of the Garden of Eden?"

This is a very important question that absolutely needs to be answered by every person on the planet. Was God absent or watching as Satan beguiled Eve?

I have had several Christians warn me about my blasphemous attitude with respect to challenging God's word, and I have been assured that one day soon God would deal with me. You can believe the Bible says that one day we will all stand before God and give an accounting for our lives.

Romans 14:12 *So, then, every one of us shall give account of himself to God.*

I preached that message, myself, and I was always concerned for what I would have to explain about my life. Today, I confess to the absolute fact that I am not afraid of what I would have to say to God if that scenario really came to pass. I would actually look forward to the meeting, and what follows is what I would ask God.

Genesis 1:27 *So God created man in his own image, in the image of God created he him; male and female created them.*

So God, if you created us in your image, placed us in the perfect setting of the Garden of Eden and together we all had good fellowship for a long time and if you had NEVER allowed Satan to come down to beguile us, do you think we would we have done something we had never done before — or even knew was a possible thing to do — to sin against you? This one question alone, and its answer would resolve a lot of confusion.

The Bible does not tell us that Adam and Eve had sinned before Eve ate of the fruit of the tree of knowledge of good and evil. If Adam and Eve had sinned before, the "original sin" would not have centered around an apple. So it would appear that in Genesis, God did have a loving, peaceful, obedient, and honoring relationship with man and woman until He allowed a heavenly creation — Satan — to come down to Earth and mess up the Garden of Eden.

The Bible states that Satan, the serpent, was subtler than all of the beasts of the field. So God allowed the one heavenly creation that showed God the least respect to come down and have his way with Adam and Eve, and then you want to declare that "Adam had it perfect and then he willfully disobeyed God?"

Isaiah 14:12-14 *12 How art thou fallen from heaven, O Lucifer, son of the morning! How art thou cut down to the ground, who didst weaken the nations! 13 For thou hast said in thine heart, I will ascend into heaven, I will exhalt my throne above the stars of God; I will sit also upon the mount of the congregation, in the sides of the north, 14 I will ascend above the heights of the clouds, I will be like the Most High.*

I guarantee that if you found yourself in Adam and Eve's situation that you would retain the best lawyer you could find and then you would shout to the heavens, "Entrapment!" You certainly would not stand there and say: "Yes God, I did wrong. My actions were willful and on purpose with a full understanding of the consequences. Sentence me to death, even if I don't know what death means. I certainly deserve your penalty for my sin, even if I don't know what sin even means."

Your basic argument that Adam and Eve were sinful "by nature," and that no matter how God explained the instructions to them, they would have sinned anyway, is just not valid!

Let me explain. I believe one major problem with the Bible in general is that the Bible is not very clear. Now, the problem is either with God who didn't know how to clearly state commandments, instructions or punishments, or the problem is with the translators who did not listen carefully to God while He was inspiring words to them, or possibly with other translators who said: "We will interpret these words our way because we want to, for whatever agenda we may have." Regardless of whether it is God's or the translator's mistakes we are now dealing with, my point is that we *converted non-Christians* are not going to be held responsible by *organized religion* for commandments, instructions, and punishments when they are not clearly laid out!

Your interpretation of God's commandments and punishments do not hold any authority with us anymore. An example is **Exodus 20:13** *Thou shalt not kill*. Most people agree the word kill means murder or intentional slaying. According to the Bible, having an abortion is an act of intentional slaying. *Organized religion* says they are against abortion, but they have not proven that they will stop their members from having them, nor are they condemning them as passionately as they condemn non-member gays and lesbians.

I do not care whether you have an abortion or do not have an abortion. But, if *organized religion* would give as much conviction and damnation to the abortions they have as they give to gays and lesbians who are really not impacting anyone's right to life, there would undoubtedly be more Christians in this world today.

My point is not about abortions, per se. My point with this example is that *organized religion* interprets their Bible to *prove its position to then serve its own purpose* about which commandments to obey.

When I command "You had better do this or I will do that" and you ignore my command, is it willful disobedience or just lack of understanding of the consequence? Is it important that you even know what my "this or that" is?

When *organized religion* tries to control others and assert that we must do what God's word says or we will be condemned — first by them and then by God — we certainly deserve to know whether *organized religion* even knows what God is commanding and demanding from us.

I believe the first unclear commandment of God's word that led to a spiritual death occurred in the Garden of Eden when God told Adam, on the day he ate of the tree of the knowledge of good and evil, that he would surely die. At least in this account, the Bible did mention the commandment and a punishment.

When God told Adam not to eat of the tree of the knowledge of good and evil or he would surely die, did Adam understand what God meant by die? The Bible does not tell us whether Adam understood what die meant. So, as a Bible reader, I am now subject to the translator's explanation — or preacher's declaration — of what die meant. I am not comfortable with any translators's definition of what I should *be or do*.

I am not making an excuse to justify Adam to disobey God, I am making the point that I believe, according to the Bible: either God or the translators of God's word were not very clear at explaining abstract ideas. Death at the time of the Garden of Eden was an abstract idea because nobody had ever died before. No human had physically died before. No human had spiritually died before. As a consequence, I would argue that Adam or Eve did not know what "die" meant.

I would accept the fact that since Satan had been around a while: **Genesis 2:1** *Thus the heavens and the earth were finished, and all the host of them,* and after Satan had been cast out of heaven for disobeying God; **Isaiah 14:12-14** *12 How art thou fallen from heaven, O Lucifer, son of the morning! How art thou cut down to the ground, who didst weaken the nations! 13 For thou hast said in thine heart, I will ascend into heaven, I will exalt my throne above the stars of God; I will sit also upon the mount of the congregation, in the sides of the north, 14 I will ascend above the heights of the clouds, I will be like the Most High,* Satan knew exactly what God meant when He said, "Surely you will die."

According to today's preachers, this was a spiritual death, not a physical death. If a commandment and a punishment are confusing and unclear, then the deception of each can be successful. I believe it was easy for Satan to twist around the words relating to the meaning of death, because Satan had already been told that if he disobeyed God, he would surely die. It only makes sense that God would have applied the same parenting skills to all of His creations, both heavenly and earthly.

After Satan rebelled and was cast out of heaven, he experienced a supposed spiritual death but not a physical death. Satan could with certainty have told Eve that she would not surely die. Satan knew perfectly well that it was another moment to declare: "Well, not exactly!"

Nakedness at the time of the Garden of Eden was also an abstract idea.

Genesis 3:7 *And the eyes of them both were opened, and they knew that they were naked, and they sewed fig leaves together, and made themselves aprons.*

The Bible states that Adam didn't even know he was naked nor what that meant. Today, without some preacher's explanation, I do not know what naked meant in the context the Bible placed on Adam and Eve's naked condition. I have heard many explanations concerning their naked condition, but I am still not sure I can agree with any of them. No biblical explanation has been presented to help clarify naked.

Is clarification from God important to you or will you go through this life and hopefully move to the next life, purely based on your blind faith? I believe it should be clear. We *converted non-Christians* want clarity, not just a vague and ambiguous explanation from some preacher with a personal agenda.

I truly am not trying to tell God what He should have written. I think enough translators have already done that. But I would have appreciated God fully explaining what death meant and then explaining clearly precisely how Adam did in fact willfully disobey God. As you read earlier in *Disorganized Christianity*, Jesus had to explain to his own disciples that the words die, death, sleep, asleep, and sleeping all ultimately meant dead. Which *infallible* words and *infallible* meanings are correct?

Every Sunday, there are preachers who preach: "Adam willfully disobeyed God and so do you."

How do they know what Adam did or didn't do? Nowhere does the Bible say that Adam willfully, and with full understanding of his actions and their consequences, disobeyed God. That verse simply does not exist in the Bible! Moreover, those Sunday preachers were not there, and God did not tell them that. "Willful disobedience" would at the very least have to include elements of an action against God with a full understanding of the consequences of that action, instead of a mystic death sentence.

Again, I am not God, but wouldn't it have been better to say: "Adam, if you eat of the tree of the knowledge of good and evil I will be upset that you disobeyed me, and I will throw you and that lady friend of yours out of the Garden, and you will have to grow your own food and go through life apart from me and all the good things I have provided for you will end. You will also have to start sacrificing animals and shed their blood on an altar to make me happy after you sin again."

If God had explained die like that, then Adam would have had some conditions he would actually be familiar with. Now, if Adam still chooses to be tempted or beguiled by Satan to eat of the tree of the knowledge of good and evil, he most certainly deserves whatever punishment God gives him.

Please don't start to tell me that you think I am being foolish and illogical and unreasonable for wanting an explanation for why God would punish Adam and Eve or me or us without a real understandable explanation.

Consider this: when that police officer — who is in authority over you — pulls you over and gets ready to punish you with a ticket, don't even start to tell me that you haven't asked him or her, "Why, what did I do?" You may have fully understood that the posted speed limit was 55 miles per hour and not 75 miles per hour and, thus understood why the officer gave you a ticket! But you may not have known, however, that when driving the posted 55 miles per hour in a 35 miles per hour work zone — even if workers are not present — that in some states it is still illegal, a "sin," to drive the posted 55 miles an hour.

Ticket? Are you guilty of breaking the law and should you be punished if you did not know it was a law, just because you are driving in a different state? As the judge told me: "You need to be aware of the traffic laws, in every state you drive."

I believe the second unclear commandment that led to a physical death in the Bible is so vague it allows a wide variety of opinions, and there have been many. This concerns the account of Cain and Abel and what eventually was to become the first murder of all time.

We were told in Sunday School that Adam and Eve had two sons, Cain the first-born son and Abel the second-born son. We were told Cain killed Abel, thereby committing the first murder. Why did Cain kill his brother?

In this example of unclear commandments or punishments, we do not have a clear explanation of God's commandment to Cain. The punishment of Cain is clear, but the reason for the condemnation is not clear. Later in the Bible there are Old Testament verses and New Testament verses concerning Cain and how he displeased God, but there is no reason given for God's displeasure in this Genesis passage.

Organized religion has an opinion, but it is not found in Genesis Chapter Four. I have heard *organized religion's* opinion, and I actually believed that opinion until I realized that the Bible does not explain Cain's disobedience of God's supposed commandment. *Organized religion* can have an opinion and then start putting random verses together that will explain its own biblical opinion for God's displeasure with Cain, but nowhere in Genesis Chapter Four does it say what led Cain to murder his brother!

Genesis Chapter Four does say that Abel brought a sacrifice of an animal for an offering to God. The animal was a sheep from the flock he tended. The verses also say that Cain brought the first fruits of the ground that he tended. The Bible says that God respected the animal offering from Abel, but not the first fruits of the ground that Cain offered.

Nowhere before Chapter Four did God explain that an animal sacrifice was better than a first fruits of the ground offering. Was Cain the victim of another abstract commandment from God or were the translators just lazy about recording more of God's inspired words? Does Chapter Four say that the better blood sacrifice was implied? Does *organized religion* say that the condemnation and damnation of us is implied? Are you going to suggest that God told Cain and Abel the differences about sacrifices, but just not then?

If that is a valid argument, then how are we to interpret **1 Corinthians 14:40** *Let all things be done decently and in order.* I believe the "decently and in order" way would be to tell someone the exact rules before you hand out an exact punishment. If you want to say that God did give them the exact rules before the exact punishment, then why not record the *infallible* word of God correctly?

Your *infallible* word of God thought it was important enough to put the creation of man before the creation of woman, the creation of the sun before the creation of the moon, and the creation of vegetation before the creation of cattle. Shouldn't the exact rules be proclaimed before an exact punishment is inflicted?

What we *converted non-Christians* are tired of is *organized religion* seemingly knowing just enough of their Bible to be dangerous. Before *organized religion* declares our condemnation using a "well, not exactly" verse and then adds a self-serving, non-biblical statement to seal our damnation in the hereafter, we *converted non-Christians* will stand up and say "Not in our house!"

God — or God's translators — did get very explicit about the details about what God commanded with regard to offerings and sacrifices, later in the Bible. So why didn't God get more explicit about what he expected from Adam, Eve, Cain, and Abel? Clarity in explaining early commandments and punishments does not appear to be a very strong Bible trait!

We were told in Sunday School and church that in the Old Testament man had to sacrifice different kinds of animals for different kinds of sins, as a basis for a blood sacrifice needed to appease God because of man's original sin.

Exodus 24:4-8 *4 And Moses wrote all the words of the Lord, and rose up early in the morning, and built an altar under the hill, and twelve pillars, according to the twelve tribes of Israel. 5 And he sent young men of the children of Israel, who offered burnt offering, and sacrificed peace offerings of oxen to the Lord. 6 And Moses took half of the blood, and put it in basins; and half of the blood he sprinkled on the altar. 7 And he took the book of the covenant, and read in the hearing of the people; and they said, All that the Lord hath said we will do, and be obedient. 8 And Moses took the blood, and sprinkled it on the people, and said, Behold the blood of the covenant, which the Lord hath made with you concerning all these words.*

We were told in Sunday School and church that Abel offered a blood sacrifice to God, and Cain gave God the best of his first fruits. The story was interpreted to mean that we must do what God commands and not what we think God should be satisfied with. The fundamental problem with this explanation is that we are not told in or before Chapter Four the exact nature of what God's directive was for offerings.

No, we are not going to accept your insistence that "Well, we all really know what God meant." Assumption is the core problem with most of your interpretations. You read a few very vague Bible verses and then you make up whatever explanation you feel sounds correct for your agenda and then you expect us to follow along. Cain gave the harvest of first fruits and God was angry, then Cain got jealous of Abel and killed him. This is what we were told, but Chapter Four of Genesis does not say that.

Genesis 4:5 *But unto Cain and to his offering he had not respect. And Cain was very angry, and his countenance fell.*

In Genesis Chapter Four we go from the birth of Cain and Abel in verses one and two, to giving offerings to God in verses three and four and then to God not respecting Cain's offering in verse five. That is a lot of life span to be covered in five verses.

Questions abound! Yes, we have a right to ask questions, and we will now start asking even more! Was this the first attempt at offerings by Cain and Abel? Had Cain or Abel each ever completed an acceptable offering before? Had Cain already given God 100 animal offerings before his rebellion, and then he presented his self-centered harvest offering as has been implied by *organized religion*? To further add to this confusion, were first fruits ever an acceptable offering to God — and if they were — could Cain have been confused by vague commandments and then been unjustly judged by God?

Exodus 23:16 *And the feast of harvest, the first fruits of thy labors, which thou hast sown in the field; and the feast of ingathering, which is in the end of the year, when thou hast gathered in thy labors out of the field.*

First fruits were not used for sin atonement offerings. First fruits had their place as a celebration offering at harvest time and were given to the priests in the temple. First fruits were a valid offering, just not a valid sin atonement offering, but Cain did not have a Bible to read that.

In the New Testament the ultimate sin atonement sacrifice would be Jesus.

Hebrews 26:26-28 *26 And as they were eating, Jesus took bread, and blessed it, and broke it, and gave it to the disciples, and said, Take, eat; this is my body. 27 And he took the cup, and gave thanks, and gave it to them, saying, Drink ye all of it; 28 For this is my blood of the new testament, which is shed for many for the remission of sins.*

I didn't write the Bible, but if I have to live by the words and commandments of the Bible, would it not be reasonable for me to expect a clear understanding of what God wants from me?

You may say that I am again being unreasonable and petty because I expect God to fully and in detail give me as much information as I need to completely understand my choices about obeying God or telling God "Don't think so!" Blasphemy?

Don't think so!

I was blasphemous quite often with *organized religion*'s easy nonsensical answers to my questions and also because they demanded so much blind faith obedience from me. In my world, *organized religion* can no longer say with any credibility: "I cannot answer that, but God has His own timing and reasons, so just let it go for now."

If the Bible is unclear in its message, is that my fault? Is the Bible entirely too vague in its message and are there instances where the message from God is very clear? My answer is illustrated in the next three examples of God's exactness in commands.

The Ark of the Covenant was a focal point of Israel's worship and obedience to God. The Ark of the Covenant was the place where God told the Israelites to put the Ten Commandments away for safekeeping. A simple box of any kind of wood could have been ample housing for the Ten Commandments, but God had a different vision for the Ark of the Covenant.

Exodus 25 gives one of the most detailed descriptions of the Ark of the Covenant.

Exodus 25:10-22 *10 And they shall make an ark of acacia wood: two cubits and a half shall be the length thereof, and a cubit and a half the breadth thereof, and a cubit and a half the height thereof. 11 And thou shalt overlay it with pure gold, within and without shalt thou overlay it, and shalt make upon it a rim of gold round about. 12 And thou shalt cast four rings of gold for it, and put them in the four corners thereof; and two rings shall be in the one side of it, and two rings in the other side of it.13 And thou shalt make staves* *of acacia wood, and overlay them with gold. 14 And thou shalt put the staves into the rings by the sides of the ark, that the ark may be borne with them. 15 The staves shall be in the rings of the ark; they shall not be taken from it. 16 And thou shalt put into the ark the testimony which I shall give thee. 17 And thou shalt make a mercy seat of pure gold: two cubits and a half shall be the length thereof; and a cubit and a half the breadth thereof. 18 And thou shalt make two cherubim of gold, of beaten work shalt thou make them, in the two ends of the mercy seat. 19 And make one cherub on the one end, and the other cherub on the other end: even of the mercy seat shall ye make the cherubim on the two ends thereof. 20 And the cherubim shall stretch forth their wings on high, covering the mercy seat with their wings, and their faces shall look one to another; toward the mercy seat shall the faces of the cherubim be. 21 And thou shalt put the mercy seat above upon the ark; and in the ark thou shalt put the testimony that I shall give thee. 22 And there I will meet with thee, and I will commune with thee from above the mercy seat, from between the two cherubim which are upon the ark of the testimony, of all things which I will give thee in commandment unto the children of Israel.*

In verses 18 and 19 God explicitly details instructions three times that the cherubim need to be on each end of the Ark of the Covenant. This placement is not only detailed instruction, but it is detailed to the point of redundancy. God tells the craftsman to build the Ark of the Covenant and overlay it with gold and then put cherubim on the ends in the most detailed fashion.

Verse 22 even alludes again to the position of the mercy seat as between the two cherubim. With all this Ark of the Covenant detail, please explain to me why the sum total of explanations and details of the commandment that led to the total damnation of mankind is this: "Don't eat the apple or you will surely die." Again, the craftsmen of the Ark of the Covenant knew exactly what acacia wood, gold, placement of the cherubims, and the mercy seat were, but Adam and Eve had no idea what die meant.

One of the best-known Bible stories is about Noah's Ark. Many people have claimed to have found Noah's Ark, but no one has produced any substantial evidence to support their claim. The Bible gives such specific details as to the size and nature of the ark that verifying any discovery of the ark would be easy.

Genesis 6:13-16 *13 And God said unto Noah, The end of all flesh is come before me; for the earth is filled with violence through them; and, behold, I will destroy them with the earth. 14 Make thee an ark of gopher wood; rooms shalt thou make in the ark, and shalt pitch it within and without with pitch. 15 And this is the fashion which thou shalt make it of: the length of the ark shall be three hundred cubits, the breadth of it fifty cubits, and the height of it thirty cubits. 16 A window shalt thou make to the ark, and in a cubit shalt thou finish it above; and the door of the ark shalt thou set in the side thereof; with lower, second, and third stories shalt thou make it.*

The size of the ark and the placement of windows and doors were explicitly clear.

How many of each kind of animal was Noah told to bring on the ark? If your answer is "two, one male and one female," you would be incorrect.

Genesis 6:19 *And of every living thing of all flesh, two of every sort shalt thou bring into the ark, to keep them alive with thee; they shall be male and female.*

Sounds like two animals. Well, not exactly!

Genesis 7:2 *Of every clean beast thou shalt take to thee by sevens, the male and his female; and of beasts that are not clean by two, the male and his female.*

God was exact in his commandment on how many animals were needed to replenish the earth and how many animals were needed for a blood sacrifice while Noah and his family were on the ark and after they got off the ark.

Genesis 8:20 *And Noah builded an altar unto the Lord; and took of every clean beast, and of every clean fowl, and offered burnt offerings on the altar.*

I am going to share the entire first chapter of Leviticus because it is so detailed with respect to burnt sacrifice. There are numerous other burnt and blood sacrifice passages, but my point will be well made that if God wants to be clear about a commandment and punishment, God is perfectly capable of being incredibly detailed.

Leviticus 1:1-17 *1 And the Lord called unto Moses, and spoke unto him out of the tabernacle of the congregation, saying, 2 Speak unto the children of Israel, and say unto them, If any man of you bring an offering unto the Lord, ye shall bring your offering of the cattle, even of the herd, and of the flock. 3 If his offering be a burnt sacrifice of the herd, let him offer a male without blemish: he shall offer it of his own voluntary will at the door of the tabernacle of the congregation before the Lord. 4 And he shall put his hand upon the head of the burnt offering, and it shall be accepted for him to make atonement for him. 5 And he shall kill the bullock before the Lord: and the priests, Aaron's sons, shall bring the blood, and sprinkle the blood round about upon the altar that is by the door of the tabernacle of the congregation.6 And he shall flay the burnt offering, and cut it into its pieces. 7 And the sons of Aaron, the priest, shall put fire upon the altar, and lay the wood in order upon the fire. 8 And the priests, Aaron's sons, shall lay the parts, the head, and the fat, in order upon the wood that is on the fire which is upon the altar; 9 But its inwards and its legs shall he wash in water: and the priest shall burn all on the altar, to be a burnt sacrifice, an offering made by fire, of a sweet savor unto the Lord. 10 And if his offering be of the flocks, namely, of the sheep, or of the goats, for a burnt sacrifice, he shall bring it a male without blemish. 11 And he shall kill it on the side of the altar northward before the Lord; and the priests, Aaron's sons, shall sprinkle its blood round about upon the altar. 12 And he shall cut* *it into its pieces, with its head and its fat: and the priest shall lay them in order on the wood that is on the fire which is upon the altar; 13 But he shall wash the inwards and the legs with water: and the priest shall bring it all, and burn it upon the altar: it is a burnt sacrifice, an offering made by fire, of a sweet savor unto the Lord. 14 And if the burnt sacrifice for his offering to the Lord be of fowls, then he shall bring his offering of turtledoves, or of young pigeons. 15 And the priest shall bring it unto the altar, and wring off its head, and burn it on the altar; and the blood thereof shall be wrung out at the side of the altar: 16 And he shall pluck away its crop with its feathers, and cast it beside the altar on the east part, by the place of the ashes. 17 And he* shall cleave it with the wings thereof, but shall not divide it asunder: and the *priest shall burn it upon the altar, upon the wood that is upon the fire: it is a burnt sacrifice, an offering made by fire, of a sweet savor unto the Lord.*

I realize this is a long passage to read, but it is full of specific words and complete instructions on how to offer a burnt sacrifice. If God had given Adam and Eve as much detail concerning the apple and kept the snake away, we may not have needed burnt sacrifices.

In these three previous examples of the Ark of the Covenant, Noah's Ark, and burnt sacrifices to God, we have read some of the most elaborate and detailed commands on exactly what God demanded from His people. The exactness of the details demanded by God while meeting His expectations is not vague in these Bible verses. Instead we have perfection and a clear understanding of what God commands, with explicit instructions and descriptions of the rewards and punishments the Israelites could expect.

My problem with the case of Adam's or Eve's ultimate sin and possibly the single most important instruction from God is that the only thing we get to go by amounts to: "Don't eat the fruit or touch the fruit or you will die!"

Genesis 3:3 *But of the fruit of the tree which is in the midst of the garden, God hath said, Ye shall not eat of it, neither shall ye touch it, lest ye die.*

It is the one verse in the entire Bible that condemns us all, and yet this single verse is not worthy of any further explanation! This rudimentary declaration may be enough for *organized religion,* but it is not enough for us anymore!

Did the Bible have a word limit for Genesis 3:3 so there wasn't enough room in the written Word of God to further elaborate on this most important instruction?

In the New Testament we in many cases have the exact same Bible story told four times, once in each of the first four gospels: Matthew, Mark, Luke, and John. No one knew what die meant, so they could not explain it any better!

Did God believe that we would eventually fully understand what this verse meant after a bunch of guys put all of God's words in a book? Using that thought process, I don't think God's expectations turned out exactly like they were supposed to. I believe *organized religion* and your translators have a lot of further explaining to do.

Genesis 3:5 *For God doth know that in the day ye eat thereof, then your eyes shall be opened, and ye shall be as God, knowing good and evil.*

Hold on to your emotions again. God knew that on the day Adam and Eve ate from the apple tree they would be like God and know the difference between good and evil or right and wrong! *Organized religion* adamantly declares Adam and Eve willfully chose to disobey God. *Organized religion* attempts to analyze Adam and Eve and their psyche in some garden thousands of years ago. According to your Bible this analysis of willful disobedience by Adam and Eve is incorrect!

A very clear and detailed verse in your Bible proves that you are incorrect about Adam and Eve's willful disobedience. Would *organized religion's* teachings agree that disobeying God's instructions is a wrong or an evil thing? Whether *organized religion* agrees or disagrees, my question is this: "How could Adam and Eve willfully choose to disobey, which is an evil trait, when it explicitly says in **Genesis 3:5** *For God doth know that in the day ye eat thereof, then your eyes shall be opened, and ye shall be as God, knowing good and evil?*"

Adam and Eve could not have known the difference between good and evil or sin because they had not eaten of the fruit of the tree of the knowledge of good and evil, yet!

There was no law to break. There was no valid sin to condemn man! Adam and Eve could not have sinned or committed evil against God because Adam and Eve did not know the difference between good and evil, yet. God even made a special point of declaring that:

Genesis 3:22 *And the Lord God said, Behold, the man is become as one of us, to know good and evil; and now, lest he put forth his hand, and take also of the tree of life, and eat, and live forever;*

The verse says that man is become as one of us, not that man was always as one of us; to know good and evil. Adam and Eve had to be tricked or beguiled by Satan in order to commit *organized religion*'s original sin. The same created being that defied God earlier in the design of man and Earth was also the one who tricked Adam and Eve. Where in this verse is willful disobedience explained or even implied?

Yes, it IS important! The beginning of Adam and Eve's knowledge of good and evil and sinful nature began *after* they ate the apple!

Satan had to beguile or trick Eve into eating the fruit of the tree of the knowledge of good and evil and only then did they know the difference between good and evil. God or God's translators used the word beguiled.

Webster's New Collegiate Dictionary defines beguiled as "1: to lead by deception, 2: a: hoodwink, b: to deprive by guile: cheat."

After eating the apple, and only then, did Adam and Eve gain the awareness that they were naked?

Where was God while Adam and Eve were being beguiled? The entire chapter of Psalm 139 describes how God knows everything. But if God knows all things, even before they happen, was God just watching Satan beguile Eve and letting it happen like He did with Job later in the Bible? Satan had already messed with God enough to get thrown out of heaven. How could God allow Satan to mess with Eve? Why would God expect Eve to withstand such a powerful force as Satan? Could God not control Satan?

Don't even try to give me that free will excuse! You have to know the difference between good and evil before you can claim the free will to do good or evil and verse five clearly says that Adam and Eve did not know the difference between good and evil, yet:

James 4:17 *Therefore, to him that knoweth to do good , and doeth it not, to him it is sin.*

How could Adam and Eve willfully disobey God? If verse five really does not mean what it actually says, because it does not fit your *organized religion* agenda and your excuse is that the translators mistranslated the verse, that is your problem, not ours.

I believe my explanation of Adam and Eve not willfully sinning against God totally shakes *organized religion's* foundation of Adam and Eve choosing to do wrong and thereby deserving their separation from God; and then passing this condemnation on to all of us. This condemnation that *organized religion* uses to *control and condemn us on this earth and then declare our damnation* in the hereafter is not valid.

Adam and Eve did not know what *die* meant. Adam and Eve did not know what *naked* meant. Ultimately, it appears that Satan was simply a better talker, salesman, or beguiler than God was a teacher, protector, or Father. God said, "Don't eat the apple." Satan said, "Go ahead and eat the apple." Satan won. God lost! Adam and Eve lost! And, according to the Bible story, we *all* supposedly lost!

If God made Earth for man and woman, and Satan was the first of God's creation to sin, why is the Bible full of condemnation for *man's* original sin but not condemnation for *Satan's* original sin? The Bible verse does not say, by one *fallen angel's* sin, all men die, it says by one *man's* sin, all men die.

Rev 20:1-3 *1 And I saw an angel come down from heaven, having the key of the bottomless pit and a great chain in his hand. 2 And he laid hold on the dragon, that old serpent, who is the Devil and Satan, and bound him a thousand years, 3 And cast him into the bottomless pit, and shut him up, and set a seal upon him, that he should deceive the nations no more, til the thousand years should be fulfilled; and after that he must be loosed a little season.*

Okay, STOP! First question: Is this thousand years only a day or is it an actual thousand years?

2 Peter 3:8 *But, beloved, be not ignorant of this one thing, that one day is with the Lord as a thousand years, and a thousand years as one day.*

I know Revelation 20 says a thousand years but with our proven translation problems, is it really a thousand years or only one day? *Your* Bible comparison not mine. Again, where is the *original* parchment that clearly states one day or a thousand years? Yes, Satan's punishment does make a difference, to us. We humans lost forever and Satan may lose only one day or what may seem to be only one day.

Second question; Why in the hell *must* Satan *be released?*

Revelation 20:7 *And when the thousand years are ended, Satan shall be loosed out of his prison.*

Organized religion preachers, explain to me why God will eventually, someday, cast Satan in prison and then after 1,000 years *(or one day?)* of prison time, release Satan? Who is *really* running this planet? Satan thoroughly ruined the planet once, and now God is going to let him try to do it again after doing a little prison time? God doesn't even try to say that Satan, the fallen angel, the host of them, the beguiler, the Devil or snake is going to be given a second chance because he could have been rehabilitated.

Revelation 20:7-8 *7 And when the thousand years are ended, Satan shall be loosed out of his prison, 8 And shall go out to deceive the nations which are in the four quarters of the earth, Gog and Magog, to gather them together to battle; the number of whom is as the sand of the sea.*

God knows and declared that Satan is coming back with the sole purpose of trying to beguile and deceive as many of us as he can, again?

If this God of the Bible — that *organized religion* worships — thinks that it is fair or loving or even *sane* to allow Satan to come back one more time to beguile us so we can have another chance to prove that we love God, you can keep *that* God!

As mentioned in the chapter *I believe in the separation of church and hate!,* we have recorded from the Bible that God of the Old Testament had no problem with killing entire civilizations, and anyone who was not killed was promptly made a slave. The Bible record of getting mad and killing the bad guys is a dominant theme in God's daily life. God even killed a man who sincerely was just trying to do a good thing.

There is a story in the Old Testament about the Ark of the Covenant and one Israelite who died because he did not follow God's clear commandment. God gave a very clear commandment that no one was to touch the Ark of the Covenant, period. The story claims oxen were pulling a cart that was carrying the Ark. As the oxen stumbled and the Ark started to tip, an Israelite named Uzzah reached out to steady the Ark and God's anger burned against Uzzah and God struck him dead.

2 Samuel 6:6-7 *6 And when they came to Nacon's threshing floor, Uzzah put forth his hand to the Ark of God, and took hold of it; for the oxen shook it. 7 And the anger of the Lord was kindled against Uzzah; and God smote him there for his error, and there he died by the ark of God.*

For an error!

Was this an act of willful disobedience, like Adam and Eve's fruit picking in the Garden of Eden, or a product of muscle memory, or just a knee-jerk response to try to protect something that needed protecting? Was Uzzah trying to cop a feel of the Ark when he thought God wasn't looking? The verses say God was so attentive and protective of the Ark that when one man out of the entire nation of Israel touched and supposedly defiled the Ark, God killed him for his error.

Why wasn't God attentive enough to Eve in the Garden of Eden when Satan was planning to touch far more than a box? Satan figuratively touched Eve and the whole world was defiled and Eve was to blame? Did God just watch?

With God's well-documented Old Testament history of killing, why not kill Satan? Satan did a lot more than just touch a box. My confusion begins when God's unknowing earthly creations, Adam and Eve, were destroyed by God's knowledgeable heavenly creation, Satan, and God takes it out on the earthly creation. God, what does Satan hold over you? Are you, as some writers say, "Equal or almost equal?"

Genesis 1:26 *And God said, Let us make man in our image.*

Is Satan one of the "in our image" beings? With God's proven ability to kill anyone, at any time, for any reason, what is keeping God from killing the one creation who has done multiple times more damage to God's ego than Adam or Eve or Uzzah ever did? Because of Satan's sin in the Garden of Eden, you have condemned not only Adam and Eve but also every living soul until the end of time, solely over an apple.

If there is a civilization the televangelists do not reach before Jesus comes back and that land has not ever heard the Jesus message, so its people have not received Jesus as their personal Savior, what have they done against God to deserve eternal damnation? Are you really going to condemn them to hell, like the Christmas children at Jesus' birth, "just because?" Satan has sinned against you multiple times, and still you play with Satan, at our expense. *You can believe* God has dominion over Satan but to judge by God's own actions to date, I do not believe God has any dominion over Satan.

In Mark 7:1-9 The Pharisees were talking to Jesus about his disciples who ate bread and food without washing their hands first. The Jews were very strict about eating with unclean hands and felt that it was a breaking of tradition of the oral law passed down by Moses. Jesus rebuked them by telling them that they were worried more about keeping traditions of man than of keeping the commandments of God. The Pharisees did not honor their mothers and fathers, which was a commandment, but did keep the traditions of man, by washing *hands, pots, and cups.*

Mark 7:8-9 *8 For laying aside the commandment of God, ye hold the tradition of men, as the washing of pots and cups; and many other such things ye do. 9 And he said unto them, Full well ye reject the commandment of God, that ye may keep your own tradition.*

If God gave *organized religion* commandments that were *infallibly* written in the Bible, why do Christians allow their "traditions of man" to override the commandments of God?

You can believe that Sunday is really the Sabbath, your holy day of worship, but why dilute *your* day? *You can continue to believe* the tradition that it is all right to work and shop and play on Sunday because that part of the Bible is outdated and today's times are different from Old Testament times. Does it really make sense for the NFL quarterback, running back or strong safety to thank Jesus that they made the winning play that was the cause for the other team to lose… on *Sunday! You can believe* that your Bible verse about keeping the Sabbath holy is a little outdated, but that the condemning homosexual Bible verses are still valid. *You can believe* that you really don't have to stop working and shopping and playing on Sunday even though it is a commandment.

Exodus 20:10-11 *10 But the seventh day is the Sabbath of the Lord thy God; in it thou shalt not do any work, thou, nor thy son, nor thy daughter, thy manservant, nor thy maidservant, not thy cattle, nor thy stranger that is within thy gates; 11 For in six days the Lord made heaven and earth, the sea, and all that in them is, and rested the seventh day; wherefore, the Lord blessed the Sabbath day, and hallowed it.*

Search the many Internet sites that declare that the Catholic Church — in order to lure the Gentiles to Christianity — changed the Jewish last day, Saturday Sabbath, to the Gentiles' first day, Sunday Sabbath. Catholic and other Internet sites use New Testament verses to absolutely prove that Sunday is the Sabbath and some Sunday Sabbath arguments seem reasonable, if you want to believe them instead of the Bible (see *gotquestions.org/ Saturday-Sunday.html*).

Let's see whether or not the Bible is clear about a Saturday, last day of the week, Sabbath.

Genesis 2:1-3 *1 Thus the heavens and the earth were finished, and all the host of them. 2 And on the seventh day God ended his work which he had made; and he rested on the seventh day from all his work which he had made. 3 And God blessed the seventh day, and sanctified it, because that in it he had rested from all his work which God created and made.*

Seems clear that God rested on the seventh day. Exodus 20, above, states that on the seventh day we should not work because it is the Sabbath.

Organized religion has known of this discrepancy for years, and yet they do nothing about living by God's commandments. Are you trying to tell us that it has been a man-made tradition for so long that it would upset the world order if we actually correctly kept the Sabbath holy? Do all Christians *really* believe that they are not breaking God's commandment when according to **Exodus 20:8-11** *8 Remember the sabbath day, to keep it holy. 9 Six days shalt thou labor and do all thy work; 10 But the seventh day is the Sabbath of the Lord thy God; in it thou shalt not do any work, thou, nor thy son, nor thy daughter, thy manservant, nor thy maidservant, nor thy cattle, nor thy stranger that is within thy gates; 11 For in six days the Lord made heaven and earth, the sea, and all that in them is, and rested the seventh day; wherefore, the Lord blessed the sabbath day, and hallowed it.*

It took God four verses to clearly and decisively *command* you to keep the Saturday Sabbath holy and yet you casually dismiss God's commandment. Are you just *willfully disobeying* God's Sabbath commandment because you are fully aware of the commandment and don't care, or are you completely oblivious to God's Sabbath commandment?

Like Adam and Eve, do you want to be condemned by God's judgment based on a willful act of disobedience or do you think you have an excuse good enough to attract God's attention and mercy? The Devil made me do it! It doesn't matter to us whether you don't want to keep God's commandments because that would make you have to change your way of life. But do not then selectively give *us* a commandment that orders us to change *our* way(s) of life.

You can believe that the Christmas tree, lights, tinsel, presents, Santa Claus, and his reindeer have their place next to the nativity scene with the baby Jesus. You have that tree and those presents in your foyer and the nativity scene on the church's lawn every year.

You can believe that there were three wise men at the birth of the baby Jesus. If Jesus was a newborn baby, why did King Herod order all first-born children up to two years of age to be killed? King Herod could have stopped even at six months and still been sure to get the baby Jesus. Was it really necessary, in order for God's ultimate plan to work, to kill all of those two-year-old innocent children?

You can believe that maybe God spared all of those children from suffering in hell because they did not have a choice to either reject Jesus as Savior or accept him. Ooops, my mistake — Jesus wasn't yet the path to salvation. Did all those one-day-old to two-year-old innocent children go to hell? What was the way to heaven for one-day-old to two-year-old children before the time of Jesus? Whatever it was, I don't think all those children fulfilled it.

Are those Christmas children in heaven or hell? There is no age of accountability where a child has to reach a certain age before he or she will be held accountable for his or her own personal decision to accept or deny Jesus. You may insist that I should just worry about whether I get to heaven or not, and that God will take care of the little children. Someone actually told me that! If God's mindset was to kill all those children to prove some point, I guess I am more worried about what kind of God I want as my Father.

You can believe that the Easter bunny, the colored eggs, the chocolate candy, your daughter's new dress and patent leather shoes, your son's first suit, tie and shoes, and the Easter egg hunt you have on the lawn where the nativity scene used to be are all scriptural. But at least maintain the *appearance* of spirituality and humbleness. Instead of all the pretty new clothes, I would actually recommend shopping for some non-descript burial cloth, just like Jesus wore on *your* Easter resurrection Sunday!

You can believe that Santa Claus and the Easter bunny are harmless, cute little celebrations you engage in once or twice a year. But these celebrations actually water down the true story of *your* Savior's birth and *your*

Savior's death. Furthermore, these celebrations water down your biblical standards, period. If *you* can water down your biblical standards about Jesus, then *we* will water down your biblical standards that allow you to *control and condemn us on this earth and then declare our damnation in the hereafter.* I am willing to stand and say: "Your loving God may condemn me at judgment time, but *organized religion* will not condemn any of *us,* anymore, on this earth!"

You can believe that it is all right to charge other Christians interest on a loan. Bible verses claim other Israelites are brothers and that anyone in surrounding countries who is not an Israelite is a foreigner. Fellow Christians are not to charge a brother a usury but, you can charge a foreigner a usury.

Deuteronomy 23:19-20 *19 Thou shalt not lend upon interest to thy brother; interest of money, interest of victuals, interest of anything that is lent upon interest. 20 Unto a foreigner thou mayest lend upon interest, but unto thy brother thou shalt not lend upon interest, that the Lord thy God may bless thee in all thou settest thine hand to in the land to which thou goest, to possess it.*

You can believe anything that makes you feel like you are being a better Christian.

You can believe what others have made up, or you can interpret words your own way. I don't care what you want to believe, but be aware that your God does. God told the Israelites they were to be given their enemies' lands and when they took those lands they were not to take in new traditions and beliefs.

Deuteronomy 12:29-32 *29 When the Lord thy God shall cut off the nations from before thee, where thou goest to possess them, and thou succeed-est them, and dwelleth in their land, 30 Take heed to thyself that thou be not snared by following them, after they are destroyed from before thee, and that thou inquire not after their gods, saying, How did these nations serve their* *gods? Even so will I do likewise. 31 Thou shalt not do so unto the Lord thy God; for every abomination to the Lord, which he hateth, have they done unto their gods. For even their sons and their daughters they have burned in the fire to their gods, 32 Whatsoever thing I command you, observe to do it; thou shalt not add thereto, nor diminish from it.*

It seems that throughout the history of Christianity, the faith has evolved from an attempt to get everyone on the same page to: "let's all add our own rules and blessings." *Organized religion* seems to be very *traditional*, but not very biblical.

You can believe that your Christmas tree and Easter basket traditions are all right, but God said they are not!

You can believe that the 66 books chosen to make up the Bible were the ordained books chosen by God. But of the 39 books of the Old Testament and the 27 books of the New Testament, how did *some* get canonized and others not? There were other books in the pile of parchments to make up the Bible that did not make the list. Why? There are also books by Mary Magdalene, Judas Iscariot, and Enoch.

Using my old time religion mentality, I could probably persuade you why we wouldn't want a prostitute or a traitor writing a book that would be canonized! But when I discovered a book written by Enoch, I was very surprised that it was not canonized.

I was surprised The *Book of Enoch* was not canonized because he was actually *perfect* in the sight of the Lord. Enoch was so *perfect* in God's sight that he did not have to die, ever.

Genesis 5:23-24 *23 And all the days of Enoch were three hundred sixty and five years. 24 And Enoch walked with God, and he was not; for God took him.*

Enoch and Elijah were the only two recorded humans who did not ever die. If God was so pleased with Enoch that he did not have to die, and he wrote a book, why wasn't the Book of Enoch canonized? If a man was found *perfect* in the sight of God, and God needed to get a message to mankind, how could you do better than to choose a perfect man like Enoch to deliver such a message — unlike Noah who was *said* to be perfect and proven otherwise?

Could it be that *organized religion* would lose control of mankind — and its followers — because of what was written in the Book of Enoch? The Book of Enoch begins with a startling declaration:

Enoch 1:1-3 *1 The words of the blessing of Enoch, wherewith he blessed the elect and righteous, who will be 2 living in the day of tribulation; when all the wicked and godless are to be removed. And he took up his parable and said-Enoch a righteous man, whose eyes were opened by God, saw a vision of the Holy One in the heavens, which the angels showed me, and from them I heard everything, and from them I understood as I saw, but not for this generation, but for a remote one which is 3 for to come.*

Enoch claimed to have been given "flying" tours of heaven and earth by angels. Enoch claimed to have seen the Son of man, Jesus, before he was even born. Many Internet sites claim that the Book of Enoch was not canonized because it has too many contradictions, that it was written by more than one person, that it has multiple mistranslations, that it has time sequences that do not match, and that there are just too many outrageous claims that no one could ever really believe. If you think about it, that sounds a lot like the *infallible* Holy Bible to me!

IT IS OKAY, FOR *YOU TO BELIEVE...*

You can believe that Jesus fed 5,000 men with five loaves of bread and two fishes and when everyone had eaten their fill, they had 12 baskets of leftovers.

You can believe that Moses parted the Red Sea and everyone walked across on dry land.

You can believe that the Israelites obeyed God and wandered around in the desert for 40 years within eyesight of the promised land until most of them died. The Israelites have a written history of disobeying God in even the smallest of circumstances or sins. They would never have accepted a 40-year death sentence, wandering on the hot sand until death, without a rebellion.

You can believe that Jesus walked on water.

You can believe that Sodom and Gomorrah were destroyed by fire and brimstone sent down from the heavens by God.

You can believe that Jesus raised people from the dead.

You can believe that Jesus rose again on whatever day you *want* or *need* him to have risen.

You can believe that Jonah stayed alive in the belly of a great fish for three days and three nights without food or fresh water.

You can believe that Noah *in one day* put eight people and two of every animal, one male and one female, on a boat with enough provisions for 150 days and then replenished the earth as we know it today.

You can believe Sunday is your Holy Sabbath.

You can believe the *baby* Jesus got three presents from three wise men in the stable.

You can believe with personal conviction — based on your special interpretation of God's *infallible* Bible — that *your* path is the only way to get to heaven. *You can also believe* every other soul on this planet, except *you* and your chosen people, from the beginning of time until the last day this planet exists, is going to hell.

You can believe that I have been too bold and brazen about my concerns about God and God's *infallible* Holy Bible.

Out of a sense of keeping *organized religion* from ever trying to condemn me and attempting to convince *organized religion* that my faith will never be shaken again, I have been very headstrong in my beliefs. But, in all humbleness, I have a final question I will try to present to *organized religion* and hopefully have God answer, someday.

My question is: If we understood — in our hearts and minds — about good and evil from the beginning of our existence; if we knew what "die" really meant; if we knew what "naked" meant; if we understood that we could live forever; and if you, God, did not allow a fallen angel (who was completely prepared to beguile us and hell bent to destroy us) to come down to Earth to beguile us; and if you truly had the power over Satan to control him, would we really have done something we did not even know how to do; to sin against you?

Until *organized religion* answers this question, you can keep your dogma. We will choose something else.

CHAPTER 12

We choose to believe...

We converted non-Christians choose to believe that a child does not come out of the womb knowing how to, nor having a plan to, break as many of the 10 commandments as soon and as often as he or she can. *We choose to believe* in the kindness and goodness of mankind before we were segmented into different religious groups that foster hatred and division.

You may say, "But look at all of the killing, stealing, cheating, prejudice, and hate."

You can believe that eating an apple started all that. *We choose to believe* that mankind was taught hatred by God or God's translators because the Bible indicts itself with its own verses. How did we get from the Old Testament recordings of a God of hate and killing to the New Testament love of Jesus?

Hebrews 13:8 *Jesus Christ, the same yesterday, and today, and forever.*

The Bible clearly says that Jesus is the same yesterday, and today and forever.

1 John 5:7 *For there are three that bear record in heaven, the Father, the Word, and the Holy Spirit; and these three are one.*

Again, Jesus has always been equated with being the Word.

I am just asking: "If the Father and the Word and the Holy Spirit have been the same in being, the same in their ideals and judgments since before the ages, how can *organized religion* possibly equate God the Father of hate in the Old Testament to the Word, Son, Jesus of love in the New Testament? The Old Testament and the New Testament do not validate in any harmonious way the Bible teaching that God is the same yesterday, and today and forever.

We converted non-Christians choose to believe that men and women were good from the beginning of their creation and according to the Bible were good, had daily chats with God, and were obedient until God introduced sin to the earth. Satan had already sinned against God in the heavens and *we choose to believe* that God allowed Satan to tempt Eve in some egotistical game he was playing with Satan. Adam was not the first sinner on earth. Eve was not the first sinner on earth. Satan was the first sinner on earth and God allowed it!

In several chapters I have discussed and attempted to offer different points of view to prove that Adam or Eve did not commit the original sin. This original sin is the focal point of *organized religion's* condemnation of all of us. If I am going to be condemned to hell because someone ate an apple, then I want to know whether they were tricked into eating the apple or if it was a willful act of disobedience; as *organized religion* states. Without this apple, there is no need for Jesus.

I believe I have provided enough evidence to convincingly prove that the Bible as we have it today cannot be the *infallible* Word of God. I will concede that once upon a time the Bible might have been the *infallible* Word of God. But, by showing that so many parts are incorrect and now wondering which parts could be correct, I choose to believe none of it. I have sincerely tried to write with as much clarity as I could for the benefit of those souls in the gray area of "I believe in God. I just don't know who he is, or she is or they are or we are." I am not dictating or expecting anyone to make a choice based on my beliefs. But I do hope *Disorganized Christianity* will help open people's eyes with a new perspective and then help them search with a different heart that guides them through their own personal choices. I do not spiritually know what you — or anyone — needs, but it seems neither does *organized religion*.

It appears that after believing that we had been given God's word and directions on how to rekindle an everlasting relationship with Him because of Adam or Eve's sin, we have actually uncovered a lot of wasted energy spent on man's dogma instead of what could have been God's true word.

There is absolutely no way the Bible can be held up in its current condition as the road map to heaven. Is there a heaven? Some people do not care whether or not there is or isn't a heaven, and they will do their thing no matter what anyone says or commands. To those of us who hope there is a heaven (whatever it may be) because right now we do not have an idea of anything better, we have a dilemma.

There have been many thoughts and religions that present heaven in various ways. Some names for alternative heavens include Paradise, Utopia, Zion, Elysium, Happy Hunting Ground, Nirvana, and Shangri-la. Christianity, although by Bible declaration it is understood to be the first and only God mandated religion, is by no means the only religion or even the largest religious group to have an idea about heaven.

Some people have asked me to come up with an alternate solution for all of the dogma I have dispelled. It is not my responsibility to provide the fix for heaven, and if I did try right now to give you my insights, then I would be no better than those I have challenged by writing *Disorganized Christianity*.

I do not have a newly discovered original parchment with God's special revelations given to me to cure the earth's spiritual problems for only $29.99. I cannot fix any problems. I believe I have been blessed with the opportunity to see beyond what I used to believe and preach, and to now see that I was wrong and then to have found a potential venue to correct it. I do not know enough about how things should be and what would happen if we followed ten new rules or what would happen if we did not follow ten new rules. I have no new rules.

Several people have expressed concern that I am creating spiritual chaos with *Disorganized Christianity* and what will we use as a barometer for right and wrong if our conventional sources are no longer valid.

Are there any other reliable "Codes," or "parchments from long ago" that we could possibly give any credibility to? Perhaps the Babylonian Code of Hammurabi written on stone around 1754 BC or the Mahabharata, one of two major Sanskrit texts from India. We could use the teachings of Buddha, including his Four Noble Truths. There are many more spiritual teaching possibilities to explore. I am not recommending any of these teachings. I am just giving examples of the more notable spiritual manuscripts that could help mankind find both peace and heaven. Having followed the Bible for thousands of years, with everything we claim to know, we are finding out we really do not know anything for certain.

If I was to venture a solution to cure the earth's spiritual problems, it would be this:

Matthew 6:14-15 14 *For if ye forgive men their trespasses, your heavenly Father will also forgive you; 15 But if ye forgive not men their trespasses, neither will your Father forgive your trespasses.*

1 Corinthians 13:13 *And now abideth faith, hope, love, these three; but the greatest of these is love.*

John 13:34 *A new commandment I give unto you, that ye love one another; as I have loved you, that ye also love one another.*

Mark 12:31 *And the second is this: Thou shalt love thy neighbor as thyself. There is no other commandment greater than these.*

Matthew 7:12 *Therefore, all things whatever ye would that men should do to you, do ye even so to them; for this is the law and prophets.*

The Golden Rule: Do unto others as you would have them do unto you.

Organized religion will always attempt to pervert information for its own purpose. Individuals on a personal quest to find God are the only chance for a true and pure movement towards God; whoever he is, or she is, or they are, or we are. In short, love one another and forgive one another and do not try and build your personal empire or kingdom on anyone else's back or through their soul.

After the many years I have spent writing, I humbly release my story for all to read and then leave it up to you to make your own decisions. The research that has gone into *Disorganized Christianity* has been extensive and the conclusions will be highly controversial to most people. My heart and my conscience have been put on a scale — by me — to make sure they are in perfect balance for all the revelations I have written. My absolute goal is not to confuse, but to inform and expose.

I hope that you too can put your heart and conscience on a balance scale now that you have read *Disorganized Christianity*. My desire is that your intellectual and spiritual scale will weigh in perfect balance for your life. We really do not need any *organized religion* to tell us how to act. We already do know how to love one another and to forgive one another, and whereas we often each miss the mark, that is no reason or justification to send anyone to HELL!

Another emotional ingredient I encountered while writing *Disorganized Christianity* was sadness and concern at knowing that there are so many people like me in this world who are constantly searching for a real God. To them, I also dedicate this book in the hope that they may find the light. For those who cannot understand or believe my true concern for them and perceive me as their enemy or as someone less than human, I offer my regrets. I am only speaking the truth: "That we do not need to be held captive by nor put in bondage by *organized religion*."

The followers of *organized religion* have created their own special dogma surrounding Christianity. They can have it. They can share it. They can believe it. They can live it. It is none of our business what they want to believe, and that is all right. With the same respect and balance, we *converted non-Christians* should be allowed by *organized religion* to not have it, not hear it, not believe it and not live it, without their condemnation.

I understand that even out of love and charity and with a very real personal desire to get me to believe in Christianity again, some followers of *organized religion* sincerely believe that their Jesus can offer me Heaven and save me from Hell. After years of investigating their Bible, I do not want their Heaven, and I am not afraid of their Hell!

Should you choose to judge me harshly because I have shared my truth, first walk in my shoes for 25-plus years and read your Bible again. Having done that, then and only then, you will discover you cannot judge me anyway.

Luke 6:37 *Judge not, and ye shall not be judged; condemn not, and ye shall not be condemned; forgive, and ye shall be forgiven.*

I used my Bible as my guide until I was 33 years old. Then my *organized religion* dogma died, and I was spiritually born-again. I choose to live within my own temple, with my own personal search for God and to honor all of it! Namaste!

After writing *Disorganized Christianity,* I now say: "I STILL BELIEVE IN GOD, but I still do not know who *he is,* or *she is,* or *they are,* or *we are!*"

However, I *do* know and believe that God is not what the fallible Bible and the moneychangers of *organized religion* are selling.